AGAINST ALL ODDS

Recent Titles in Contributions in Women's Studies

Women as Interpreters of the Visual Arts, 1820-1979
Claire Richter Sherman, editor, with Adele M. Holcomb

Flawed Liberation: Socialism and Feminism
Sally M. Miller, editor

Wartime Women: Sex Roles, Family Relations, and the Status of Women
During World War II
Karen Anderson

Women Writers in Black Africa
Lloyd W. Brown

The Paradise of Women: Writings by Englishwomen of the Renaissance
Betty Travitsky, compiler and editor

The Origins of the Equal Rights Amendment: American Feminism
Between the Wars
Susan D. Becker

European Women on the Left: Socialism, Feminism, and the Problems
Faced by Political Women, 1880 to the Present
Jane Slaughter and Robert Kern, editors

Toward the Second Decade: The Impact of the Women's Movement on
American Institutions
Betty Justice and Renate Pore, editors

A Conflict of Interest: Women in German Social Democracy, 1919-1933
Renate Pore

The Second Assault: Rape and Public Attitudes
Joyce E. Williams and Karen A. Holmes

Oppression and Resistance: The Struggle of Women in Southern Africa
Richard E. Lapchick and Stephanie Urdang

Separated and Divorced Women
Lynne Carol Halem

AGAINST ALL ODDS
The Feminist Movement in Mexico to 1940

Anna Macías

CONTRIBUTIONS IN WOMEN'S STUDIES,
NUMBER 30

Greenwood Press
WESTPORT, CONNECTICUT
LONDON, ENGLAND

Library of Congress Cataloging in Publication Data

Macias, Anna.
  Against all odds.

  (Contributions in women's studies, ISSN 0147-104X ;
no. 30)
  Bibliography: p.
  Includes index.
    1. Feminism—Mexico—History. 2. Women—Mexico—
Social conditions. I. Title. II. Series: Contributions
in women's studies ; no. 30.
HQ1462.M32   305.4'2'0972   81-6201
ISBN 0-313-23028-5 (lib. bdg.)   AACR2

Library of Congress Catalog Card Number: 81-6201
ISBN: 0-313-23028-5
ISSN: 0147-104X

First published in 1982

Greenwood Press
A division of Congressional Information Service, Inc.
88 Post Road West, Westport, Connecticut 06881

Printed in the United States of America

10 9 8 7 6 5 4 3 2 1

Copyright Acknowledgment

Eight lines of Robert Graves's translation of the poem "Hombres necios" by Sor Juana Inés
de la Cruz have been reprinted from Robert Graves, "Sor Juana Inés de la Cruz,"
Encounter 1, no. 3 (December 1953): 11, by permission of Robert Graves.

For
Isabel, Concha, and Beatriz

and to the memory of my mother
Josefa González Macías (1890-1963)

CONTENTS

Acknowledgments   ix

Introduction   xi

1. The Roots of Feminism in Mexico   3

2. Women and the Mexican Revolution, 1910-1920   25

3. Yucatán and the Women's Movement, 1870-1920   58

4. Felipe Carrillo Puerto as Champion of Women's
    Rights in Yucatán, 1922-1923   87

5. Mexican Women on Their Own, 1924-1930   104

6. The Feminist Movement in the 1930s   125

Conclusion   152

Bibliographical Essay   159

Index   183

ACKNOWLEDGMENTS

Without the encouragement and support of many friends and colleagues, this work would never have been written. First I would like to thank Lewis Hanke, Emeritus Professor of Latin American history at the University of Massachusetts, for urging me, in 1970, to present a paper on Mexican women at the 1971 American Historical Association annual meeting. Professor Hanke then published an abbreviated version of the paper entitled "The Mexican Revolution Was No Revolution for Women" in his *History of Latin American Civilization: Sources and Interpretations*, 2 vols. (Boston: Little, Brown and Co., 1973).

The many supportive comments I received about that first effort led to my decision to prepare a monograph on Mexican feminism. With the help of a Social Science Research Council/American Council of Learned Societies grant, I spent 1973-74 doing research at libraries in Mexico; New York; Chicago; Washington; Bloomington, Indiana; Columbus and Delaware, Ohio. A generous leave policy and a grant from Ohio Wesleyan University made it possible for me to complete the research and write the text.

My friends of many years, Edith Boorstein Couturier and Jean Jacques Couturier, have encouraged and supported my work at every step of the way, introducing me to scholars working on Latin American women, locating sources, and critically reading the text. I am also grateful to Asunción Lavrin of Howard University for bringing a number of sources on Mexican women to my attention and for offering excellent suggestions for improving the manuscript.

In Mexico Anita Fisher de Aguilar of the American School included me in all her weekend trips to the state of Morelos to interview surviving

Zapatistas. These trips were a welcome respite from long hours of reading at libraries in Mexico City and a magnificent opportunity to participate in a crucial oral history project. Mrs. Aguilar also located written sources for me on female teachers who helped Zapata's cause. In addition, in 1973-74 both Anita and her husband, Fernando Aguilar, constantly encouraged my research in the face of some discouraging and skeptical remarks by other Mexicans, who questioned the validity of my study.

In April 1974 talks with a contemporary feminist, María Antonieta Rascón, who was researching feminism in the 1930s, provided a useful exchange of information and ideas on the outstanding Marxist feminists of the 1930s. In 1973-74 Valerie Campbell of the American School in Mexico City shared her apartment with me and patiently listened to my excited account of each day's discoveries at the Biblioteca de México, the Biblioteca Nacional, or the Hemeroteca Nacional. Joan Cunningham de Zamora and her husband, Dr. Carlos Zamora González of Mexico City, made me confront my own feminist bias and helped me to view the situation of Mexican women more objectively.

I was given courteous attention at the many libraries I consulted in Mexico City; Mérida, Yucatán; Delaware and Columbus, Ohio; New York; Washington; Chicago; and Bloomington, Indiana. I would like to give special thanks to Concepción Alonso Sellés of the Biblioteca de México for her limitless efforts on my behalf in locating sources and for her serious interest in my subject. Through her efforts I was able to interview the distinguished educator, Doctora María Teresa Chávez, the successor of José Vasconcelos as Director of the Biblioteca de México.

I am grateful to the generous assistance of Libuse Reed of Ohio Wesleyan University and Justus Doenecke of New College, Sarasota, Florida, for reading the entire manuscript and for making excellent suggestions for improving the text. Fred Bronner of the Hebrew University of Jerusalem and Corinne Lyman of Ohio Wesleyan University also gave generously of their time in a critical reading of various chapters. I am, of course, solely responsible for whatever errors may appear in the text.

I am deeply grateful to my family for their support and encouragement of my scholarly efforts over the years. I also owe a debt of gratitude to Robert E. Shimp, other colleagues in the history department at Ohio Wesleyan University, and many friends and neighbors in Delaware, Ohio, for their interest in my work. My thanks to Lyn Shimp for typing most of the manuscript, and to Linda McVetty Roberts for typing chapter 4.

INTRODUCTION

Early in 1971 I was invited to present a paper at the American
Historical Association sessions in New York on "Mexican Women in the
Social Revolution." I knew something about the subject in an experien-
tial way. I had first visited Mexico in 1954, had lived in the capital, and
had travelled widely in the country in 1956-57 and again in 1961-62. As a
teacher of Latin American history and as a Mexicanist with a specialization in the independence period, I made it a point to visit Mexico at least
every two years but usually each summer. As the years went by Mexico
underwent enormous changes that have been documented well by econ-
omists, sociologists, historians, political scientists, and others. However, it could not escape my notice that the role and situation of most
Mexican women I knew, whether of the upper, middle, or lower class,
had not changed dramatically from 1954 to 1971, despite their attainment
of suffrage in 1953.

It was also clear that in the period from 1954 to 1971, with a few
exceptions, notably the work of Oscar Lewis and other anthropologists
and sociologists, there was relatively little scholarly interest in what
Mexican women thought, said, wrote, or did. Most Mexican women
worked in their own homes or someone else's and devoted much of their
time to the bearing and rearing of children. Before 1971 most historians
of Mexico were not interested in the home or in children and were
therefore not interested in women. Even when Mexican women had
played a significant role in national crises such as the independence
movement of 1808-21, the reform movement of 1855-76, or the Revolution of 1910-20, most historians, myself included, had little to say about

their participation in Mexico's cyclical struggle to be free of foreign domination.

I commenced work on the subject of "Mexican Women in the Social Revolution" with some trepidation, for I feared that it would be difficult to document the role of Mexican women in the revolution that began in 1910. To my surprise, I soon discovered that there had been an important attempt to foster a feminist movement in Yucatán from 1916 to 1923, that five feminist congresses had been held in Mexico in the 1920s and 1930s—all organized by women—and that Mexican women had almost achieved the vote in 1939. Yet, up to 1971 only one work that touched on the subject of feminism in Mexico had appeared in English: Ward M. Morton's *Woman Suffrage in Mexico* (Gainesville, Fla.: University of Florida Press, 1962). However, as the title suggests, Morton's study centers almost exclusively on the issue of female enfranchisement. A careful analysis of the feminist congresses held in Mexico from 1916 to 1940 reveals that suffrage was only one of a number of issues that agitated Mexican feminists in the period from the earliest stirrings of feminist consciousness in the nineteenth century to 1940, the year that women were temporarily thwarted in their fight for suffrage. The present study attempts to analyze all the major issues, including suffrage, that concerned Mexican feminists from about 1890 to 1940.

There are two reasons why I chose to prepare a history of the feminist movement in Mexico from 1890 to 1940. On the one hand, research from 1971 to 1975 in libraries and archives in Mexico and the United States turned up an enormous number of books, pamphlets, newspaper articles, and other printed sources on Mexican women and on feminism, much of which had never been utilized before. On the other hand, despite all the documentary evidence to the contrary, at the start of my research many Mexicans insisted that a feminist movement had never existed in Mexico. For example, when I arrived in Mexico City in September of 1973 to begin a year of research, I was told with considerable vehemence by a rather pompous banker that "there never has been a feminist movement in Mexico," after I had answered his inquiry about the subject I was researching. I knew then that I had to prove to the banker and to everyone else who shared his view that such was not the case. In a very real sense, this study is an attempt to piece together lost, neglected, and forgotten history.

One can easily argue that feminism originated in Mexico when Sor Juana Inés de la Cruz (1648-95) penned her famous poem, "Hombres necios'' (''Foolish Men''). However, it is harder to prove that feminism has had a significant following in Mexico in the twentieth century, in part because of the paucity of widely disseminated works on the subject before 1971 in any language, and in part because prior to 1971 there were few visible signs that feminist thought and action had had any impact on the attitudes of most men and women in Mexico.

When Mexican women voted in a presidential election for the first time in 1958 I was there, and I shared the prevailing view that women had been granted the right to vote because the conflict between church and state of the 1920s and 1930s had been defused and the government no longer feared that women would overwhelmingly support Catholic opposition candidates. I also accepted the commonly held notion that Mexican women themselves had done little or nothing to obtain the vote. I believe that the first assumption is correct, but I hope to demonstrate in the following pages that thousands of Mexican women made a determined effort in the 1930s to win the franchise.

The object, then, of the present work is to demonstrate that a significant feminist movement, involving thousands of women of every social class and whose origins go back to the seventeenth century, developed from approximately 1890 to 1940. Yet the reader has every right to be skeptical and to ask why it is that Mexican feminists had so little impact on changing traditional attitudes about women during these fifty years. The answer is both simple and complicated. Between 1890 and 1940 and until very recently, Mexican feminists have had to struggle against severe odds to be heard and to change the role, the image, and the opportunities of women. Their contribution has been limited to the narrow yet crucial sphere of the home.

First, one must briefly examine the problem of machismo in Mexico. Cuban, Argentinean, Chilean, and other Latin American men will insist that the machismo that the embittered Consuelo Sánchez so eloquently denounced in Oscar Lewis's *The Children of Sánchez* does not exist in their respective countries, but this writer has experienced machismo in Spain, in Argentina, and in other Latin countries. Still, one cannot escape the impression that until recently machismo was especially pronounced in Mexico. Feminists have never had an easy time combating machismo in any country, but the writings of Mexican feminists give testimony to the overwhelming difficulties they encountered in trying to educate Mexican men to view women as persons and not as symbols or objects.

Second, while the Mexican church was in conflict with the state between 1890 and 1940, it still had an enormous influence on most Mexicans, and the church hierarchy discouraged even the most moderate brand of feminism, refusing to countenance the establishment of any feminine organizations not controlled by the hierarchy. Much ink was spilled by articulate priests such as José Castillo y Pina and José Cantú Corro in the 1920s and 1930s, for example, condemning feminist ideas as destructive of traditional values. As a result, most pious Mexican women of every class steered clear of feminism, and the ranks of Mexican feminism were filled with women who came from families that generally departed from traditional religious values. A large number of Mexican feminists were liberal anticlericals, Protestants, agnostics, freethinkers, atheists, anarchists, socialists, and Communists. Students of feminism in other Latin American countries have observed the same phenomenon.

Third, Mexican feminists, like feminists elsewhere, seldom agreed on issues, tactics, and programs; and every feminist congress from 1916 to 1940 was an exhausting battle among left, right, and center factions that only the very tenacious could endure or survive. Women who aspired to leadership of the fractious movement ''burned out'' after a few years. There were only a few women, such as the schoolteacher and writer, Julia Nava de Ruisánchez, who could continuously be involved in feminist organizations from 1904 to 1940. Mrs. Ruisánchez, it should be pointed out, never aspired to leadership; those who did, such as the teacher Elena Torres and the journalist María Ríos Cárdenas, became exhausted and embittered and dropped out of feminist organizations and activities after about three to five years. As a result, there was little continuity of leadership in the period under discussion.

Fourth, Mexican feminists received little support and encouragement from government leaders, especially from 1900 to 1934. As I note in examining the feminist programs of two governors of Yucatán, Salvador Alvarado (1915-18) and Felipe Carrillo Puerto (1921-23), these two men, exemplary revolutionaries in many respects, tried to manipulate the very feminists they championed in order to further their own political ambitions. On the other hand, Mexico's presidents from 1910 to 1934 were indifferent to feminism and suspicious of all women because of prevailing male attitudes. These national leaders believed that most Mexican women were politically unreliable due to their attachment to the church.

A fifth reason why Mexican feminists faced overwhelming odds is that they received little support but much ridicule from the press. The widely read Mexico City daily, *Excelsior*, for example, was bitterly antifeminist from 1916 to well into the 1930s. Feminists were seldom interviewed by the press or given any opportunity to make their views known on such questions as legal equality, education for women, the double standard, and divorce. In addition, the press seldom reported on feminist organizations and activities unless women held a congress, and even then coverage was minimal. Lacking funds to publicize their activities and ignored by the press much of the time, Mexican feminists were very nearly invisible.

Lastly, it needs to be stressed that most Mexican feminists came from the middle class and had to work for a living. Most of them were elementary schoolteachers, and after a hard day's work, they had little time or energy to devote to organizing a movement and raising the consciousness of the masses of abysmally poor Mexican women. The extreme poverty and the social, economic, and political instability that characterized Mexico in this period made it all but impossible for feminism to have much impact on the masses of Mexican women. Yet, despite the terrible odds against them, Mexican feminists began organizing in 1904 and by 1939 had almost won the right to vote, not just because they had won the support of President Lázaro Cárdenas, but because they had organized meetings; held congresses; published books, articles, and journals; taken part in demonstrations; and picketed the seats of power. Their pioneering efforts are worth examining and worth remembering.

AGAINST ALL ODDS

1

THE ROOTS OF FEMINISM IN MEXICO

Feminism in Mexico? In that land where male dominance and female subordination have, according to a vast literature, always been so conspicuous? For example, Mexican sociologist, María Elvira Bermúdez, claims that "if Spain has her Don Juan, and England her Othello, Mexico has her machos. And these, without a doubt, are more punctilious than Othello and less satiable than Don Juan."[1] Similarly, a contemporary writer, Juana Armanda Alegría, asserts that the vast majority of Mexican women, now and in the past, accept and have accepted without protest their role as "champions of suffering" at the hands of demanding and domineering men.[2] Undoubtedly *machismo* ("extreme male dominance") and its counterpart, *hembrismo* ("extreme female submission"), have been pervasive in Mexico, in part because of the Aztec subordination of women and even more because of the Spanish colonial experience. As one writer notes, after the Spanish conquest of Mexico "the great disparity [between the] sexes already existing in Spain and Mexico was increased by the gulf of caste and race."[3]

Yet what Gerda Lerner observes about American society can also be applied to pre-Columbian and colonial Mexico: "Women are subordinate, yet central; victimized, yet active."[4] Women in pre-Columbian and Spanish colonial society played a crucial role in the economy, ran large households, and participated actively in religious life. In addition, women found emotional support from the network of female relationships within the extended family that mitigated feelings of subordination and victimization.[5]

At the same time, however, not all females were submissive, and some women protested against the most oppressive aspects of patriarchal society. For example, evidence shows that there was protest against the sexual double standard in Aztec society.[6] A series of poems addressed to females reveal that adultery by married women, though supposedly punishable by death, was a source of concern in Aztec Mexico.[7] In Spanish colonial society, both the existence of a sexual double standard and the prejudice against a learned woman was to occasion protest. The most celebrated critic of machismo was Sor Juana Inés de la Cruz (1648-95), one of the greatest poets of the Hispanic world.[8] In her plea for a single sexual standard and equal educational opportunity for men and women, Sor Juana prefigured the modern feminist movement in Mexico.

Honored in her lifetime as the "Tenth Muse of Mexico," Sor Juana has long exercised an extraordinary fascination over literary critics.[9] Alfonso Reyes, the renowned Mexican writer, observed that it was impossible to study Sor Juana without falling in love with her,[10] while Manuel Toussaint, the distinguished Mexican art historian, noted with deep feeling that "esta mujer fue mucha mujer"("this woman was very much a woman").[11] Amado Nervo, one of Mexico's most popular poets, has written a most sensitive and appreciative biography of Sor Juana.[12] None of these Mexican male writers were in the least affronted by Sor Juana's feminism. They and the Mexican people are and always have been most proud of the fact that Sor Juana is a precursor of the modern women's movement, as evidenced by her famous poem "Hombres necios" ("Foolish Men") and in her autobiographical "Letter to Sor Filotea." In the former, she denounced the sexual double standard; in the latter, she defended the right of women to study the liberal arts and theology.[13] It was not a Mexican, but a German writer, Ludwig Pfandl, who, in his Freudian interpretation of Sor Juana, charged her with "a compulsive desire to compete with men in their special preserves."[14]

In her poem "Hombres necios," Sor Juana denounced those male seducers who incited women to break the moral code and who then, having achieved their objective, denounced them as "bad." Here Sor Juana rejected the notion of some early Christian and medieval theologians that women were the impure ones, who had brought sin to the world and who corrupted men. Instead, she argued:

> Which has the greater sin when burned
> By the same lawless fever:
> She who is amorously deceived,
> Or he, the sly deceiver?

Or which deserves the sterner blame,
Though each will be a sinner:
She who becomes a whore for pay,
Or he who pays to win her?[15]

Sor Juana's disenchantment with men and her insistence that they corrupt women is also clear in her "Letter to Sor Filotea," a celebrated *apologia pro vita sua* written to the Bishop of Puebla. Here she argues that women have a right to study both liberal arts and theology. Indeed, virtuous and learned women should teach females these subjects. Male teachers, warned Sor Juana, would take advantage of their situation and, as Abelard had seduced Heloise, would sexually exploit their students. Sor Juana argued that St. Paul's remark that "women should be quiet in church" was misinterpreted; the apostle never meant that women were to be ignorant in religious matters. She did concede that St. Paul probably opposed public preaching by women, but she saw no scriptural evidence that he had frowned on private study. On the contrary, she quoted St. Paul's approval of "bene docentes," or female teachers of the good, and insisted that he advocated personal female study, writing, and teaching.[16] Sor Juana also noted that St. Jerome, in his work, "To Leta, concerning the education of her daughter," counseled Leta to teach her daughter the Scriptures.[17]

Using St. Paul and St. Jerome as her authorities, then, Sor Juana defended her right and the right of all women to master the same curriculum as men. Her plea for equality was not revolutionary, for this ideal developed during the Middle Ages—Heloise, Eleanor of Aquitaine, and Christine de Pisan are notable examples—and flowered during the Renaissance. Highly educated women were not unknown in Sor Juana's day either, with Queen Christina of Sweden, the Duchess of Aveyro, and the Countess of Villaumbrosa—the latter two of the Iberian peninsula—cited by the Mexican nun as examples of truly Renaissance women.[18]

In one passage that few students of Sor Juana have commented on, she notes that many parents preferred an ignorant daughter to one exposed to frequent and close contact with a male teacher.[19] The only solution to this problem, Sor Juana said, was to select a group of self-educated women to teach young females, instructing them not only in elementary subjects, but in literature, history, science, and theology as well.

Sor Juana's ideal of educating an elite class of women made some headway during the century following her death, and between 1700 and

1810, a number of educational institutions for women were established, the most famous of which was Las Vizcaínas in Mexico City.[20] However, contrary to Sor Juana's goal, most educational institutions down to the twentieth century directed their teaching toward making women better wives and mothers, toward training them as artisans, or toward preparing them to teach only in primary school. As the noted historian of colonial Mexican women, Asunción Lavrin, has observed, "a woman 'in the world' would always fall into sin."[21]

When we turn to Mexico's struggle for independence, we find that it is no mere coincidence that the two most famous women of the 1810s—Josefa Ortíz de Domínguez, also known as La Corregidora, and Leona Vicario— were well educated. Vicario's uncle and guardian, a highly respected lawyer, took particular care in the education of his ward, while Josefa Ortíz studied at Las Vizcaínas until her marriage to the royal official, the Corregidor Miguel Domínguez.[22] La Corregidora is well known to every Mexican schoolchild, for this forthright and decisive woman gave Father Hidalgo, the initiator of the Mexican independence movement, a timely warning of his imminent arrest.[23] Leona Vicario left the comfort and security of an upper middle-class urban household first to give material aid and then to join the embattled insurgents in rural Mexico.[24]

After the American and French revolutions, organized activity in favor of equal rights for women developed in those countries which accepted, at least in theory, the idea of the equality of all citizens before the law. Crucial to the realization of equality was the promotion of free, public education. In Mexico the idea of the equality of all citizens—without reference to gender—was first proclaimed in Article 24 of the 1814 Apatzingán constitution, written during the struggle for independence from Spain.[25] Article 39 of that same document stated: "As education is necessary for all citizens, society should favor it with all its power."[26]

With the establishment of a republican form of government in Mexico by 1824, liberal-minded officials who desired to see Mexico ranking among the world's most advanced nations stressed the need to end elitist education and to replace it with fundamental education for all, regardless of one's sex, race, or economic class. A good example of a plan for public education is the 1826 "Project of a Decree Concerning Public Education in the Free State of Jalisco." The authors stated that they had not forgotten women in organizing public schools in Jalisco, and that given the neglect of female education in the past, municipal schools for girls were now to be established where they would study the three r's, draw-ing, and "those occupations suitable for their sex."[27] But the authors went on to hope that: "The happy day will come in which this amiable sex, schooled in the august temple of the sciences, shall produce the remarkable spectacle of [Mesdames de] Staëls amongst us. In the mean-time, the Commission is pleased to cast its vote to improve the advance-ment of their education."[28]

The Jalisco educational project called upon the municipalities to set up separate elementary schools for boys and girls, with the girls to be taught by "preceptoras," or women teachers selected and paid by the munici-pality. The plan even specified that male and female teachers should receive a decent remuneration, suggesting a minimum of three hundred and a maximum of five hundred pesos a year.[29]

Unfortunately, the transition from a royal colony to an independent republic was not smooth, and soon after independence Mexico was plunged into chaos. Enmity between liberals and conservatives, conflict between church and state, military uprisings, the misrule of General Santa Anna, and the loss of half of Mexico's territory to the United States between 1835 and 1848 left her institutions shattered and her people demoralized. Yet despite this grim picture, there were forces at work that aimed at creating an egalitarian society, one that would unleash the country's economic potential and create a prosperous and productive society.

In spite of Mexico's troubles, by the 1840s more and more liberal men—they were still a political minority—realized that women needed training beyond the fundamentals and that secondary schools for women should be established.[30] Although women's views were not recorded before the 1850s, it is worth speculating why men of liberal ideas increasingly came to advocate the need for female secondary education.

The advocates of female education seldom spelled out the reasons for their interest in the education of women. It is clear from their remarks, however, that since the state was weak and the church was under attack, only the family held the social fabric of Mexico together. For the family to survive amid the economic decline and political instability, liberals argued that skilled, energetic, and decisive wives and mothers were necessary, because Mexican men had traditionally exercised power but had seldom assumed domestic responsibility.[31] Yet many nineteenth-century observers of the social milieu believed that Mexican women fell all too easily into the stereotype of the helpless, indecisive, inept, uncomplaining, and submissive female. The gifted writer Guillermo Prieto (1818-97) complained bitterly in *Contigo Pan y Cebolla* (*Bread and Onion With You*) that the image of the self-abnegating Mexican woman "was a comedy which is presented with more frequency than is convenient."[32]

Champions of female education maintained that a weak, dependent, and uneducated woman could not run a household, nor raise a family of strong, active, and decisive children. In addition, abandoned or widowed women lacked the skills needed to support themselves and their offspring and were frequently reduced to doing needlework as a means of staying alive. But as the nineteenth-century novelist José T. de Cuellar pointed out in *Ensalada de pollos* (*Chicken Salad*), "the needle spells hunger."[33]

Until 1855 women who did not marry had the option of entering a convent. However, when the liberals came to power in 1855 they were intent on ending monasticism in Mexico, and eventually they banned all convents and monasteries in the country. As a result of these measures, women who did not marry and who had previously found support in a convent now added to the ranks of females in need of an education and a way to earn a living.

Prostitution was a severe but unacknowledged problem throughout the nineteenth century, but only novelists gave it serious attention.[34] We do not have figures for the middle of the century, but as will be discussed below, later statistics indicate that many women—reduced to becoming domestic servants, or ill-paid seamstresses, cigarette makers, and textile workers—fell into prostitution out of need and out of ignorance.[35] Advocates of female education insisted that schooling, if open to women of all classes, would reduce the incidence of prostitution.

Other advocates of female education argued that many upper- and middle-class women were frivolous, flighty, imprudent, indiscreet, improvident, and vacuous; they found these qualities rooted in the lack of solid and adequate education.[36] Such views were expressed by the editors of a weekly journal, the *Semanario de las Señoritas Mexicanas*, which began publication in December 1840. Since no secondary schools were available for women, they began publishing a weekly intended to improve the minds of their female readers by including "artículos de religión, de sana moral, de ciencias, literatura y artes, educación, economía doméstica... e historia...."[37] One of the contributors to this weekly, which survived until at least April 1841, was the aforementioned writer Guillermo Prieto, a consistent feminist who, speaking in the guise of "Doña Quiteria," wrote in the *Semanario*: "Our defects are due exclusively to our neglected and badly applied education, for which reason we do not yet know what Mexican women will or will not be capable of accomplishing."[38]

Yet for all the interest of the Liberal minority in promoting public education and in improving the education of women, very little was accomplished from 1824 to 1855. The resistance of the Conservatives to modernization and the aggrandizing expansion by the United States distracted Mexico from the task of nation building. In fact, in the chaotic years that extended from 1810 to 1867, educational opportunities for all Mexicans probably regressed from the levels achieved during the Bourbon Renaissance of 1730 to 1810.[39]

In 1855 the Revolution of Ayutla brought to an end the Santa Anna syndrome and propelled the Liberals to national power. However, it took Ignacio Comonfort, Benito Juárez, the Lerdo de Tejada brothers, Melchor Ocampo, and other outstanding liberal leaders another twelve years to dislodge their conservative enemies. The Conservatives, now in a minority status, allied themselves with Napoleon III and the ill-fated Maximilian of Austria, in order to prevent the Liberals from governing the country.

When the Liberals came to power in 1855, neither they nor most of their adherents anticipated the tenacious resistance of Mexican traditionalists and European adventurers. Instead, the liberals immediately began the task of reconstruction, first by abolishing the special privileges of the army and the church, then by breaking up large church estates and closing down monasteries, and finally by turning their attention to public education. In this heady atmosphere of reform, Mexican women finally began to demand an adequate education. On April 5, 1856, when the interim president, Ignacio Comonfort, entered Mexico City, he was crowned with a laurel wreath by a group of young women. Seizing a golden opportunity to address the president before a large gathering, they petitioned him to establish a secondary school open to young women of all social classes.[40]

Comonfort graciously answered that, foreseeing such a petition by the "bello sexo," he already had issued a decree establishing a secondary school for young women in Mexico City.[41] Neither President Comonfort nor his successor, Benito Juárez, were immediately able to make good on their promise. However, Juárez, in outlining his program to the Mexican Congress on January 20, 1861, was probably the first president in Mexican history to state in an annual message to Congress that "the education of women will also be attended to, giving it the importance it deserves because of the influence women exercise over society."[42]

It was not until 1867 that the Liberals could begin the task of reconstruction interrupted in 1856. The long-promised secondary school for girls opened its doors in 1869, followed in the next five years by a number of such establishments in provincial cities.[43] The school in Mexico City had no sooner been established when its female director requested that faculties in medicine, pharmacy, and agriculture be set up within that institution. But, as social historian Luis González y González laconically observes, "La idea no prosperó."[44] However, in Mexico City a vocational school for women, the Escuela de Artes y Oficios de Mujeres, was first established in 1871 and offered fifteen courses in arts and crafts, including embroidery, watchmaking, bookbinding, photography, tapestry making, and telegraphy. The school also offered some eight courses in basic scientific subjects.[45]

Apparently liberals were willing to countenance the idea of women studying the humanities, some science, and some vocational subjects deemed "appropriate to their sex," so that they might earn their living without competing economically with men. Women were especially encouraged to become primary schoolteachers, because teaching of young children required enormous dedication but received minimal compensation. During the Porfiriato, from 1876 to 1910, when the regime of Porfirio Díaz brought peace and some modernization to Mexico, elementary schoolteachers, of whom over two-thirds were women, received less than two pesos a day, a sum that barely supported one person.[46] In tributes paid to outstanding female elementary schoolteachers on their retirement or at their funerals, they were referred to as "verdaderas sacerdotistas," veritable priestesses of learning.[47] It is clear from the fulsome praise these women received that in their self-sacrificing devotion to their young students they were conforming to the role that had always been expected of women in Mexican society. At the death of the schoolteacher María de Jesus Soto, for example, schools in Pachuca were closed for a day of mourning and her funeral was attended by the secretary of the interior. From the governor on down to all the local teachers, every important citizen of the state of Hidalgo was present.[48]

That Mexican women were eager to study and earn their living is clear from the data on education included in each annual presidential message in the period from 1860 to the end of the Porfiriato in 1910.[49] We have already noted that women publicly requested the establishment of a secondary school for females in 1856 and that when it opened its doors in 1869 its female director, having discovered that not all her pupils wanted to be schoolteachers, requested that the curriculum be enlarged. Women, she maintained, could study to be doctors, agronomists, and business agents. The presidential messages of Porfirio Díaz from 1895 to 1905 note that each year more women than there were places available for sought to attend both the Escuela Nacional Secundaria de Niñas (changed to Normal de Profesoras in 1889) and the Vocational School for Women.[50] The former started with 40 students in 1869; in 1874 it had 100 students, and by 1905 it had 284 students. In September 1910, on the eve of the Mexican Revolution, the Normal de Profesoras had 401 students.[51] The vocational school, whose students came primarily from working-class families, started out with a small number of students in 1871, but by 1874 its enrollment had jumped to five hundred.[52] By 1899 there were over one thousand women enrolled in the vocational school.[53]

The unwillingness of the leaders of Porfirian society to permit women to teach beyond the primary grades became evident after 1889, when the Secondary School for Women in Mexico City became the "Normal de Profesoras."[54] Until 1889 the graduates of the secondary school were certified to teach in primary and secondary schools, but after that date the course of study at the normal school was reduced from six to four years, and its women graduates were certified to teach in primary schools only.[55]

There was also considerable resistance to women becoming licensed doctors. Courses in obstetrics were available, for women had delivered babies in Mexico from Aztec times down through the colonial period, but there was real opposition to women receiving the same medical training given to men. Matilda Montoya was the first woman who, spurred on by the need to support her widowed mother, was determined to break down the prejudice against women studying medicine.[56] As the government of Porfirio Díaz was financially unable to establish a separate school of medicine (or commerce, law, or dentistry) for women, in 1880 Montoya was finally permitted to attend classes at the National School of Medicine with male students.[57] Her example inspired another middle-class woman,

Columba Rivera, to register at the School of Medicine and to graduate as Mexico's second woman doctor.[58] By 1904 there were at least three women doctors practicing in Mexico City, with twice that many enrolled in medical school. Resistance to this development ceased when it became apparent that there was a real need for women doctors. Both Montoya and Rivera discovered that women who refused to see a male doctor would consult them, so both specialized in women's diseases. However, because a respectable woman could not go out alone or at all hours, neither of them made house calls.[59]

The first woman to receive a law degree, María Sandoval de Zarco, met even more resistance. She positively scandalized "la gente decente," ("the respectable element") when she agreed to represent a male defendant in a criminal case. After that she was obliged to practice civil law only, as Mexico's lawyers deemed it highly inappropriate for a woman to practice criminal law.[60]

By the end of the Porfiriato thousands of middle-class women worked outside the home as schoolteachers, with another 1,785 women working for the government.[61] Between 1888 and 1904 the first women were accepted, however reluctantly, in the schools of medicine, law, and commerce in Mexico City, and by 1910 a number of females began to work in commercial establishments without jeopardizing their reputation as respectable women.[62]

When one considers that up to 1856 Sor Juana's dream of higher education for women had never been realized, the advances made by Mexican women between 1869 and 1910 are really remarkable and parallel the other positive achievements of the Porfirian era, such as the building of railroads and a telegraph system, the rehabilitation of old mines and the opening of new ones, the growth of the textile and other industries, and the increase in agricultural exports.

But there was another side to the Porfirian coin as well, and much of the economic progress achieved between 1876 and 1910 was at the expense of the general populace. Many country peasants were reduced to peonage, while urban workers were mercilessly exploited in the mines, on the railroads, and in the textile mills. While more middle-class women were studying and working during the Porfiriato than ever before, the number of poorer women who became domestic servants or fell into prostitution increased considerably from 1877 to 1910. In 1895, with a population of 12.7 million, Mexico had over 275,000 domestic servants, most of them women and most of them living in virtual servitude.[63] In 1907, with only one-fifth the population of Paris, Mexico City had twice as many *registered* prostitutes, and Paris was supposed to be the sin city of the West.[64] Another sign of dysfunction in Mexican society is that about 30 percent of Mexican mothers were single parents. In addition, about 80 percent of the adult population lived in *amasiato*, or free union, yet illegitimate children had no legal rights to inheritance and could not investigate their paternity.[65]

While most lower-class women lived on the edge of misery or in its abyss, the middle and upper classes had problems of a different order. The Civil Code of 1884 accorded to adult single woman almost the same rights accorded all adult males, but a married woman really was treated as *imbecilitas sexus* ("an imbecile by reason of her sex").[66] A leading feminist in the revolutionary era, Hermila Galindo (active between 1916 and 1919), nicely summed up the legal discriminations against married women in the 1884 code:

The wife has no rights whatsoever in the home. [She is] excluded from participating in any public matter [and] she lacks legal personality to draw up any contract. She cannot dispose of her personal property, or even administer it, and she is legally disqualified to defend herself against her husband's mismanagement of her estate, even when he uses her funds for ends that are most ignoble and most offensive to her sensibilities. [A wife] lacks all authority over her children, and she has no right to intervene in their education. . . . She must, as a widow, consult persons designated by her husband before his death, otherwise she can lose her rights to her children.[67]

Why a woman should have her legal personality erased upon marriage mystified the few lawyers who favored the legal emancipation of women; presumably the legislators thought that absolute power by the husband over his wife and children would make for domestic happiness.[68]

An incipient feminist movement began in Mexico in 1904 when Dr. Columba Rivera, María Sandoval de Zarco, and the normal schoolteacher, Dolores Correa Zapata, founded a feminist monthly, *La Mujer Mexicana*.[69] Owned and edited exclusively by women, it was continuously published until 1908, when it apparently fell victim to the economic depression that had begun the previous year. With the founding of *La Mujer Mexicana*, female teachers, writers, doctors, lawyers, bookkeepers, telegraphists, and other white-collar workers whose ranks had swelled to the thousands from 1880 to 1904 began to speak out on social and economic problems. Any reader of that pioneer publication did not have to ask, as Freud once did, "What do women want?" Articles by editors and contributors, a group which included such gifted women writers and poets as Laureana Wright de Kleinhans and Rita Cetina Gutiérrez, made it clear what educated middle-class women sought for themselves and for other women as well.

In the second issue of *La Mujer Mexicana,* dated February 1, 1904, Profesora Esther Huidobro de Azua wrote that feminists wanted to see more trained women taking part in Mexico's progress. She noted that, in general, most Mexican women were not well trained either to be efficient housewives or to earn an honest living if male support was insufficient.[70] Idealization of middle- and upper-class Mexican women as selfless, helpless, dutiful, and good was not enough, she said,[71] and middle-class families with a large number of children, many of them girls, would be economically better off if daughters were trained to make their own living. Another writer in *La Mujer Mexicana* stated that Mexican feminists wanted to be better daughters, wives, and mothers. They did not want to destroy the home, a fear possessed by males suspicious of feminism. Indeed, they did not want to break family ties, but to strengthen them.[72]

Profesora Azua argued that while middle-class women could benefit most from feminism, women already trained and educated had an obligation to help those who were working in low paying jobs such as textile laborers, hatters, and seamstresses. Unless educated women came to their aid, she said, many such women would swell the already large ranks of prostitutes. Shortly after Profesora Azua's article was published, the staff of *La Mujer Mexicana* formed the Sociedad Protectora de la Mujer, one of the earliest feminist societies in Mexico intended to help working-class women. Their first action was to establish a school-factory for embroiderers and hatters, one that could train unemployed women and pay them a just wage.[73]

While such suggestions did not threaten male prerogatives, the second most important feminist demand, that only a single sexual standard prevail, most certainly did. In November 1904, the editors of *La Mujer Mexicana* reproduced an article by the Spanish writer Concepción Gimeno de Flaquer in which she stated that "una moral para los dos sexos es el constante anhelo de los feministas" ("a single standard is the constant desire of feminists").[74] She and Mexican feminists objected to the fact that, in Spanish and Latin American culture, polygamy was more general than monogamy and that this order of things was tolerated by the church and, even worse, given legal sanction in the Civil Code of 1884. That code, inspired by Napoleonic legislation of the early nineteenth century, forbade the investigation of paternity, but permitted the investigation of maternity. Adultery by a wife under any circumstances was grounds for legal separation, but she could seldom sue for legal separation. Only if a husband committed adultery in the home, kept a mistress, or created a public scandal by mistreating or permitting his mistress to mistreat his wife could a spouse seek legal redress.[75] When feminists protested against this inequity, critics insisted that they were advocating sexual license for women. Feminists countered that elevating the moral level of men and women was at stake.

Feminists also objected to the 1884 Civil Code because it deprived married women of any rights to administer or dispose of their personal property. It will be recalled that married women could not take part in civil suits, draw up any legal contract, or even defend themselves against husbands who squandered their money. A husband had complete authority in the home and over the children, and if widowed, the wife's right to act as the guardian of her children was severely limited.[76]

The editors of *La Mujer Mexicana* wanted the civil code reformed, but they did not suggest that Mexican women agitate for suffrage. Although feminists did not indicate explicitly how they expected to have the laws changed, they apparently hoped that enlightened men would lead the way. Yet the few women who sought political rights received very little male encouragement. Even Minister of Public Education Justo Sierra, a relatively enlightened man who favored greater educational and economic opportunities for women, was indifferent.

Addressing his remarks to teachers, Sierra said:

I do not want [to see you] pursue your feminism to the extreme of wishing to convert yourselves into men; that is not what we desire; [for] then all of life's enchantment would be lost. No; let men fight over political questions, [let them] form laws; you ought to fight the good fight, that of feeling, and form souls, which is better than forming laws.[77]

In summary, before the outbreak of the Mexican Revolution, an incipient feminist movement, which was led primarily by middle-class, educated women, wanted greater educational opportunities for all women, decent wages for working women, and reform of the civil code. The Mexican feminists believed that advances in all these areas would end both the double standard and the legal inferiority of married women. Yet the question of suffrage interested few women since feminism was in its infancy in Mexico and very few females had the vote anywhere in the world in 1910.

That feminism was making some headway in Mexico by 1910, however, is clear from the public alarm expressed by a number of men, including some well-known ones. As early as 1856, an anonymous but frankly misogynistic writer published an article in *El Monitor Republicano* stating that there were only five kinds of women, all bad and all guaranteed to be vexatious to their husbands. Women were either "lacrimosas, dinerosas, artifisacias, santacias, o talentacias," the writer warned prospective husbands. The first are whiners and crybabies, the second spendthrifts, the third think only of their appearance, and the fourth are forever praying and attending mass. The fifth, the "talentacias" or the bluestockings, are the worst of all. They eat little, pay no attention to their appearance, constantly bemoan the ignorance of the masses, and consider themselves unfortunate because one lifetime is not enough to read even a millionth part of what has been written. These *literatas* cannot even dress or undress themselves without the help of maids.[78]

In a less humorous vein were the attacks on feminism by the anthropologist, Manuel Gamio, who accused feminists of being unfeminine in a book published in 1916.[79] In 1904, an extremely conservative Yucatecan writer named Ignacio Gamboa had been even more explicit than Gamio. He had stated in his book, *La mujer moderna*, that feminism represented the suicide of the race. Feminists, he maintained, were against reproduction.[80] He insisted that "los divorcios, las asociaciones femeniles contra el matrimonio, el vicio lésbico, que por una inmensa desgracia toma gigantescas proporciones en los grandes centros de la población..." ("divorce, feminine associations against matrimony, and the vice of lesbianism, which, by an immense misfortune assumes gigantic proportions in the largest cities...") all resulted from the women's movement.[81] Continuing the theme that feminism masculinized women, the sociologist José Hernández predicted that Mexican women would lose "100 percent of their charms as a result of the triumphal entrance of feminism into Mexico."[82]

In 1904 a journalist who signed himself *Pistache* identified all feminists with "bad" women. "Women who speak of feminism are not good," he asserted, "and wish to call themselves 'progressive' and 'liberal' because that sounds better than what they really are."[83] Even Felix Palavicini, the writer and educator who in 1916 championed woman suffrage at the Querétaro Constitutional Convention, opposed feminism before the revolution. In a book published in 1910, Palavicini, while expressing great admiration for self-abnegating elementary schoolteachers, railed against feminism, and stated bluntly that an intellectual woman would produce physically weak or degenerate children.[84] He was quoting Herbert Spencer, who claimed that mental effort overtaxed women's brains, resulting in "a serious reaction on the physique" of women and a "diminution of reproductive power."[85]

In conclusion, the key to the development of feminism in Mexico, as elsewhere, has been the acceptance of the concept of the equality of all citizens and of the need for an educated citizenry. The adoption of a republican form of government in 1824 committed Mexican liberals to public education for all. By the middle of the nineteenth century these same liberals recognized the need for secondary education for women for social, economic, and ideological reasons. Due to internal conflicts and external threats, however, few schools were founded in the first fifty years of Mexico's history as an independent nation. Progress in developing a system of national education began in approximately 1867 and continued during the long era of Porfirio Díaz's rule from 1876 to 1910. During that period women eagerly sought secondary and vocational training. In addition, during the 1880s and 1890s the first women doctors, commercial agents, pharmacists, and other professionals received their education.

By 1904 these educated women of primarily middle-class origin began to band together. They founded Mexico City's first feminist journal, *La Mujer Mexicana*, and in its pages they demanded greater educational opportunities for all women and an end to the sexual double standard. They also formed an organization designed to help women less fortunate than themselves.

The appearance of feminism in the early twentieth century was an unexpected and largely unwelcome by-product of modernization in Porfirian Mexico. Not a few men were alarmed, and Mexico's earliest feminists— like their sisters in other countries—had to endure considerable ridicule and not a little malice from men who feared that any change or improvement in the status of women would somehow diminish male rights and prerogatives. These opponents of women's rights did not take into account that the roots of feminism lie deep in Mexican soil, going back to Sor Juana's eloquent plea in the seventeenth century for the education of women and an end to the double standard. How women fared during the Mexican Revolution is our next concern.

NOTES

1. María Elvira Bermúdez, *La vida familiar del mexicano*, México y lo mexicano, vol. 20 (México: Antigua Librería Robredo, 1955), p. 86.

2. Juana Armanda Alegría, *Psicología de las mexicanas* (México: Editorial Samo, 1974), p. 180.

3. Ernest Gruening, *Mexico and its Heritage* (New York: D. Appleton-Century Company, 1928), p. 623.

4. Gerda Lerner, *The Majority Finds its Past* (New York: Oxford University Press, 1979), p. xxi.

5. For evidence of the active role of women in Aztec society, see Anna-Britta Hellblom, *La participación cultural de las mujeres indias y mestizas en el México precortesiano y postrevolucionario*, Monograph Series, no. 10 (Stockholm: The Ethnographical Museum, 1967), pp. 299-300. For recent research on the active role of women in Mexican colonial society, see the essays by Asunción Lavrin, Edith Courturier, and Ann M. Gallagher in Asunción Lavrin, ed., *Latin American Women: Historical Perspectives*, Contributions in Women's Studies, no. 3 (Westport, Conn.: Greenwood Press, 1978).

6. Miguel León-Portilla, "La mujer en la cultura nahuatl," *Nicaragua Indígena* 2d. epoch, no. 21 (July-August 1958): 11-12.

7. Ibid., pp. 11-12 and Hellblom, *La participación cultural*, p. 91.

8. Earlier studies of Sor Juana gave 1651 as the year of her birth, but recent research reveals that she was born in 1648. See, for example, the handsomely illustrated work of Margarita López Portillo, *Estampas de Juana de la Cruz* (México: Bruguera Mexicana de Ediciones, 1979), p. 12. Gerard Flynn, *Sor Juana Inés de la Cruz*, Twayne's World Author Series, no. 144 (New York: Twayne Publishers, 1971), has a good selected bibliography of primary and secondary Spanish sources on the Mexican nun. For appreciative essays on Sor Juana in English, see Robert Graves, "Sor Juana Inés de la Cruz," *Encounter* 1, no. 3 (December 1953): 5-13; Irving A. Leonard, "A baroque poetess," in his *Baroque Times in Old Mexico* (Ann Arbor, Mich.: University of Michigan Press, 1959), pp. 173-89; and Jean Franco, *An Introduction to Spanish-American Literature* (Cambridge, Eng.: Cambridge University Press, 1969), pp. 21-23.

9. According to Flynn, *Sor Juana*, p. 11, "no other writer of colonial Latin America has received more praise than Sor Juana Inés de la Cruz." However, an edition of her complete works did not begin to appear until 1951. See Sor Juana Inés de la Cruz, *Obras completas*, eds. Alfonso Mendez Plancarte and Alberto G. Salceda, 4 vols. (México: Fondo de Cultura Económica, 1951-57). A one volume paperback edition of her complete works is Francisco Monterde, ed., *Obras completas*, 2d ed., Sepan Cuantos, no. 100 (México: Editorial Porrua, 1972).

10. See Germán Arciniegas: *América mágica*, 2 vols. (Buenos Aires: Editorial Sudamericana, 1961), 2:43.

11. Ibid., 2:42.

12. Amado Nervo, *Juana de Asbaje* (Madrid: Hijos de M. G. Hernández, 1910).

13. For a fine translation into English of "Hombres necios" see Robert Graves, "Sor Juana Inés de la Cruz," pp. 10-12. A much abbreviated English translation of her letter to Sor Filotea is in Benjamin Keen, ed., *Readings in Latin American Civilization*, 3d ed., 2 vols. (Boston: Houghton Mifflin Co., 1974), 1: 308-13. For the complete letter in Spanish see Sor Juana Inés de la Cruz, *Poesía, teatro y prosa*, 2d ed., Antonio Castro Leal, Colección de Escritores Mexicanos, no. 1 (México: Editorial Porrua, 1965), pp. 251-302.

14. Ludwig Pfandl, *Die zehnte Muse von Mexico* (Munich, 1946), as described by Jean Franco, *An Introduction to Spanish American Literature*, pp. 21-22.

15. The translation is by Robert Graves, "Sor Juana Inés de la Cruz," p. 11.

16. "Respuesta a Sor Filotea de la Cruz," in Sor Juana Inés de la Cruz, *Poesía, teatro y prosa*, pp. 281, 285.

17. Ibid., p. 283.

18. Ibid., p. 280.

19. Ibid., pp. 284-85.

20. In 1790 there were some 56,932 women in Mexico City, and those aged eight to sixteen numbered 8,753. There were six schools for young women at the time, with a total enrollment of 759. Of these, 266 attended Las Vizcaínas. At about the same time Madrid also had six schools for girls, but with a total of only 455 students, considerably less than in the colony. Genaro García, *Leona Vicario, heroína insurgente*, Biblioteca Enciclopedia Popular, no. 36 (México: Secretaría de Educación Pública, 1945), p. 10.

21. The quotation is from a letter to the author, 1971.

22. For information on Doña Josefa Ortíz de Domínguez, see Luis Rubio Siliceo, *Mujeres célebres de la independencia de México* (México: Talleres Gráficos de la Nación, 1929), pp. 12-16. For material on Leona Vicario, see the aforementioned work by Genaro García, and C. A. Echánove Trujillo, *Leona Vicario: La mujer fuerte de la independencia*, Vidas Mexicanas, no. 21 (México: Ediciones Xochitl, 1945).

23. Rubio Siliceo, *Mujeres célebres*, p. 12.

24. Echánove Trujillo, *Leona Vicario*, p. 167. The nation's veneration of Leona Vicario was not shared by Lucas Alamán, the distinguished but staunchly conservative historian of the independence movement who believed that the rupture with Spain was a tragic mistake. In a typical put down, Alamán asserted that Leona Vicario was moved to join the insurgents simply and solely out of love for the young Yucatecan lawyer and patriot, Andrés Quintana Roo, one of the authors of Mexico's first constitution. According to Alamán, a woman was incapable of disinterested patriotism; he further insisted that emotion, not reason, governed the actions of Leona Vicario and all women. In a spirited reply that is generally overlooked, even by students of the independence movement, Leona Vicario chided Alamán and wrote:

> Admit, Sr. Alamán, that it is not love alone which is the mover of the actions of women; that they are capable of a lively interest in all matters, and that the desire for the glory and liberty of one's country are not sentiments alien to women; rather, such sentiments act on them with greater force, because the sacrifices of women are always, no matter what their object or cause, the most disinterested, and it appears that women seek no more recompense for their sacrifices than acceptance. [Ibid.]

25. Ernesto de la Torre Villar, *La constitución de Apatzingán y los creadores del estado mexicano* (México: Universidad Nacional Autónoma de México, Instituto de Investigaciones Históricas, 1964), p. 382.

26. Ibid., p. 383.

27. *Proyecto de decreto sobre enseñanza libre en el estado libre de Jalisco. Formado por una Comisión nombrada al efecto por el gobierno, presentada a su honorable Congreso y mandado imprimir de orden del mismo* (Guadalajara, Jal: Imprenta del C. Urbano Sanroman, 1826), p. 24.

28. Ibid., p. 25.

29. Ibid., p. 27.

30. Prospectus of the *Semanario de las Señoritas Mejicanas. Educación científica, moral y literaria del bello sexo*, vol. 1 (México: Imprenta de Vicente G. Torres, 1841), pp. 2-7.

31. On this matter see Oscar Lewis, "Husbands and Wives in a Mexican Village: A Study in Role Conflict," *American Anthropologist* 51 (October-December 1949): 602-10.

32. Quoted in Moisés González Navarro, *El porfiriato: La vida social*, vol. 5 of *Historia moderna de México*, ed. Daniel Cosío Villegas (México: Editorial Hermes, 1957), p. 410.

33. Quoted in Barbara Ann Bockus, "La mujer mexicana en el siglo XIX a través de la novela" (M.A. Thesis, Universidad Nacional Autónoma de México, Escuela de Verano, 1959), p. 36.

34. Ibid., pp. 37-45. "Si queremos evitar la prostitución. . .eduquemos a la mujer," ("If we wish to avoid prostitution. . .let us educate women") wrote the Socialist José Romero Cuyas in an essay entitled "La emancipación de la mujer," which originally appeared in the newspaper *La Comuna Mexicana* in 1874. It is reprinted in *La mujer y el movimiento obrero en el siglo XIX: Antología de la prensa obrera* (México: Centro de Estudios Históricos del Movimiento Obrero Mexicano, 1975), pp. 73-74.

35. González Navarro, *El porfiriato*, p. 413.

36. *Semanario de las señoritas mejicanas*, pp. 2-3.

37. Ibid., pp. 6-7.

38. Ibid., p. 14. At a very early age Guillermo Prieto was left penniless. He came to the attention of the eminent jurist, Andrés Quintana Roo, who aided the young man in finding employment and in continuing his education. Prieto's feminism may have been inspired by the example of Quintana Roo's wife, Leona Vicario, the independence heroine mentioned earlier.

39. In 1857, for example, only 187,757 of Mexico's school age population of 1,557,403 were attending any kind of educational establishment in the republic. Of those attending school, 98,151 were males and 87,279 were females. The remaining 2,327 were adults of both sexes. See Luis González y González, Emma Cosío Villegas, and Guadalupe Monroy, *La república restaurada: La vida social*, vol. 4 of *Historia moderna de México*, ed. Daniel Cosío Villegas (México: Editorial Hermes, 1957), p. 701.

40. *El Monitor Republicano*, 14 April 1856, p. 2.

41. Ibid., p. 3. An original copy of the *Decree of President Comonfort Establishing a Secondary School for Girls in Mexico City* (México: Secretaría de Gobernación, 1856), is in the Lilly Library at the University of Indiana in Bloomington.

42. Secretariat of Public Education, *La educación pública en México a través de los mensajes presidenciales desde la consumación de la independencia hasta nuestros días* (México: Secretaría de Educación Pública, 1926), p. 13. There is no mention of female education in the annual presidential messages from 1823 to 1860. See ibid., pp. 1-13.

43. González y González, *La república restaurada*, p. 709. Actually, the state of Jalisco, where liberal officials set up a comprehensive elementary school system in the 1820s, established a secondary school for young women—the *Liceo de Niñas*—in Guadalajara in 1862. In that year over three hundred pupils were in attendance, according to the *Memoria de la Junta Directiva de Enseñanza Pública sobre el estado que guarda este ramo en fin del año de 1862* (Guadalajara, Jal.: Tipografía de José María Brambila, 1863), p. 18. After French troops occupied Mexico and installed Habsburg Maximilian as emperor, the Guadalajara Liceo de Niñas was patronized by the Empress Carlota. In 1866 the Liceo had 248 students who were instructed in sewing, embroidery, writing, calligraphy, gram-

mar, religion, drawing, music, piano and guitar, and French. See Angélica Peregrina, "Noticia de establecimientos para la educación de niñas en el Departamento de Jalisco en 1866," *Boletín del Archivo Histórico de Jalisco* 2, no. 3 (September-December 1978), pp. 18-19. Documentary information about the school in the 1870s and 1880s is found in the *Colección de los decretos, circulares y ordenes de los poderes legislativo y ejecutivo del Estado de Jalisco*, 38 volumes in two series (Guadalajara, Jal.: Tip. de M. Pereztete [and others], 1874-1910); vol. 6 (1874-76), pp. 3-11; vol. 7 (1878-80), pp. 166-82; and vol. 9 (1884), pp. 372-85. This collection of published documents is found in the Archivo Histórico de Jalisco. It registers all the legislation passed in Jalisco from 1823 through 1910. I am grateful to Dr. Asunción Lavrin for bringing to my attention materials on the Guadalajara secondary school for girls.

44. González y González, *La república restaurada*, p. 709.

45. Ibid., p. 735. There is an excellent description of this school by Juan de Dios Peza, "La beneficencia en México," *Boletín de la Sociedad Mexicana de Geografía y Estadística*, 3d epoch, 5 (Mexico, 1881), pp. 684-93. For data on early vocational education for women in Jalisco, see Mario Aldana Rendón, "La escuela de Artes y Oficios y la educación artesanal en Jalisco, 1867-1877," *Boletín del Archivo Histórico de Jalisco* 2, no. 3 (September-December 1978):2-10.

46. Gruening, *Mexico and its Heritage*, p. 630. That elementary education attracted more women than men is indicated by the data for 1905 on the number of normal school graduates in Mexico City. The Normal School for Men graduated ten students, while fifty-eight women graduated from the women's normal school. Secretariat of Public Education, *La educación pública*, pp. 133-34. And in 1917 there were 993 male and 2,237 female teachers imparting primary education in the Federal District. Ibid., pp. 192-93.

47. *La Mujer Mexicana. Revista mensual, científico-literaria, consagrada a la evolución, progreso y perfeccionamiento de la mujer mexicana*, March 1, 1904, p. 9.

48. Ibid.

49. Secretariat of Public Education, *La educación pública*, pp. 13-165.

50. On April 1, 1895, Díaz noted that "the normal schools, especially the one for females, have had to end registration because there are no more places left." Ibid., p. 60. In 1905 he remarked that more women than ever could be accommodated wanted to study at the normal school. Ibid., p. 136. In 1906 Díaz noted that enrollments in the vocational school continued to grow, but he did not provide figures. Ibid., p. 142.

51. Ibid., p. 163.

52. González y González, *La república restaurada*, p. 735.

53. Secretariat of Public Education, *La educación pública*, p. 88.

54. Ibid., p. 42.

55. González Navarro, *El porfiriato*, p. 627.

56. Biographical data on Matilda Montoya is found in Laureana Wright de Kleinhans, *Mujeres notables mexicanas* (México: Tipografía Económica, 1910), pp. 534-41.

57. Ibid., p. 539.

58. *La Mujer Mexicana*, 1 August 1904, p. 1.

59. Advertisements on the end pages of *La Mujer Mexicana* 1 April 1904. Thirty years before, the Socialist journalist José Romero Cuyas argued that Mexico needed women doctors to attend the many female patients who refused to be examined by male doctors. See his essay, "La emancipación de la mujer," in *La mujer y el movimiento obrero*, pp. 74-75.

60. *La Mujer Mexicana*, 1 October 1904, pp. 1-2; and González Navarro, *El porfiriato*, pp. 414-15.

61. José E. Iturriaga, *La estructura social y cultural de México* (México: Fondo de Cultura Económica, 1951), p. 14n.

62. González Navarro, *El porfiriato*, p. 415.

63. Iturriaga, *La estructura social*, p. 16. In 1900 Mexico City had 25,074 maids out of a female population of 195,251. See Luis Lara y Pardo, *La prostitución en México* (México: Librería de la Vda. de Charles Bouret, 1908), p. 25.

64. Lara y Pardo, *La prostitución en México*, pp. 19, 29. Lara y Pardo estimated that from 1900 to 1906 an average of 3,600 unregistered prostitutes were arrested each year in Mexico City. Most of the registered prostitutes who stopped at the Health Inspection Office for regular checkups said that they became prostitutes out of economic need and out of ignorance. Only five percent were literate. See González Navarro, *El porfiriato*, p. 413.

65. González Navarro, El *porfiriato*, pp. 409-10. In 1906 the Liberal party included in its platform a plan for ending the legal discrimination against illegitimate children. González Navarro comments that "acaso estas discusiones resultaron un tanto bizantinas en un país de tan abrumador predominio del concubinato," (perhaps these discussions were somewhat Byzantine in a country where concubinage was so overwhelmingly prevalent); p. 412.

66. Genaro García, *La desigualdad de la mujer* (Thesis presented by the student Genaro García in his professional examination as a lawyer; México: Imprenta de Francisco Díaz de León, 1891), p. 11.

67. *Estudio de la señorita Hermila Galindo con motivo de los temas que han de absolverse en el segundo congreso feminista de Yucatán* (Mérida, Yuc.: Imprenta del Gobierno Constitucionalista, 1916), p. 14.

68. Genaro García, *La condición de la mujer* (México: Compañía Limitada de Tipográficos, 1891), p. 47.

69. *La Mujer Mexicana*, 1 February 1904, p. 1.

70. Ibid., p. 2.

71. This idealization of women was also common in the United States in the nineteenth century. See David M. Kennedy, *Birth Control in America: The Career of Margaret Sanger* (New Haven, Conn.: Yale University Press, 1970), pp. 51-63.

72. *La Mujer Mexicana*, 1 April 1904, p. 2.

73. Ibid., 1 March 1904, p. 9.

74. Ibid., 1 November 1904, p. 11.

75. García, *La condición de la mujer*, pp. 77-78.

76. García, *La desigualdad de la mujer*, pp. 9-19.

77. Quoted by González Navarro, *El porfiriato*, p. 415.

78. "Memorias de ultratumba de un viejo," *El Monitor Republicano*, 14 April 1856, p. 2.

79. Manuel Gamio, *Forjando patria* (México: Librería de Porrua, 1916), pp. 211-12.

80. Ignacio Gamboa, *La mujer moderna* (Mérida, Yuc.: Imprenta Gamboa Guzmán, 1906), p. 51.

81. Ibid., p. 37.

82. Quoted in Paula Alegría, "La educación de la mujer," (Tesis: Escuela Nacional de Maestros, México, 1930), p. 47.

83. Quoted in Angeles Mendieta Alatorre, *La mujer en la revolución mexicana*, Biblioteca del Instituto Nacional de Estudios Históricos de la Revolución Mexicana, no. 23 (México: Talleres Gráficos de la Nación, 1961), p. 36.

84. Felix Palavicini, *Problemas de educación* (Valencia: F. Sempere y Cía., 1910), pp. 54-64.

85. Kennedy, *Birth Control in America*, p. 48.

2

WOMEN AND THE MEXICAN REVOLUTION, 1910-1920

Women played a significant but, until recently, largely overlooked role in the complex and destructive civil war known as the Mexican Revolution of 1910-20.[1] A number of women who were trained and educated in the vocational and normal schools and molded by the incipient feminist movement of the Porfirian era actively sought involvement in the struggle during its various phases. A much larger number of rural and urban lower-class women found themselves caught up in the struggle and had no choice but to become actively involved, especially in the military aspects of the revolution. Still others, numbering in the hundreds of thousands, and including women of every class, were among the victims and casualties of that conflict.[2] Lastly, women of primarily but not exclusively middle- and upper-class origins who strongly identified with the Catholic church became active and bitter enemies of the decidedly anticlerical leadership of the revolution.

There were many precedents for the active involvement of women in the armed struggle of 1910-20. Mexican writers interested in the female role in the epic revolution have accentuated the fact that women had given aid and comfort and had also, when necessary, fought alongside their men in all the wars the country had previously experienced. This included the independence movement of 1810-20, the North American invasion of 1846-48, and the Reform War and French intervention of 1857-67.[3] However, the educational and vocational opportunities offered to and

This chapter originally appeared in *The Americas* in July 1980 and is reprinted here, with changes, by permission of *The Americas*.

accepted with such alacrity by women between 1876 and 1910 added an intellectual dimension to their participation in their country's crisis. Three persons who best exemplify the intellectual contributions of women to the Mexican Revolution are the journalist Juana Belén Gutiérrez de Mendoza (1875-1942), the schoolteacher Dolores Jiménez y Muro (1848-1925), and the feminist private secretary of President Carranza, Hermila Galindo de Topete (1896-1954).

The journalist, poet, and political radical Juana Belén Gutiérrez de Mendoza was born in 1875 in Durango of an Indian mother and a mestizo father who worked at such varied jobs as blacksmith, horse tamer, and farm worker.[4] Trained as a typographer, in 1901 Juana joined the Precursors or early critics of Don Porfirio who called for an anticapitalist revolution by Mexico's peasants and workers against the Díaz regime.[5] Angered by the foreign domination of Mexico's banks, insurance companies, mines, textile mills, and railroads; aroused by the increasing impoverishment, exploitation, and debasement of the country's landless peasants and workers; and disturbed by the resurgence of the Catholic church in Mexico, in May of 1901 Juana established an anti-Díaz newspaper, *Vesper*, in the extremely traditionalist provincial capital of Guanajuato.[6]

Fearless, combative, and an uncompromising foe of social injustice, political tyranny, and religious obscurantism, in her little newspaper Juana Gutiérrez passionately defended the wretchedly treated miners of Guanajuato. She attacked, with equal vehemence, the clergy of one of the most religiously conservative states in all of Mexico.[7] Contradicting the stereotypes of the timid and religious Mexican woman, and attacking head-on the reactionary milieu of Guanajuato, Señora Gutiérrez early developed an inimitable style that led the anarchist journalist and editor of *Regeneración*, Ricardo Flores Magón, to hail her newspaper as "virile".[8] A later admirer, Santiago R. de la Vega, stated that, like the Spanish feminist novelist Emilia Pardo Bazán, Juana Gutiérrez had "trousers in [her] style."[9]

A few copies of *Vesper* and other newspapers that Juana edited between 1901 and 1941 survive in the Hemeroteca Nacional (Newspaper Archives) in Mexico City, and all of them attest to the refreshing candor, incisiveness, and vigor of her writing. She castigated Díaz for failing to carry out his obligations as leader of the Mexican people, but pointed out to her readers that they and all Mexican citizens had also failed to exercise their rights.[10]

While millions of supposedly enfranchised Mexican men silently endured the abuses of the Díaz regime, Juana Gutiérrez protested against the harshness and brutality of Don Porfirio's government, especially against workers.

Díaz's response was to treat Juana Gutiérrez as he treated the male foes of his regime. She was thrown into jail several times between 1904 and 1920. The horrors of the women's section of the prison of Belén in Mexico City fortified rather than broke this extraordinary woman's spirit, and she celebrated the beginning of the tenth year of *Vesper* in May 1910 by assuring her readers that she was back at her post, ready once again to do battle against a tottering dictatorship.[11]

In May 1910, sensing that the fall of Don Porfirio was imminent (he left Mexico for exile a year later), Juana warned her readers that "the fall of a tyrant is not the end of tyranny."[12] She endorsed and supported Francisco I. Madero, the leader of the Anti-Reelectionist party, for president in two editorials in the May 8, 1910, edition of *Vesper*. This brought the wrath of Díaz down upon her once again. As prison had not silenced her, her press was confiscated. Later, in July of 1911, Angela Madero, the politically active sister of the Anti-Reelectionist opponent of Díaz, secured for Doña Juana, never in her life a woman of means, two-thousand pesos to compensate her for the earlier seizure of her printing press by the recently deposed government.[13]

In time Señora Gutiérrez became disillusioned with Madero, who ignored her warning that Díaz's fall was not the end of tyranny once he had been elected to the presidency in October 1911. Don Francisco retained many Díaz holdovers in the government and in the military and turned against his early supporters, including the agrarian leader Emiliano Zapata. The latter wanted land reform and an end to local political tyranny immediately and not, as Madero promised, at some vague date in the future.

In early 1919, when the most violent phase of the revolution was over, with Madero dead since 1913, Zapata recently assassinated, and Venustiano Carranza soon to meet a bloody end for attempting to perpetuate a new tyranny, Doña Juana surveyed the revolutionary panorama from 1900 to 1919 in the pages of her new weekly, *El Desmonte*. The title *Vesper*, she said, had to go. "It was too visionary, too idealistic. . . . [Now] the countryside is bristling with old logs; one must dismount."[14]

In her editorial of June 15, 1919, entitled "Desmontada," Juana Gutiérrez spoke for a war-weary and exhausted people who hungered for the social and economic justice that nine years of fratricidal strife had failed to bring about. "In general," she wrote, "the situation is not better nor worse than it was in 1900, when the movement [against Díaz] began. . . . As for the so-called principles that have been inscribed on the flags of combat, with the exception of that part of. . . [Zapata's] 'Plan de Ayala' dealing with the agrarian question, there has been nothing that scarcely merits the name of principle."[15]

As for leadership, the situation was disheartening after so much struggle. One could expect little from Mexican labor, she asserted, for it was plagued by bad leadership and demagoguery. In fact, the Mexican labor movement was so disoriented from within that agents of the United States's AFL were succeeding in drawing the Mexican unions into the orbit of a country which Juana believed exploited not only workers but whole nations.

One could expect even less leadership from political parties, for in Mexico, Juana wrote, "the name of party is applied to any half dozen individuals who have some very special and determined interests, interests they wish to protect by gaining office."[16] And there was nothing to expect or hope for from the regime of President Carranza, for Carrancismo or constitutionalism was pictured by Juana Gutiérrez as a cadaver "that has produced nothing but impurities, monstrosities and bastardies."[17] Nor could one expect anything from Pancho Villa, who was now a captive of reactionary forces.

For Juana Gutiérrez, Emiliano Zapata had been the most authentic voice of revolutionary Mexico, of Indian Mexico, and of village Mexico. But Zapata was dead, assassinated on orders of Carranza. All the good Zapata had sought to do for the disinherited peasants of Morelos was being undone by the enemies of land and liberty.

The picture that Doña Juana painted of Mexico in 1919 was very grim, but it was realistic, as realistic as the classic novels Martín Luis Guzmán and Mariano Azuela wrote about the revolution. Juana Gutiérrez did not despair, however, and all her life she urged workers and peasants to participate in the electoral process, "not," as she wrote, "to integrate power, but to disintegrate it, as a means of forming, not a new oligarchy, but of transforming the oligarchies into truly public administrations."[18] Juana Belén Gutiérrez de Mendoza could not be bought, could not be intimidated, could not be frightened, and could not be broken. Yet, except for the handful of Mexicans who have read her vigorous prose, she has been forgotten, while her exhortations are ignored by those who govern Mexico.

Dolores Jiménez y Muro had much in common with Juana B. Gutiérrez. She too was a political radical (a socialist by conviction), a poet by avocation, a contributor to left-wing journals, and a fervent admirer of Emiliano Zapata.[19] She too was jailed in the Belén penitentiary in the days of Díaz and during the counterrevolutionary government of Victoriano Huerta in 1913-14. And Dolores Jiménez y Muro was also hailed as a "viril escritora de combate" ("virile, combative writer") by her male revolutionary colleagues.[20]

If we know little of Juana Belén Gutiérrez's private life, we know hardly more about that of Dolores Jiménez y Muro, except that she was an unmarried schoolteacher who was born in Aguascalientes on June 7, 1848, and died in Mexico City on October 15, 1925. We also know that Profesora Jiménez contributed poems and articles to various journals under assumed names and was a member of the editorial staff of the feminist journal *La Mujer Mexicana* in 1905. She was also active in the Precursor Movement from 1900-1910 and in the Revolution from 1910 until the death of Zapata.[21]

In March 1911, Dolores Jiménez y Muro became involved in the "Complot de Tacubaya," a conspiracy intended to bring Madero to power by a rebellion near the nation's capital.[22] Like all projected uprisings in Mexican history, it was preceded by a "plan," which served to morally justify armed rebellion and which also explained the goals of the conspirators. The principal ideas of the plan were agreed upon by the revolutionary leaders, who then turned to their esteemed colleague, Profesora Jiménez, to give form to these ideas.[23] The political and social plan that she put together and that was published on March 18, 1911, is of great interest to students of the ideological currents of the Mexican Revolution. Unlike the party platforms of early 1910 or Madero's Plan de San Luis Potosí of October 1910, the schoolteacher's plan recognized the need for far-reaching social and economic reforms and not simply the need for a political change at the top.[24]

James D. Cockcroft, in *Intellectual Precursors of the Mexican Revolution, 1900-1913*, correctly points out that the "Political and Social Plan Proclaimed by the States of Guerrero, Michoacán, Tlaxcala, Campeche, Puebla, and the Federal District (March 18, 1911) was . . . a forthright continuation of the principles set down in the *Partido Liberal Mexicano* (PLM) [Mexican Liberal Party] Program of 1906, with only slight modification.''[25] Both documents insisted on the need for agrarian reform, maximum hours of work, and improved wages and working conditions for rural and urban workers. Both documents also called for educational reform, the restoration of municipal autonomy, and the protection of the indigenous race.[26] They also favored a strong economic nationalism, a crucial point on which all anti-Díaz revolutionaries agreed. Profesora Jiménez's plan stipulated that at least half the employees of any foreign firm operating in Mexico were to be Mexican nationals, whether in blue-or white-collar positions, and that Mexicans were to be paid the same salaries as their foreign counterparts.[27]

At the same time, Profesora Jiménez proposed other reforms in her plan which are not found in the July 1, 1906, PLM program drawn up by her friends and colleagues, the Flores Magón brothers, Juan Sarabia, Librado Rivera, and other important intellectual precursors of the revolution.[28] For example, point seven of her plan called for decentralization of Mexico's educational system. Carranza may very well have had Señorita Jiménez's idea in mind when he assumed leadership of the revolution and was in control of Mexico City by mid-1915. Beginning in that year he sought to abolish the highly centralized educational system in Mexico and to substitute one that allowed the localities to finance and control their own schools. The noble experiment came to an end when Alvaro Obregón succeeded to the presidency in 1920. Before 1915, only the federal government had collected enough taxes to finance schools, inadequate as they were. From 1915 to 1920, a further decline in the already low educational standards evidently led to a return to the highly centralized system of the prerevolutionary period.

Profesora Jiménez also diverged from her colleagues' 1906 platform in devoting one of the fifteen points of her plan to what is still one of Mexico's most serious problems—expensive and inadequate housing for the vast majority of Mexican urban dwellers. In her many years as a schoolteacher in urban institutions, Profesora Jiménez was no doubt deeply distressed by the wretched housing available to the families of the children she taught. She was also probably very conscious of the relationship between unsanitary housing and poor health. In point thirteen of her revolutionary plan, Dolores Jiménez y Muro urged that as soon as circumstances permitted, the value of urban properties was to be revised in order to establish equitable rents and in order to ensure that poor people were no longer forced to pay relatively high rents to real estate speculators. She hoped that eventually real estate taxes would be used "to construct comfortable and hygienic housing for the working classes, to be paid for in long-term installments."[29]

Dolores Jiménez y Muro left her personal imprint on the March 1911 Social and Political Plan by specifying in it, as no other contemporary revolutionary plan did, that the daily wages of rural and urban workers of *both* sexes were to be increased. The schoolteacher, herself a wage earner, seems to have been more aware than her male colleagues that large numbers of women worked outside of the home. Although the 1910 census judged that women made up only 8.8 percent of the "economically active" population in the republic, in 1902 at least 17 percent of the workers in the textile industry, most of it foreign-owned, were women.[30] What was happening in Mexico by 1910 was a phenomenon to be observed in every industrializing country. "Once economic production moved to the factory," observes Mirra Komarowsky in *Women in the Modern World*, "women were forced to follow their work beyond the confines of their homes."[31] Señorita Jiménez was keenly aware of this fact and was also conscious that, contrary to the conclusions drawn by the 1910 census, many women in the rural areas also worked outside of the home.

The 1910 Mexican census's determination that females made up only 8.8 percent of the economically active population bears examination, since at least one writer interested in the role women played in the 1910 Revolution has cited these census figures as evidence that until the coming of the revolution women lived in seclusion at home.[32] What the directors of the 1910 census did was to imagine that a clear-cut division of labor between the sexes existed in Mexico, that men were the providers and women, the homemakers.[33] Actually, in 1910 about 80 percent of the population had been largely unaffected by the modernization that took place between 1876 and 1910, and in Mexico, as in all other preindustrial societies, "women were also economic providers through the multitude of goods and services supplied by home industry."[34] The 1910 census ignored the fact that in rural areas women spent most of their time outside the home, raising animals, fruits, vegetables, and flowers for sale in town and village markets when they could,[35] or working as peons alongside the men when they were landless. The 1910 census takers also ignored the women living in the vicinity of railroad stations who spent a large part of the day preparing food to sell to hungry passengers travelling on second- and third-class coaches on the nation's 15,000 kilometers of railroads. This phenomenon is still observable when one travels by train in Mexico today.

Other economically active women who escaped the attention of the census takers were artisans, pieceworkers, street vendors, boardinghouse owners, and many others deemed "economically inactive" by short-sighted bureaucrats in Mexico City. Naturally, working women did nothing to correct the erroneous impressions held by the census takers. An admission that they earned money might have led unwelcome tax collectors to their door and, in addition, would have deflated male pride. Since most of the questions asked by the census takers were probably answered by or in the presence of male members of the household, it is understandable that few men were willing to admit to outsiders that their wives or daughters or sisters were providers. Instead, they told the census takers what they wanted them to hear and which the latter were predisposed to believe anyway. Profesora Jiménez y Muro was more attuned to reality and sought to bring the problem of working women to the attention of the revolutionary leaders.

When Emiliano Zapata was shown a copy of Profesora Jiménez's plan and saw that point nine called for the restitution of usurped village lands, he said to Gildardo Magaña: "That is exactly what we are fighting for—so that the lands we were robbed of shall be returned."[36] When Zapata was told that the plan was written by a very "enthusiastic, cultivated, and revolutionary señorita," the agrarian leader said he had need of such people in his ranks, and he expressed the wish that she and other intellectuals would join his cause in the state of Morelos. After the death of Madero, Dolores Jiménez y Muro joined the legendary leader of the south and remained in Morelos until Zapata's assassination in 1919.[37] An active revolutionary since 1900, by then Señorita Jiménez had passed her seventieth birthday. Despite her contributions to the Mexican Revolution, she has received little attention from students of that conflict.

Of all the women who participated in the Mexican Revolution between 1915 and 1919, none was better known nor more influential than Hermila Galindo.[38] She was the author of several feminist and political tracts, editor from 1915 to 1919 of the feminist journal *Mujer Moderna*, and one of Carranza's most energetic propagandists in Veracruz, Tabasco, Yucatán, Campeche, and other Mexican states.[39] In addition, Galindo represented Carranza abroad, and in September 1916, gave a series of public lectures explaining Carranza's doctrine in Havana, Cuba.[40] Then, in 1919, her public career came to an abrupt end, and though she lived until 1954, Hermila Galindo took no part in the feminist movement of the 1920s and 1930s, a movement she helped to inspire.

Her spectacular rise and enigmatic fall raise a number of questions about Hermila Galindo that have not been pondered before. How is it that such a young woman—she was only fifteen when the revolution broke out—became the most prominent exponent of feminism in Mexico during the Carranza era? Why did her career come to such a sudden end in 1919, and why was it followed by complete silence and oblivion for the remainder of her life? What specific ideas and strategies did she contribute to the women's movement that developed during and after the Mexican Revolution?

Hermila Galindo was the most prominent exponent of feminism in Mexico between 1915 and 1919 because she had skills and abilities that Carranza was shrewd enough to recognize and exploit. Born in Lerdo, Durango, in northern Mexico in 1896, Hermila Galindo was a precocious and diligent student. She studied English and became an accomplished stenographer and typist by the time she was fifteen.[41] Moving to Mexico City in 1911, she joined the liberal ''Abraham González'' Club in that city. As a gifted speaker, she was named orator of the club and was selected to give a welcoming speech to Carranza upon his triumphal entry into the capital after the fall of the counterrevolutionary government of General Victoriano Huerta.[42]

Carranza was impressed with the young woman's enthusiasm and oratorical skill and invited her to join his government, which was temporarily moved to Veracruz in late 1914 when his rivals, Zapata and Pancho Villa, drove him out of Mexico City. In an effort to build up political support in his unrelenting drive for the presidency and to counter the popularity of Zapata and Villa among the masses, in 1914-15 Carranza wooed representatives of worker and peasant groups. Similarly, he sought the support of women, or hoped at least to reduce their enmity against his conspicuously anticlerical positions. He found a willing ally in Galindo, who wrote newspaper articles and gave numerous speeches before women's groups extolling Carranza's leadership abilities. She also urged women to join revolutionary clubs, no doubt to counter the influence of Catholic women's groups, which were becoming bastions of antirevolutionary sentiment. Galindo also began publication of the journal *Mujer Moderna*, which had the twin aim of promoting feminist ideas and supporting Carranza's bid for power. She steadfastly supported Carranza after he was elected president in 1917 and remained loyal to him despite mounting criticism of his venality, duplicity, and bad faith as the supposed leader of Mexico's peasantry and urban working classes.[43]

There are a number of reasons why Hermila Galindo's career came to an abrupt end in 1919. First of all, her continued association with Carranza and her well-known role of propagandist for his cause made all of his enemies her enemies. Second, in 1919 she supported the wrong man to succeed Carranza in the presidency (General Pablo González), thus losing Carranza's confidence without gaining that of the men who were to wield power in Mexico after Carranza's demise.[44] Third, her ideas were anathema to most "revolutionaries," not to speak of conservative Mexicans. Emboldened by Carranza's support, between 1915 and 1919 Hermila Galindo adopted advanced positions on divorce, sexuality, religion, prostitution, and politics, which shocked even secular-oriented middle-class women with some education.[45]

After General Alvaro Obregón succeeded to the presidency in 1920, Galindo no doubt discovered that she was "*quemada*" ("burned"), one of the "outs" whose attempt to regain influence would be blocked. In 1923 she married Manuel de Topete, and we hear no more of her after that.[46] Presumably she settled down to the busy life of housewife and mother. Her feminism, it would appear, had been a youthful fling. And her sudden fall from favor in 1919 was a warning to other feminists that close association with an incumbent president was not the most effective way to pursue feminist goals in Mexico.

Yet despite the brevity of Hermila Galindo's career as a feminist, she left her mark on the women's movement in Mexico. A number of the ideas she championed were endorsed by prominent feminists in the 1920s and 1930s, and at least one of her strategies for drawing attention to the feminists' demand for political equality was to be used over and over again by activists from 1925 until 1940.

Hermila Galindo was one of Mexico's first feminists to frankly state that the Catholic church was the chief obstacle to the promotion of feminism in the country. She maintained that the Mexican church, which had remained impervious to change throughout the nineteenth and early twentieth centuries, was the principle agent for the subjection of women. Galindo was convinced that the hierarchy would oppose the movement for women's rights in Mexico through its control of Catholic women's organizations and its influence among conservative newspaper editors. Feminists of the Porfirian era had made no references to religion in public, for although they might have privately held views similar to those of Galindo, they knew that any expression of anticlericalism would offend public sensibilities, especially at a time when Don Porfirio was busy reducing church-state antagonisms.[47]

However, a new surge of extreme anticlericalism did develop during the revolution. The church had become so identified with the Porfirian regime that the revolutionaries, whether liberals, socialists, anarchists, or nationalists, all agreed that the power and influence of the church had to be curbed. As a result of this near unanimity among revolutionaries, a number of articles of Mexico's 1917 constitution went beyond the anticlerical measures of the 1850s and 1870s and sought, among other things, to drastically reduce the number of clergy in Mexico and to prohibit church schools from functioning.[48] Hermila Galindo's anticlerical stance reflected the mood of this period. While feminists after Galindo avoided references to religion and the church in their public utterances to gain as wide a following as possible, most of them had no allegiance to the Catholic church, while a few became prominent in the Protestant YWCA.[49]

One of the chief challenges to the Catholic church in the revolutionary period was Carranza's proposal, which was adopted by most Mexican states in 1915-17, that divorce be permitted in Mexico. Until his divorce decree of January 29, 1915, only legal separation was in force in the country. After that date remarriage was legal. Hermila Galindo staunchly endorsed the Carranza decree, agreeing with him that divorce would have a "moralizing effect" in Mexico.[50] She believed that it would be a great boon to unhappily married women, and her position was adopted by the more advanced and secular-oriented feminists of her day and by mainstream feminists in the late 1920s and 1930s. If feminists objected to the divorce decree, it was in large part because Carranza's law discriminated blatantly against women.

Hermila Galindo was also very frank in her endorsement of sex education in the schools, arguing that the major reason why women were held in subjection was because of religious preoccupations, ignorance, and an absurd lay education. She shocked the country's more moderate feminists when, in her "La mujer en el porvenir" ("Woman in the Future"), read at Mexico's first feminist congress in Yucatán in January 1916, she argued that women have a strong sex drive. She insisted that women needed to understand the nature of their sexuality and that schools needed to include a study of the human reproductive system in a required course in biology. Once again she brought up the relation of women and the church by asserting that "religion has wanted woman to ignore her sexuality in order to always keep her in ignorance and in order to exploit her."[51] Her plea for recognition and understanding of female sexuality and for the need for sex education in the public schools received little support at the time. However, the need for sex education in the schools became a consistent part of feminist demands in the succeeding decades, and during the presidency of Lázaro Cárdenas (1934-40) sex education in the public schools was first introduced.[52]

Hermila Galindo insisted that women should enjoy the same rights and privileges as men, and to achieve equality females needed a modern, relevant, and well-rounded education. Galindo affirmed that a woman had to get rid of the pervasive idea that she was useful only for bearing and raising children; she had to break away from the yoke of ignorance that reduced her to "a being without consciousness and without aspirations."[53] With a proper education, Galindo maintained, women "would appreciate the advantages of independence and the beauties of truth."[54]

Hermila Galindo also joined the prerevolutionary feminists in insisting that the first step to achieving equality of the sexes was to drastically revise the civil code, since it extinguished the legal rights of women when they married.[55] Pressure for revision of that code led Carranza to issue the Law of Family Relations in 1917. He also campaigned steadily for a revised civil code, which was finally completed in 1926.

Hermila Galindo was one of the earliest feminists to insist that, to achieve legal equality, women first had to be given the right to vote.[56] Before 1910 few feminists talked about female suffrage, no doubt because effective use of the vote had never been a reality in Mexico. But Madero's revolution and his insistence on "effective suffrage and no reelection" kindled a new interest in the need for democratic procedures in Mexico, and with it came an interest in woman suffrage among the more advanced feminists.[57] Galindo argued that women pay taxes and contribute to society when they work for a living. A woman is as liable to the law as any man, she noted. Galindo added that if women were guilty of breaking the law they received the same penalties as men. This being the case, she concluded, there were no rational grounds to deny women the right to vote and to run for office.[58]

When Carranza called a constitutional convention to meet at Querétaro to revise the 1857 constitution, Hermila Galindo and a number of other women petitioned its members to provide for woman suffrage.[59] However, Felix Palavicini, Carranza's education director, was the only member of the Querétaro convention to seriously champion the feminists' cause. His colleagues simply ignored or laughed at his proposal that they at least debate the question of woman suffrage.[60]

Shortly after the 1917 constitution was completed and its provisions were made public, Hermila Galindo informed the leading newspapers in Mexico City, including Palavicini's *El Universal*, that she intended to run for a seat in the Chamber of Deputies in the coming elections.[61] She was backed by hundreds of supporters. Galindo made it clear that she had no hope of being elected, but that she had two other objectives in mind. One was to bring to the attention of the nation and its leaders the large number of women who wanted to vote. The other was to set a precedent for the next generation.[62]

The electoral law of 1918 dashed the hopes of Hermila Galindo and other feminists by limiting the vote to males. However, during the 1920s and 1930s feminists employed Ms. Galindo's tactics by showing up at the polls on election day and by campaigning for office in order to force the Mexican Congress to change the electoral law. Their efforts were not rewarded until after World War II. In Mexico, as in France, it was the fear that the vast majority of women would vote for church-endorsed candidates that delayed woman suffrage.

Unlike her contemporaries, Juana Belén Gutiérrez de Mendoza and Dolores Jiménez y Muro, Hermila Galindo did not suffer imprisonment for expressing her ideas. However, she did have to face a great deal of hostility, scorn, and ridicule from both men and women for expressing unpopular views and for speaking up on subjects that still remain taboo in Mexico.[63] Her willingness to face strong opposition encouraged many feminists of her own generation and of the succeeding one as well.

In addition to these three outstanding women of the revolutionary era, many other educated, middle-class females, the greater part of them schoolteachers, took an active part in the Revolution of 1910-20. When Francisco I. Madero decided to run for the presidency against Díaz in the 1910 elections, women established their own liberal, antireelectionist clubs or were invited to participate in Maderista political clubs established by men.[64] Typical of these women was Julia Nava de Ruisánchez, a teacher and writer who was also an active feminist all her adult life. She participated in the prerevolutionary feminist movement and was one of the founders of the Sociedad Protectora de la Mujer (Women's Protective Society) in 1904.[65] She was an early critic of Díaz and joined the Precursor Movement at the same time that she affiliated with feminists seeking to help working-class women.[66]

Another normal school graduate who joined the political opposition to Díaz was Profesora Elisa Acuña y Rossetti. In 1903 she was made a member of the Mesa Directiva (Executive Board) of the opposition "Ponciano Arriaga" Confederation of Liberal Clubs. Profesora Acuña aided Juana Gutiérrez in publishing *Vesper*, and she too was imprisoned in Belén prison for opposing Don Porfirio's government. After Madero's assassination, she followed the example of Profesora Jiménez and joined Zapata in Morelos.[67]

A third normal school graduate, María Arias Bernal, was also a fervent Maderista. After Madero's death, she was jailed by Huerta for holding periodic demonstrations against his government at the grave of Madero.[68] A fourth woman to join the political opposition to Díaz and later to Huerta was María Hernández Zarco, a typesetter who worked at various printing establishments in Mexico City from 1910 to 1913. When her employer refused to print Senator Belisario Domínquez's speech denouncing Huerta as a tyrant, the young woman agreed to print the speech that night, knowing full well that her action might cost her her job as well as her freedom.[69] She printed the speech and delivered it to the senator, and on October 7, 1913, Belisario Domínquez, who was to pay with his life for his courageous denunciation of Huerta, stated in his last speech in the Senate:

My fellow senators, I am happy to tell you that I found someone willing to print this speech. Do you wish to know, gentlemen, who printed it? I shall tell you, for the honor and glory of the Mexican woman. A young lady printed it.[70]

That night Senator Domínquez was murdered, but as a street in Mexico City named after him attests, he was not forgotten. However, María Hernández Zarco has been completely forgotten.[71]

In the period from 1909 to 1913 large numbers of women also signed public protests and took part in dangerous demonstrations. For example, on September 6, 1910, a number of women in Mérida, Yucatán, sent a petition to the wife of Porfirio Díaz asking her to intercede with her husband on their behalf in requesting a national amnesty for political prisoners.[72] A few days later, members of a feminist club in Mexico City, the Hijas de Cuauhtémoc (Daughters of Cuauhtémoc), were part of a peaceful group of anti-Díaz demonstrators who were arrested as they sought to place floral wreaths at the tomb of the heroes of independence. This same group had previously collected one-thousand signatures calling for Díaz to step down and requesting that a truly free election take place.[73]

When armed rebellion proved to be the only means of removing Díaz from office, middle-class women participated in the struggle in a number of ways. They gave money to various revolutionary groups and engaged in a number of undercover activities, including the gathering of arms and ammunition, expediting letters, and passing on information to revolutionaries.[74] During the fighting, a number of women served as nurses, both on the battlefield and behind the lines.

One of the most celebrated nurses of the revolutionary period was Beatriz González Ortega (born in 1873), who was director of the normal school in Zacatecas at the outbreak of the revolution. In June of 1914 she turned the school into an emergency hospital when Pancho Villa and his army attacked the city. She and her associates tended the wounded of both sides, whether federal troops or Villistas. When Pancho Villa triumphed, he demanded to know who among the wounded were federal troops, as it was his practice, as well as general practice among most of the guerrilla leaders, to routinely execute prisoners. Profesora González, who had previously burned the telltale uniforms of the wounded, answered that she made no distinction between federals or revolutionaries and that "here I tend only wounded Mexicans."[75] Pancho Villa immediately ordered that she and the doctor who was helping her be whipped until they identified the federal troops. They received the lashing with stoicism, but still refused to talk. Villa was furious and ordered that she and the doctor be shot. At the last minute friends of the teacher intervened, and Villa relented. Beatriz González Ortega apparently taught Pancho Villa a lesson in the quality of mercy, for he treated her with the greatest respect for the remainder of the revolution. The courage and humanity of Profesora González was not forgotten, and in 1955 a school bearing her name was inaugurated at Fresnilla, Zacatecas.[76]

While sheltered middle- and upper-class Mexican women could avoid involvement in the revolution, this was not true for most rural and urban lower-class women. These women of the popular classes became the famed *soldaderas* of the revolution, the women who accompanied the military units. José Clemente Orozco immortalized them in his paintings of Zapatistas, the graphic artist José Guadalupe Posada glamorized them on the covers of widely distributed popular ballad sheets, and the lens of the photographer Casasola captured their true image.[77] The *soldadera* peoples the novels of the Mexican Revolution and is the subject of such revolutionary songs as "Valentina," "Adelita," and "Marieta." Foreign observers of the revolution, including John Reed and Rosa E. King, made her a familiar figure to the English-speaking world.

Yet the word *soldadera*, as it applies to a clearly observable phenomenon in Mexican history, is not to be found in standard dictionaries of the Spanish language, not even in dictionaries that include Spanish-American colloquialisms.[78] This may account, in part, for the varied translations of the word into English. Robert Quirk insists on calling *soldaderas* "camp followers,"[79] while Frederick C. Turner refers to them politely as "lady soldiers."[80] However, the most accurate translation of the term is supplied by Rosa E. King, whose *Tempest Over Mexico* records this remarkable Englishwoman's experience in revolutionary Mexico. Mrs. King refers to the *soldadera* as simply "the Mexican soldier's woman."[81] Francisco L. Urquizo, who fought in the revolution and later wrote novels about it, concurs with Mrs. King's description and adds: "Si es soldadera tiene que seguir a su hombre, sea donde sea." ("If she is a *soldadera*, she must follow her man, wherever that may be.")[82]

The Mexican *soldadera* followed her man when he left home and joined a large fighting force. When and if he died, she became another soldier's woman, as John Reed pointed out in his poignant account of Elisabetta in *Insurgent Mexico*.[83]

The *soldadera* made her first appearance in Mexican history during the independence movement. In that conflict, as in all subsequent wars in Mexico, the opposing armies had no commissary or medical corps. They depended on women to forage for and prepare the soldiers' food, wash their clothes, and tend their wounds.[84] In 1901, Julio Guerrero provided a vivid description of *soldaderas* in *La génesis del crimen en México*:

[They are the women] who accompany the husband or lover on his military marches, carrying a child, a basket filled with clothing, and working utensils. In the abandoned battlefield they carry water to their wounded masters and despoil the dead of their clothing. . . . They are jealous and courageous. . . and their moral code has two precepts. . . absolute fidelity to and unconditional abnegation for the husband or lover, and respect for the officers of the battalion or regiment.[85]

Rosa E. King had many opportunities to observe *soldaderas* in the state of Morelos, for as she noted, "the Zapatistas were not an army; they were a people in arms."[86] She praised their patience, stoicism, resignation, resourcefulness, and perseverance; qualities that made it possible for them and the men they tended to survive. Mrs. King wrote:

The wonderful soldiers' women—none like them in the world for patience and bravery at such times—combed the town [Cuernavaca] for food, and when they could not get it any other way they stole, whatever and wherever they could, to nourish their men. These were the type of women who one day, in the north, when their men ran short of ammunition, tied their *rebozos* (shawls) to the ammunition cart and hauled it to them. I bow in respect to the Mexican women of this class. . . . The Mexican women who marched with the Mexican soldier, who went before him to the camping place to have refreshment ready, who nursed him when sick and comforted him when dying, were helpers and constructionists, doing their part in laying the foundation of this liberal government of today.[87]

To be sure, not all the women who accompanied the military units were self-abnegating angels of mercy. The fighting, as Charles Cumberland reminds us, was vicious and bloody,[88] and some women, already hardened by a life of misery and degradation before the revolution, turned vengeful and sadistic. A good example is La Pintada (The Painted Woman) in Mariano Azuela's realistic novel of the Mexican Revolution, *The Underdogs.* Although Azuela does not tell us anything about La Pintada's life before the revolution, she conforms exactly to R. H. Mason's 1849 description of Mexican women among the unemployed poor in urban centers. He noted that such women "are accustomed to brawls and warfare, and are in the habit of carrying concealed knives with them as a matter of course."[89]

Except in emergencies, the *soldaderas* did not normally bear arms or participate in the actual fighting. In addition, *soldaderas* were to be found only in the *columnas gruesas* ("heavy military columns") that usually, but not always, travelled by train.[90] Gustavo Casasola notes, however, that some women joined *columnas volantes* ("flying columns") as *soldados rasos* ("privates") and, if they proved themselves in battle, were made officers and leaders of men.[91] He noted that such women

needed to masculinize themselves completely; both inwardly and outwardly: dress like a man and act like a man; go on horseback, like the rest, be able to endure long marches and, at the hour of combat, prove with weapon in hand that she was no longer a *soldadera*, but a soldier.[92]

Rosa E. King observed the phenomenon of women soldiers among the Zapatistas, and early on in her book she noted that when President Madero met Zapata in Cuernavaca on July 12, 1911, "Zapata arranged a 'review' in his honor. . . . Among the troops were women soldiers, some of them officers."[93] One of these women might very well have been Coronela María de la Luz Espinosa Barrera of Yautepec, Morelos, whose service record shows that she was on duty as a Zapatista from 1910 to 1920.[94] In 1973 La Coronela was eighty-six years old and in failing health, but despite age and infirmity, she remained a gifted raconteur with a phenomenal memory. Her remarkable narrative of her rise from *soldado raso* to colonel in Zapata's army, which was taped over a period of many hours in 1973-74, is the stuff of which novels are made. In fact, La Coronela of Yautepec bears some resemblance to "La Negra Angustias" of the novel of the same title by Francisco Rojas González. Rojas modelled his character on a real woman, Remedios Farrera, who, like María de la Luz Espinosa Barrera, rose to the rank of colonel during the revolution.[95] There are some interesting parallels in the lives of both women before the revolution. In both cases, their mothers died at their birth. Neither father remarried, and both women felt sharply the pain and loneliness of being a motherless child. Both took care of goats as children, and the goats provided them with both nourishment and companionship. On December 8, 1973, at a party celebrating her eighty-sixth birthday, La Coronela tearfully recalled that when she was very small other children asked her who her mother was; who nourished her. She pointed to a favorite goat amid the peals of laughter of her insensitive peers.

Each woman also killed someone. La Negra Angustias killed a man who tried to rape her; and La Coronela, the woman who was having an affair with her husband. Convicted of murder, La Coronela of Yautepec spent five years in Belén prison. She was released in 1910 and returned to Morelos with her father just at the time that Zapata was mounting his rebellion against the landlords in Morelos who had seized what remained of village and communal lands.

At loose ends and hardened by some five years in prison, María de la Luz Espinosa Barrera volunteered for service with the Zapatistas. She, as did La Negra Angustias, donned male attire and wore male clothing for the duration of the revolution. La Coronela, vividly recounting her first battle, remembered as if it were yesterday how she and her comrades could hear nothing but the chattering of their teeth and the nervous jingling of their spurs. As they waited for the enemy to approach, they tried to swallow but found that the saliva would not flow. Others were embarrassed by their incontinence.

In the end María de la Luz Espinosa Barrera proved herself in battle over and over again, and Emiliano Zapata himself signed the papers promoting her to lieutenant colonel. After his assassination, like many of his loyal followers, she stopped fighting and returned to the ruins of her home in Morelos. A restless soul, La Coronela became an itinerant vendor of clothing and found it impossible to conform to the accepted passive and timid female role. Like the notorious Ensign Nun of the seventeenth century, La Coronela smoked, drank, gambled, and feared no man. Her eccentricities were always accepted by her neighbors in Yautepec.[96]

La Coronela is but one of many admittedly unusual women who became officers and led men in battle during the revolution. There was also Rosa Mójica Bobadilla of Jojutla and Amelia Robles, "El Güero" (The Blond) of Río Balsas, who still wore male attire and still carried pistols in 1973. There were also other women soldiers and officers known by nicknames such as "La Chata" (Flatnose), "La Güera Carrasco" (The Blonde Carrasco), and "La Corredora" (The Scout).[97] Few of them received official recognition for their services during the revolution and La Coronela was one of the few to live long enough to qualify for a modest pension as a veteran of that epic struggle.[98]

In sharp contrast to the tough and hardened *soldaderas* and women soldiers of the revolution were the women who became the revolution's victims. These were the timid and passive women, like Camila in Azuela's *The Underdogs*, who could not fend for themselves. During the worst years of the fighting, rape followed by murder became as commonplace as the routine shooting of prisoners. Hundreds of thousands of women (it is believed that as many as two million Mexicans perished between 1910 and 1920) died in the gratuitous slaughter that marked the period or perished as a result of disease, exposure, and hunger.[99]

There was a drastic decline in the food supply during the revolution,[100] and as Turner notes, "hunger, the specter that stalked all Mexican cities and especially Mexico City, forced women into prostitution."[101] Even before the Revolution of 1910, Mexico City (the only city in the republic for which we have figures) had a disproportionately large number of prostitutes. For instance, Dr. Luis Lara y Pardo found that in 1905 Mexico City had 11,554 registered prostitutes, while an additional 4,371 unregistered prostitutes were apprehended that same year.[102] This was out of a total population of 195,251 women, of whom 71,737 were in the age group of fifteen to thirty. Since 95 percent of the known prostitutes in Mexico City were in this age group, Lara y Pardo calculated that 120 women per thousand between the ages of 15 and 30 were prostitutes, probably one of the highest figures of any city in the Americas or Europe at that time.[103] These figures make clear the dreadful social imbalances in Mexico that led to the revolution.

With food supplies declining from 1910 to 1917 to the levels of the late eighteenth century,[104] it is very possible that during the revolution more than half the female population turned to prostitution in order to stay alive. The problem was so rampant that José Clemente Orozco did a particularly gruesome series of watercolors on prostitutes in Mexico City called "The House of Tears."[105] Degas and Toulouse Lautrec had treated prostitutes with some sympathy and understanding in their work, but in Orozco's series "the misogynist joins company with the uncompromising moralist who hates the sinner far more than the sin."[106] Orozco's attitude mirrored that of society in general, and prostitutes were treated as criminals rather than as victims by all but a handful of enlightened men and women.[107] Only a few revolutionaries, including Salvador Alvarado, the profeminist governor of Yucatán from 1915 to 1918, sought to help these despised women. The problem of exceedingly large numbers of prostitutes persisted in Mexico into the 1920s and 1930s, and the need to recognize and deal with this social malaise was emphasized by leading feminists in the postrevolutionary era.

It is not difficult to see why many Mexicans, alienated by the brutality and thirst for revenge that was unleashed between 1910 and 1920, became enemies of the revolution. This was especially true of middle-and upper-class Catholics, men and women alike, who were horrified at the way churches were desecrated, statuary burned or used for target practice, and bishops, priests, and nuns abused and packed off to exile aboard freight cars.[108]

The anticlericalism which erupted in the 1910-1920 Revolution had its origin in the church-state conflict of the 1830s to the 1870s. Between 1876-1910 Porfirio Díaz found it politically prudent to make a truce with the church, and during his rule he agreed to ignore the restrictions on the church written into the 1857 constitution. That document had prohibited the taking of monastic vows and monastic establishments in Mexico.[109] It had also prohibited the church from owning property other than church buildings[110] and had given the federal authorities exclusive power to "exercise, in matters of religious worship and outward ecclesiastical forms, such intervention as [is] by law authorized."[111] Lastly, the Constitution of 1857 defined marriage as a civil contract, which meant that persons married in a church service alone were not considered legally married by the civil authorities.[112]

The Constitution of 1857 was the work of an anticlerical intelligentsia bent on modernizing Mexico. A distinct minority, these intellectuals did not reflect the beliefs and practices of the majority of mostly rural Mexican men, women, and children. For the ordinary people, religion was a pervasive force and an integral part of their lives. While religious influence undoubtedly declined between 1857 and 1910 among the 10 percent of the male and female population educated in laical schools, the rest of the nation continued in the old ways. The masses flocked to the shrines of the Indian Virgin of Guadalupe and to the Black Christ of Chalma.[113] They continued to venerate the saints, celebrating their feast days with colorful fiestas, processions, and ceremonies. Whether there were priests available to say mass or hear confession did not matter much; folk Catholicism could survive without the presence of clergy.[114]

This was not true for the elite conservatives, who were formal and orthodox Catholics. Despite their political defeat by 1867, they retained or regained their economic power and social prestige during the Porfiriato. Under their leadership and aided by the strong religious sentiments of the masses, the Catholic church experienced a revival in the period from 1876 to 1910. Monastic establishments reopened discreetly, and foreign clergy flocked to Mexico to minister to the needs of the more affluent Mexicans, whose children were sent to religious schools. The prohibitions against church ownership of property were circumvented, and the contributions of the faithful made it possible for the hierarchy to live in relative splendor and for the church to run hospitals, orphanages, asylums, and other charitable institutions.[115]

The circumvention of the religious provisions of the 1857 constitution, the revival of church influence and prestige, and the identification of the clergy with the rich and powerful and with the Porfirian regime angered the Mexican liberals and radicals, who together brought down the dictatorship. The result was a new surge of anticlerical and, indeed, antireligious sentiment that once again tore the country apart from 1910 to at least 1935. Martín Luis Guzmán stated in *The Eagle and the Serpent* that he knew only one revolutionary general who was a believer.[116] The rest were either enemies of priests, like Villa, or enemies of religion altogether, like Obregón, Calles, Pablo González, Alvarado, Diéguez, Mújica, Jara, and countless other revolutionary generals.[117]

The influence of these generals was paramount in the writing of the articles dealing with religious matters for the 1917 constitution. The new constitution reiterated all the provisions of the 1857 document mentioned earlier, and in addition prohibited any religious corporation from imparting primary instruction.[118] Churches were declared to be national property, and the state legislatures were given the exclusive power "of determining the maximum number of ministers of religious creeds, according to the needs of each locality."[119] The 1857 liberals had sought to curb the power of the church and to reduce its influence among the people. The 1917 radicals were determined to succeed where their forebears had failed, even if it meant the complete destruction of religious freedom in Mexico.

Radical women like Juana Belén Gutiérrez, Dolores Jiménez y Muro, and Hermila Galindo shared the anticlerical and antireligious sentiments of their revolutionary colleagues. In addition, a large number of public schoolteachers and socially aware women workers were either neutral, indifferent, or hostile to the Catholic church, and it was from the ranks of these women that the feminist movement of the 1920s and 1930s was to draw its strength. While not necessarily enjoying numerical superiority over secular-oriented women, women from conservative families, who were staunch defenders of the Catholic faith and its clergy, were much more conspicuous than the latter in defense of their ideas. The revolutionaries were united only by their hatred of Díaz and Huerta, but were otherwise at odds. Sometimes they were divided over ideas but oftentimes by purely personalistic considerations. In this situation, it was difficult for women who abhorred what Díaz and Huerta represented to be as noticeable as the women who were united in defense of something as concrete and palpable as the institutional church and specific members of its clergy.

The important state of Jalisco in western Mexico provides a good example of the active role conservative women played in defense of the church between 1910 and 1920. Jalisco was one of the most religious states in the republic, and when free elections were held there in 1912, the voters, who were all male, of course, gave 43,000 votes to congressional candidates of the recently formed Catholic party and only 12,900 votes to all other candidates.[120] Given these figures, it is not surprising that the Association of Catholic Women of the Archdiocese of Guadalajara (capital of Jalisco) which was established on April 26, 1913, at a meeting presided over by Archbishop Francisco Orozco y Jiménez, had 10,200 *socias* ("members") within a year.[121] By mid-1914 there were at least sixteen Catholic women's organizations in Guadalajara made up of teachers, white-collar workers, maids, students, and housewives.[122] As was true of all Catholic lay organizations in Mexico, these groups were controlled and directed by the hierarchy.[123] When Archbishop Orozco y Jiménez was forced into exile from May 1914 to November 1916 another clergyman, Canon Luis Navarro, took over as director of the women's religious groups.[124]

Between 1913 and 1918, when the conflict between the civil authorities and the church came to a head, the Association of Catholic Women of Guadalajara established a number of *Circulos de Estudios Femeninos* ("Feminine Study Circles") to prepare middle- and upper-class young women for social action. This social action consisted of establishing catechism classes to prepare children for first communion and of setting up day and night schools to provide religious education for working-class children and working adults, respectively.[125] Helped by a friendly press in Jalisco's capital, the *socias* distributed one-hundred-thousand copies of proclerical newspapers among their sympathizers. At Christmas in 1913, the *socias* also distributed nine-thousand pieces of used clothing among the poor of Guadalajara. In May of 1914, just before Archbishop Orozco y Jiménez left Guadalajara, they set up a soup kitchen for the destitute adjoining Calvary Church in that city.[126]

Troubled times for Catholics in Jalisco began when the Constitutionalist army, led by Carranza's chief military strategist, Alvaro Obregón, occupied Guadalajara in mid-1914. Obregón, soon to march on Mexico City, left a garrison there under the command of the rabidly anticlerical General Manuel Diéguez. As happened in city after city occupied by the revolutionaries after the collapse of Victoriano Huerta's government, in late 1914 and early 1915 all the priests in Guadalajara were arrested and detained and then shipped out of the country. Nuns also were forced into exile.[127] Diéguez closed every church in Guadalajara, and the city remained "for many months without priests or Catholic schools."[128]

While the women of Jalisco were in a state of shock for months, on Sunday, February 21, 1915, Catholic women in Mexico City organized a demonstration protesting the arrest of all the clergy in the capital. They clashed with a counterdemonstration led by radical workers of the Casa del Obrero Mundial, affiliated with the Industrial Workers of the World, which resulted in two deaths and in many injuries.[129] Tragic confrontations like this were to occur over and over again for the next fifteen years.

Between mid-1915 and early 1917, with Carranza now in full command of the constitutionalist armies, the religious persecution lessened and Diéguez permitted some churches to reopen in Guadalajara and some clergy to return to their parishes. The conflict erupted again, however, in 1917 and 1918, and Catholic women played a prominent role in the events of those two years. At the end of July 1917, for example, several committees of Catholic women, lawyers, and students went to Mexico City to protest in person to Carranza the closing of churches in Guadalajara where the pastoral letter of Archbishop Orozco y Jiménez against the new constitution had been read.[130] Then, in July 1918, Governor Diéguez issued Decrees 1913 and 1927, which were intended to enforce Article 130 of the new constitution by requiring that priests register with the public authorities. In addition, only one priest would be permitted to minister to each five-thousand inhabitants.[131]

At the same time that Decrees 1913 and 1927 were being issued and approved by the state legislature, Archbishop Orozco y Jiménez was arrested and exiled again, and this time he was packed off in a cattle car to the border. The protests against Orozco y Jiménez's second exile and Decrees 1913 and 1927 merged,[132] and while the clergy ended all church services in Jalisco on September 1, 1918, the women of Jalisco directed an economic boycott in the state. The economic boycott proved so successful that on February 8, 1919, Governor Diéguez rescinded Decrees 1913 and 1927. When the legislature approved his actions in March, the six-month-old economic paralysis came to an end, and church services resumed. The crucial role women played in this first test of Article 130 was to be repeated in 1926, when the same tactics employed in Jalisco were attempted on a national scale.[133] No wonder that all but a few male revolutionaries looked upon Mexican women as a threat to their cause. The positive contributions of women to the revolution were ignored, while the activities of Catholic women against revolutionary leaders were constantly kept in mind.

Women, then, played a very important and varied role in the Mexican Revolution. They were active on the front, behind the lines, and in favor of or against one of the most significant social revolutions of the twentieth century. Yet, except for occasional references to *soldaderas*, most historians of that revolution have ignored the active role of Mexican women as precursors, journalists, propagandists, political activists, and soldiers. Only artists and novelists have given serious attention to the way the revolution victimized millions of women and, outside of religious publications, there has been a vast silence concerning the active role women played in opposing the anticlerical aspects of the Mexican Revolution. In addition, to date very few historians have noticed that the revolution acted as a catalyst for the women's movement in Mexico.[134] This was especially true in the state of Yucatán, which was to host the first two feminist congresses in Mexican history. Why and how Yucatán became a center of feminist activity during the revolution will be examined next.

NOTES

1. Only one monograph has appeared on the subject. See Angeles Mendieta Alatorre, *La mujer en la revolución mexicana*, Biblioteca del Instituto Nacional de Estudios Históricos de la Revolución Mexicana, no. 23 (México: Talleres Gráficos de la Nación, 1961). See also Frederick C. Turner, "Los efectos de la participación femenina en la revolución de 1910," *Historia Mexicana* 16 (1966-67); 603-20; and Shirlene Ann Soto, *The Mexican Woman: A Study of Her Participation in the Revolution, 1910-1940* (Palo Alto, Cal.: R & E Research Associates, 1979), pp. 22-48.

2. It is believed that as many as two million Mexicans lost their lives in the revolution. Charles Cumberland, *Mexico: The Struggle for Modernity* (New York: Oxford University Press, 1968), pp. 245-46. He calculates "that from the first three censuses and the last an approximation of a growth-rate curve may be

constructed, and on such a curve the population of 1921 should have fallen between 17 and 16 million—but the census of that year counted slightly less than 14.5 million.'' The actual figure was 14,334,780. The 1910 census counted 15,160,369 Mexicans, so that if both sets of figures are correct the nation had 825,589 fewer inhabitants in 1921 than in 1910. See Estados Unidos Mexicanos. Secretaría de Industria y Comercio, Dirección General de Estadística, *Censo general de población, 1960: Resumen general* (México: Secretaría de Industria y Comercio, 1962), p. xxii.

3. This is noted by Mendieta Alatorre in *La mujer en la revolución mexicana*, pp. 22-26; and by Miguel Alessio Robles in *Voces de combate* (México: Imp. Manuel León Sánchez, 1929), p. 151. Earlier, José María Vigil, director of the Biblioteca Nacional de México and a strong supporter of women's rights in the last quarter of the nineteenth century, noted the activist role women played during the French intervention. See his *La mujer mexicana* (México: Secretaría de Fomento, 1893), pp. 27-29. For a modern study of the role of women during the French intervention, see Adelina Zendejas, *La mujer en la intervención francesa*, Colección del Congreso Nacional de Historia para el Estudio de la Guerra de Intervención, no. 2 (México: Sociedad Mexicana de Geografía y Estadística, 1962).

4. Mendieta Alatorre, *La mujer en la revolución mexicana*, p. 33.

5. For an excellent study of the Precursor Movement, see James D. Cockcroft, *Intellectual Precursors of the Mexican Revolution, 1900-1913* (Austin: University of Texas Press, 1968).

6. *Vesper* 1, no. 1 (May 1901).

7. Mendieta Alatorre, *La mujer en la revolución mexicana*, p. 33.

8. Ibid., p. 31.

9. Ibid.

10. *Vesper* 3, no. 34 (July 1903), p. 1.

11. *Vesper*, 8 May 1910, p. 1.

12. Ibid.

13. Mendieta Alatorre, *La mujer en la revolución mexicana*, p. 32.

14. *El Desmonte*, 15 June 1919, p. 4.

15. Ibid., p. 1.

16. Ibid.

17. Ibid.

18. Ibid., p. 2.

19. Mendieta Alatorre, *La mujer en la revolución mexicana*, p. 96.

20. Ibid., pp. 96-103.

21. Ibid., p. 96. Cockcroft mentions her twice in his *Intellectual Precursors of the Mexican Revolution*, pp. 80, 189. She was a member of the editorial staff of *La Mujer Mexicana* from July 15, 1905, until the end of that year.

22. Gildardo Magaña, *Emiliano Zapata y el agrarismo en México*, 2 vols. (México: n.p., 1934), 1:119-20.

23. Ibid., 1:121.

24. See ibid., 1:122-24 for the full text of the plan. It is also reprinted in Mendieta Alatorre, *La mujer en la revolución mexicana*, pp. 97-100.

25. Cockcroft, *Intellectual Precursors of the Mexican Revolution*, pp. 188-89.

26. The full text of the Partido Liberal Mexicano 1906 platform is found in ibid., pp. 239-45.

27. Point 12 in the 1911 Plan Político Social in Mendieta Alatorre, *La mujer en la revolución mexicana*, p. 97.

28. Cockcroft, *Intellectual Precursors of the Mexican Revolution*, pp. 129-33.

29. Mendieta Alatorre, *La mujer en la revolución mexicana*, p. 97.

30. Donna M. Wolf, "Women in Modern Mexico" (unpublished essay, 1975) quoting Antonio Peñafiel, *Estadística industrial* (México: Secretaria de Fomento, 1902), pp. 2-72, *passim*. See also Ana María Hernández, *La mujer mexicana en la industria textil* (México: Tipográfica Moderna, 1940), pp. 27-38, for the active role of women in the textile workers' strikes of 1907 and in the Precursor Movement.

31. Mirra Komarowsky, *Women in the Modern World: Their Education and Their Dilemmas* (Boston: Little, Brown & Co., 1953), p. 50.

32. Frederick C. Turner, *The Dynamic of Mexican Nationalism* (Chapel Hill: University of North Carolina Press, 1968), p. 185.

33. Komarowsky, *Women in the Modern World*, p. 50.

34. Ibid.

35. Of women's lot in the rural community of San José de Gracia, Michoacán, between 1861 and 1882, Luis González observes that "most of the hard work fell to the women: grinding corn on the metate, making tortillas, cooking meals for the men, keeping the fire going, cleaning, washing clothes, sewing, darning, carrying water, scolding their husbands and children, taking care of the pigs and chickens, bleaching wax, making cheese, weaving—in short, keeping so busy with household chores and home industries that they got no rest. It was only the men who could allow themselves the vice of idleness." Luis González, *San José de Gracia: Mexican Village in Transition*, The Texas Pan American Series (Austin: University of Texas Press, 1974), p. 49. For examples of the work rural women perform outside the home in contemporary Mexico see Mary L. Elmendorf, *La mujer maya y el cambio*, SEP-SETENTAS, no. 85 (México: Secretaría de Educación Pública, 1972), pp. 21-22, 24-26, 28, 35, 42, 52, 59-63, 69, 74, 79-80, 93-94, 103, 105-106, 114-121, 145.

36. Magaña, *Emiliano Zapata y el agrarismo en México*, 1:125.

37. Ibid., 1:126.

38. For an interesting evaluation of her own career, see Hermila Galindo, *La*

doctrina Carranza y el acercamiento indolatino (México: n.p., 1919), pp. 159-61.

39. Ibid., pp. 160-61, and Mendieta Alatorre, *La mujer en la revolución mexicana*, pp. 79-80. No copies of *Mujer Moderna* were found in the Hemeroteca Nacional in Mexico City, but two essays Galindo prepared for the first and second feminist congresses in Mérida summarize her views on women. The first is *La mujer en el porvenir* (Mérida, Yuc.: Imprenta y Litografía de "La Voz de la Revolución," 1915). The second is *Estudio de la Srita. Hermila Galindo con motivo de los temas que han de absolverse en el segundo Congreso feminista de Yucatán* (Mérida, Yuc.: Imprenta del Gobierno Constitucionalista, 1916), (hereafter cited as *Estudio*).

40. Galindo, *La doctrina Carranza y el acercamiento indolatino*, p. 161.

41. Mendieta Alatorre, *La mujer en la revolución mexicana*, p. 79.

42. Ibid., pp. 79-80.

43. Galindo, *La doctrina Carranza y el acercamiento indolatino*, pp. 1-16, *passim*.

44. Hermila Galindo, *Un presidenciable. El General don Pablo González* (México: Imprenta Nacional, 1919). Carranza chose Ignacio Bonillas, Mexican ambassador to the United States, to succeed him, while Alvaro Obregón led the successful revolution to oust Carranza. See Charles Cumberland, *Mexican Revolution: The Constitutionalist Years* (Austin: University of Texas Press, 1974), pp. 404-13.

45. Galindo notes in her November 1916 *Estudio* (see footnote 39 for the complete title) that her *La mujer en el porvenir* aroused a storm at the First Feminist Congress of Yucatán because her ideas "afectaban hondas preoccupaciones que tienen su raíz en el pasado" ("affected deep prejudices rooted in the past"), p. 5.

46. Mendieta Alatorre, *La mujer en la revolución mexicana*, p. 80. Mendieta states that Hermila Galindo continued to write books and articles after Carranza's death, most of which were never published.

47. Galindo's views on women and the church are most fully explored in her November 1916 *Estudio*, pp. 14-18.

48. For an article by article comparison of the 1857 and 1917 constitutions, see H. N. Branch, ed. and trans., "The Mexican Constitution of 1917 Compared with the Constitution of 1857," in *The Annals of the American Academy of Political and Social Science* 69-71 (January-May 1917). Article 3 of the 1917 constitution prohibited any church or minister from directing schools of primary education. Article 130 forbade foreign clergymen in Mexico and permitted the states to limit the number of clergy who could officiate within their boundaries. See ibid., pp. 2, 103-6.

49. A good example was the feminist Elena Landázuri, who was president of the YWCA in Mexico in the early 1920s. See Ida C. Clarke and Lillian B.

Sheridan, eds., *Women of 1924 International* (New York: Women's News Service, Inc., 1924) pp. 253-54.

50. Galindo, *Estudio*, pp. 18-20.

51. Galindo, *La mujer en el porvenir*, pp. 1-12.

52. José Castillo y Pina, *Cuestiones sociales* (México: Impresores, S.A., 1934), pp. 162-64.

53. Galindo, *Estudio*, p. 12.

54. Ibid.

55. Ibid., p. 14.

56. Ibid., p. 25.

57. At the First Feminist Congress held in Mérida, Yucatán, in January 1916, the majority of the delegates approved a motion that women be permitted to vote in municipal elections. See Congreso Feminista de Yucatán, *Anales de esa memorable asamblea* (Mérida, Yuc.: Talleres Tipográficos del "Ateneo Peninsular," 1916), p. 127.

58. Galindo, *Estudio*, p. 25.

59. Mendieta Alatorre, *La mujer en la revolución mexicana*, p. 80.

60. Fernando Romero García, ed., *Diario de los debates del congreso constituyente*, 2 vols. (México: Imprenta de la Cámara de Diputados, 1917), 2:708-9.

61. *La Voz de la Revolución* (Mérida, Yuc.), 15 March 1917, p. 1.

62. Ibid.

63. Galindo, *La doctrina Carranza y el acercamiento indolatino*, p. 159.

64. Mendieta Alatorre, *La mujer en la revolución mexicana*, pp. 34, 79, 93, 174.

65. *La Mujer Mexicana*, 1 March 1904, p. 9; 5 July 1907, pp. 61-62.

66. Mendieta Alatorre, *La mujer en la revolución mexicana*, p. 111.

67. Ibid., pp. 30, 31, 34, 40.

68. Ibid., p. 93; and Alessio Robles, *Voces de Combate*, pp. 151-52.

69. Aurora Fernández, *Mujeres que honran a la patria* (México: n.p., 1958), pp. 67-70.

70. Ibid., p. 71.

71. Ibid.

72. David A. Franz, "Bullets and Bolshevists. A History of the Mexican Revolution and Reform in Yucatán, 1910-1924" (Ph.D. diss., University of New Mexico, 1973), p. 36.

73. Turner, "Los efectos de la participación femenina en la Revolución de 1910," p. 611.

74. Mendieta Alatorre, *La mujer en la revolución mexicana*, pp. 173-74.

75. Fernández, *Mujeres que honran a la patria*, pp. 121-30.

76. Ibid., p. 130.

77. Turner in *The Dynamic of Mexican Nationalism*, p. 197 notes: "Depicting *soldaderas* in individual portraits, battle scenes and on the covers of widely distributed popular ballad sheets, José Guadalupe Posada uniformly portrayed them as beautiful, well-groomed, and determined young ladies." For photographs of real *soldaderas*, see Gustavo Casasola, *Historia gráfica de la revolución mexicana: 1900-1960*, 4 vols. (México: Editorial F. Trillas, 1960), 2:720-23.

78. See, for example, Real Academia Española, *Diccionario de la lengua española* (Madrid: Espasa Calpe, 1956); Martín Alonso Pedraz, comp., *Diccionario del español moderno* (Madrid, Aguilar, 1968); Mariano Velázquez de la Cadena, et al., comps., *Velázquez Spanish and English Dictionary* (Chicago: Follett Publishing Company, 1964); and Arturo Cuyas, comp., *Appleton's New English-Spanish, Spanish-English Dictionary* (New York: D. Appleton-Century Co., 1940).

79. Robert E. Quirk, *The Mexican Revolution and the Catholic Church, 1910-1920* (Bloomington, Ind.: University of Indiana Press, 1973), p. 58.

80. Turner, *The Dynamic of Mexican Nationalism*, p. 183.

81. Rosa E. King, *Tempest Over Mexico: A Personal Chronicle* (New York: Howes Publishing Co., 1944), p. 183.

82. Quoted by Mary L. Scalise Regoli, "La mujer en la novela de la revolución" (M.A. thesis, Escuela de Verano, Universidad Nacional Autónoma de México, 1963), p. 106.

83. John Reed, *Insurgent Mexico* (New York: D. Appleton & Co., 1914), pp. 99-109.

84. Casasola, *Historia gráfica de la revolución mexicana*, 2:720.

85. Julio Guerrero, *La génesis del crimen en México* (México: Librería de la Vda. de Charles Bouret, 1901), pp. 163-64, as quoted in Donna M. Wolf, "Women in Mexico, 1810-1910," (unpublished essay, 1974), p. 5.

86. King, *Tempest Over Mexico*, pp. 93-94.

87. Ibid., p. 183.

88. Cumberland, *Mexico: The Struggle for Modernity*, p. 245.

89. R. H. Mason, *Picture of Life in Mexico, 1849* (London: Smith, Elder and Co., 1851), p. 62, as quoted in Wolf, "Women in Mexico, 1810-1910,", p. 5.

90. Casasola, *Historia gráfica de la revolución mexicana*, 2:720. Turner observes that "the Mexican soldiers in both federal and revolutionary ranks took their women along with them in the railway cars that carried belligerents from one part of Mexico to another. The *soldaderas*... provided a commissariat for Mexican troops, and both federal and revolutionary chieftains regularly provided for their transportation along with the troops in the major campaigns." Turner, *The Dynamic of Mexican Nationalism*, p. 185.

91. Casasola, *Historia gráfica de la revolución mexicana*, 2:720.

92. Ibid.

93. King, *Tempest Over Mexico*, p. 69.

94. I am grateful to Mrs. Anita Aguilar and Dr. Rosalind Rosoff Beimler of the American School in Mexico City and authors of *Así firmaron el Plan de Ayala*, SEP-SETENTAS, no. 241 (México: Secretaría de Educación Pública, 1976), for introducing me to La Coronela. I attended three tape recording sessions in 1973 and 1974 in which Mrs. Aguilar and Dr. Beimler interviewed La Coronela of Yautepec to record the testimony of surviving Zapatistas in Morelos as part of an oral history project. La Coronela died in 1977.

95. Mary Scalise Regoli, "La mujer en la novela de la revolución," p. 77.

96. All the material on La Coronela is based on her own account as related in October 1973 in Yautepec, Morelos.

97. I am grateful to Dr. Rosalind Rosoff Beimler for providing information on these women. See also Mendieta Alatorre, *La mujer en la revolución mexicana*, pp. 87, 89-92.

98. Ibid., p. 109.

99. Cumberland, *Mexico: The Struggle for Modernity*, pp. 245-46.

100. Ibid., pp. 247-48.

101. Turner, *The Dynamic of Mexican Nationalism*, p. 191.

102. Luis Lara y Pardo, *La prostitución en México* (México: Librería de la Vda. de Charles Bouret, 1908), pp. 19-20, 26-27.

103. In 1906 there were four thousand known prostitutes in Paris, in a population five times larger than that of Mexico City. Ibid., pp. 19, 22, 29. Lara y Pardo's calculations are incorrect. The figure is closer to 210, not 120 per thousand.

104. Cumberland, *Mexico: The Struggle for Modernity*, p. 247, notes that "corn, that great and necessary staple of the populace, had fallen to a point well below the 2-million mark—a total production not significantly greater than that in the late eighteenth century and far less than the earlier period on a per capita basis."

105. See James B. Lynch, "Orozco's House of Tears," *Journal of Inter-American Studies*, 3 (July 1961):376-77.

106. Ibid., p. 376.

107. Dr. Luis Lara y Pardo demonstrated hostility and hatred toward the prostitutes he studied in his *La prostitución en México*. He did not believe them when they testified that they became prostitutes because of poverty, seduction, or abandonment and insisted that most streetwalkers willingly gave up their virginity and then entered a life of vice with no qualms whatsoever. See pp. 104 ff.

108. See Quirk, *The Mexican Revolution and the Catholic Church*, pp. 54-60, for details of the ill-treatment of clergymen and nuns by such revolutionaries as Villa, Fierro, Obregón, Villarreal, and others. A contemporary account of the mistreatment of nuns by Carrancistas is provided by P. R. Planchet, a priest in

Devine, Texas, in *La persecución a las religiosas y señoras, era Carrancista* (n.p.: 1922).

109. Article 5 of the 1857 constitution in Branch, ed., "The Mexican Constitution of 1917 compared with the Constitution of 1857," p. 3.

110. Article 27 in ibid., pp. 15-16.

111. Article 123 in ibid., p. 103. In seeming contradiction to this provision, the following section of Article 123 stated that "the church and state are independent of each other." The contradiction was noted by the constituent assembly in 1916-17 and the phrase was dropped. See ibid.

112. Ibid., p. 104.

113. The masses still flock to the Guadalupe and Chalma shrines. The architect of the new basilica of Guadalupe in Mexico, Pedro Ramírez Vázquez, observed that the Guadalupe shrine "receives 1,500 pilgrimages and six million visitors per year. Even during Holy Year in 1975, St. Peter's in the Vatican only had six million visitors." Quoted in the *New York Times*, 12 October 1976, p. 10.

114. For an illuminating review of religion and church-state relations in Mexico, see Frank Tannenbaum, *Peace by Revolution. An Interpretation of Mexico* (New York: Columbia University Press, 1933), pp. 34-67.

115. Quirk, *The Mexican Revolution and the Catholic Church*, p. 17.

116. The general was Ramón F. Iturbe. Martín Luis Guzmán, *The Eagle and the Serpent* (Garden City, N.Y.: Dolphin Books, 1965), p. 84.

117. Quirk, *The Mexican Revolution and the Catholic Church*, pp. 54-60, *passim*.

118. Branch, ed., "The Mexican Constitution of 1917 Compared with the Constitution of 1857," p. 2.

119. Article 130 in ibid., p. 104.

120. Quirk, *The Mexican Revolution and the Catholic Church*, p. 32.

121. J. Ignacio Dávila Garibi, *Memoria histórica de las labores de la Asociación de Damas Católicas de Guadalajara* (Guadalajara, Jal.: Tipografía, Litografía y Encuadernación; J. J. Yguiniz, 1920), pp. 3, 5.

122. Ibid., pp. 23-24.

123. Speaking of the Confederation of Catholic Associations of Mexico, Quirk observes that "laymen were permitted to hold titular positions, but the key offices remained in the hands of the clergy, with most important posts being filled by episcopal appointments." Quirk, *The Mexican Revolution and the Catholic Church*, p. 126.

124. Dávila Garibi, *Memoria histórica*, pp. 3, 9.

125. Ibid., pp. 5-6.

126. Ibid., p. 6.

127. Quirk, *The Mexican Revolution and the Catholic Church*, p. 59.

128. Ibid.

129. Ibid., p. 75.

130. Ibid., p. 106.

131. Ibid., p. 107.

132. Ibid., p. 109.

133. Ibid., pp. 110-11. The crucial role women played in the Jalisco boycott is fully explored in the anonymous booklet, *La cuestión religiosa en Jalisco* (México: n.p., 1918), pp. 48-74.

134. On this point see Turner, *The Dynamic of Mexican Nationalism*; Mendieta Alatorre, *La mujer en la revolución mexicana*, p. 15; and Anna Macías, "The Mexican Revolution Was No Revolution For Women," in *History of Latin American Civilization: Sources and Interpretations*, ed. Lewis Hanke, 2nd ed., 2 vols. (Boston: Little, Brown & Co., 1973) 2:459-69.

3

YUCATÁN AND THE WOMEN'S MOVEMENT, 1870-1920

In 1923 the Mexican secretary of the interior, Plutarco Elías Calles, told Ernest Gruening, who was writing a book on Mexico, that "if you wish to understand the Mexican Revolution do not fail to visit Yucatán."[1] Calles, like most of the leaders of that struggle, came from northern Mexico; yet he and his colleagues recognized that the state of Yucatán, some one thousand miles away from the center of power in Mexico and accessible only by sea, had become a sort of laboratory for testing radical ideas on social reform during and immediately after the Mexican revolution.[2] Among the radical ideas tested in Yucatán was the concept of women's liberation, and in 1916 two feminist congresses were held in Yucatán's capital city, Mérida, the first such congresses to be held in Mexican history.

Why did Yucatán, a largely rural area isolated from the rest of Mexico, and possessing a large and traditionalist Maya population, become a center for social reform and feminist activity? The quality of revolutionary leadership has been heavily emphasized in the literature on Yucatán in answer to this question.[3] However, one must also consider Yucatán's unique geography, resources, and historical development to 1910 in order to understand why the revolutionary leadership found the region a propitious place for implementing a wide variety of reforms.

The peninsula of Yucatán, a projection of Middle America between the Gulf of Campeche on the west, the Gulf of Mexico on the north, and the Caribbean Sea on the east, was and still is the home of lowland Maya Indians.[4] The state of Yucatán comprises the northern part of the peninsula, a dry limestone plain formed ages ago by crustacean deposits. Although the peninsula as a whole receives abundant rainfall, the soil is thin on this stony plain, with most of the precipitation absorbed by underground rivers and caverns. The thin soil of northern Yucatán supports primarily mesquite, cactus, and the henequen or sisal plant. The latter became the state's principal source of wealth during the Porfirian era.[5]

Despite the thin soil and lack of surface water, the ancient Mayas, through imaginative and efficient organization of their resources, cultivated corn, beans, and squash in addition to henequen fiber in enough abundance to build large ceremonial cities. Richly endowed with limestone, the Mayas built their oldest city at Dzibilchaltun (near modern Mérida), followed later by the large and awesome cities of Chichén-Itza, Uxmal, Sayil, Labna, and others. The Spaniards came upon the Yucatecan Mayas at least two generations after the great cities had fallen into decay, and precisely because the population was dispersed, it proved more difficult to conquer these people than the highly concentrated Aztecs. The spoils of war proved meager for the Spanish conquerors, however, for Yucatán lacked rich soil or mineral wealth. As a result, Yucatán remained a backwater in the colonial era, with most of the desirable lands divided into large estates devoted to cattle raising.

By the end of the colonial era, Yucatán had a disproportionately large number of *haciendas* (''agricultural estates'') and *estancias* (''cattle estates'') in comparison to the rest of the Kingdom of New Spain, as Mexico was called before independence. In 1794, for example, Yucatán had 26.7 percent of all the *haciendas* and *estancias* of the vast kingdom, but only 9.5 percent of its total population.[6] The relatively large number of estates in Yucatán made it possible for a small number of Ladinos (whites and mestizos) to exploit and acculturate a much more numerous indigenous population. As elsewhere in New Spain, once the encomienda system declined in the seventeenth and eighteenth centuries, debt peonage became the principal device for attaching the indigenous population to the large estates in Yucatán. However, because it was impossible to attract voluntary labor to work under the scorching sun of the peninsula, debt peonage there became indistinguishable from slavery long before the *hacienda* system reached its peak of development between 1880 and 1910.[7]

Under Spanish rule, little economic development took place, with only modest exports of hides, tallow, logwood, and some tobacco and sugar.

Northern Yucatán's only unique resource was henequen (*Agave fourcroydes*), a drought-resistant perennial whose sword-like leaves produce long, coarse, and elastic fibers.[8] The Mayas made hundreds of articles for daily use from this fibrous plant. These included mats, hammocks, cordage, sandals, bags, and hats; but henequen had little commercial value for the Spaniards, and it figured only modestly in the colonial export trade. Indeed, as late as 1845 henequen accounted for only six percent of the total commercial production of Yucatán.[9]

Yucatecan Ladinos eagerly joined the independence movement after 1808 because they believed that for centuries the Spaniards had deliberately neglected the region in favor of the mineral-rich areas of Mexico. In 1824 the Yucatecans, who had developed a strong separatist spirit during the colonial era, reluctantly joined the Mexican federation. They did so because they received "a greater degree of local autonomy and lighter national obligations than did the other political units of the country."[10] When this special relationship was violated by the central government in the 1840s, Yucatán briefly seceded from the union. Although the secessionist movement ended by 1848, a strong regional spirit and a hearty dislike of "outsiders," that is, all other Mexicans, were to remain constant features of Yucatecan history.[11]

Once independence was achieved and local autonomy assured, the Ladino population sought radical change. Leading Yucatecans wanted to end the peninsula's isolation from the modernizing nations of the world and hoped to transform Yucatán into both an economically active and culturally progressive region. As early as 1833 a native Yucatecan, Pedro Sainz de Baranda y Borreiro, formed plans to establish a completely mechanized cotton textile factory using steam power in Valladolid.[12] Other Yucatecans invented metal mechanical devices for removing the fibers of the henequen leaves to replace the wasteful and slow wooden raspers in use since colonial times.[13] As H. F. Cline notes, "by the first third of the nineteenth century there was [in Yucatán] a climate of opinion saturated with the spirit of enterprise."[14] Cline also notes that in the 1830s and 1840s "impulses to change and novelty were surging strong in many fields," and that by the 1840s Yucatán had an intellectual life of its own.[15] In 1846 a reporter for the *Registro Yucateco* noted with pride that

we have literary and scientific periodicals, as well as mercantile and political ones. There are philharmonic societies, reading groups, and scientific academies.

Progressive enterprises have been successful; now established is a brilliant line of coaches, and also cafés, hotels, and recreational associations. Primary education has been perfected; government improves; agriculture is fostered; roads are built and repaired. In fine, there is movement, advance, down a path of progress that has no end. . . . Yucatan is going to be an important place. . . .[16]

Ladino women of Yucatán began to figure in this atmosphere of enterprise and change as early as 1846, when the first public primary school for girls was established at Mérida. Until then there had only been a few private schools for girls, usually run by self-taught women.[17] The interest in female education by women continued, and in 1870 a feminist society named La Siempreviva was founded by a group of women in Mérida.[18] The organization was led by Rita Cetina Gutiérrez (1846-1908), a poet and teacher who since the 1860s had been composing highly regarded poems for public occasions in Mérida, and it sought to awaken a female interest in literature and education. It raised funds for the establishment of a new school for girls, and on May 3, 1870, the new school opened its doors. La Siempreviva school, which functioned privately until 1886 (when it merged with the government-supported Instituto Literario de Niñas), was the first school in Mérida to offer young women a secondary education.[19]

On the same day that the new school was inaugurated, La Siempreviva society published the first issue of a newspaper of the same name—one written, edited, and printed entirely by women.[20] Rita Cetina Gutiérrez became its editor and director, and she celebrated the opening of the new school and the appearance of the new newspaper in a poem she wrote on the occasion of both events. She asked her readers to:

Listen with attention: *the hour has arrived*
for woman to ennoble her name!

Come, all [women], come. La Siempreviva
reclaims your enthusiastic support. . .

The hour has arrived, and today begins
the regeneration of woman![21]

Aided by her friends and fellow poets, Gertrudis Tenorio Zavala and Cristina Farfán, Cetina Gutiérrez soon attracted sixty students to the new school. She and her associates designed a curriculum that, on the lower level, included reading, writing, sewing, grammar, and arithmetic and, on the upper, geometry, geography, constitutional law, astronomy, music, and speech.[22] Among La Siempreviva's more celebrated students was Consuelo Zavala y Castillo, a descendant of the historian Lorenzo de Zavala. Until her death in 1956, Consuelo Zavala y Castillo devoted her life to the education of women.[23] She and Dominga Canto y Pastrana, another graduate of La Siempreviva and also a distinguished educator in the twentieth century, were later the organizers of the first feminist congress of January 1916.[24]

In 1886 Rita Cetina Gutiérrez became the director of the Instituto Literario de Niñas, the state primary, secondary, and normal school for women first established at Mérida in 1877.[25] The Instituto had 218 students when Cetina became its director, and under her dedicated and enthusiastic leadership the school's enrollment rose annually. By the time ill health forced her to retire in 1902, the Instituto had 550 students.[26] Cetina took a particular interest in poor but able students, for she herself owed her education to the generosity of a private citizen who aided her family when her father was assassinated in 1860. In her sixteen years at the Instituto between 1886 and 1902 Cetina and her associates educated practically all the female public schoolteachers in the state of Yucatán. After her forced retirement from teaching, she contributed poems to *La Mujer Mexicana* in Mexico City. The feminist monthly reported in 1904 that after thirty-two years of teaching, Rita Cetina Gutiérrez was ill, alone, and forgotten by all but a handful of her former students. At her death in 1908, however, it was reported that all of Mérida attended her funeral.[27]

Yucatán made great strides in the education of both men and women from approximately 1870 to 1910. By 1910 the city of Mérida, which rivalled the national capital in its modern improvements, could boast of a literacy rate of 59 percent.[28] The entire state had one of the highest literacy rates in the country. In 1910, for example, Yucatán had 339,613 inhabitants, of whom 74,063 could read and write Spanish and another 3,080 who could read Spanish.[29] In that same year, 62,026 children, or 18.4 percent of the total population, were attending school.[30] Yucatán had 430 official schools and 14 private schools, with 34,968 male and 27,058 female students taught by 1,132 teachers, of whom 635, or more than half, were women.[31] That there were so many literate women in the peninsula was due in large part to their own unremitting efforts over a period of forty years.

In contrast to Yucatán, the mountainous state of Chiapas, inhabited by highland Mayas, had only 6,579 youngsters or about 1.5 percent of the state's total population of 436,800 attending school.[32] Clearly, Yucatán had certain advantages over Chiapas that account for the differences in educational levels.

Yucatán's biggest advantage was henequen. There was an enormous expansion of commercial henequen after 1880, when a mechanical binder was added to the McCormick reaper. The demand for a strong but inexpensive binder twine for the reapers to use in the wheat lands of the United States, Australia, Canada, and Argentina brought great wealth to Yucatán.[33] The "green gold," as the henequen came to be called, built the lavish French Empire mansions of the "henequen kings" on the elegant Paseo Montejo in Mérida, but it also built railroads, the port of Progreso, hospitals, asylums, schools, and libraries.[34]

Yucatán's geographical position was highly favorable for worldwide contacts by sea, and the flat terrain of the peninsula made it easy to build cart roads and then railroads to transport the henequen cheaply from the plantations to the ports of Sisal and Progreso.[35] While Chiapas and other mountainous Mexican states lacked internal improvements and remained cut off from world trade, Yucatán was in frequent contact with the modern industrial nations of the world. With the exchange of goods came an exchange of ideas, and Yucatán, receptive since independence to new ideas, was one of the more advanced regions in Mexico at the outbreak of the revolution in 1910. It was therefore a logical center for further experiments in social and economic change.

Yucatán was also a region in which the sharp contradictions between progress and poverty of the Porfirian era were most painfully evident. Henequen generated wealth and stimulated cultural development among the Ladinos, but this wealth and progress were achieved at the expense of the Indian population. From 1830 onward, the self-sufficient Maya villages, protected by the Crown before independence, lost ground against the encroaching plantations,[36] and compliant state legislatures passed debt peonage laws that forcibly attached the Maya population to the estates created after independence.[37] By 1910, out of a population of 339,613 there were 76,896 agricultural workers and some 99,058 domestic servants in Yucatán.[38] Most of these men and women lived in a status of virtual slavery.

Ladinos had always maintained that the Indian population would work only when forced to do so, but what they really meant was that the Mayan people would work for the whites and mestizos only under compulsion. And compulsion was used. "It was said that the Indio could hear only through his back," Nelson Reed observes, "so the whip was kept handy and used frequently."[39] John Kenneth Turner, the muckraking North American who saw at first hand the conditions on the henequen plantations, found this to be the case. Passing himself off as a prospective investor in henequen in early 1910, Turner saw how frequently and unmercifully the "debt servants" were whipped, how poorly they were fed and housed, and how impossible it was for them to recover their freedom.[40] "Service for debt," he soon discovered, was a subterfuge for slavery, as workers were transferred from one master to another, "not on any basis of debt, but on the basis of the market price of a man."[41] Turner reported that "slaves are not only used in henequen plantations, but in the city, as personal servants, as laborers, as household drudges, and as prostitutes."[42] Such extreme social injustice cried out for remedy, and the coming of the Mexican Revolution promised a new day for the oppressed of Yucatán.

The earliest leaders of the revolution in Yucatán, Pino Suárez and Eleuterio Avila, timidly advocated establishment of rural schools for the children of the henequen workers, termination of debt peonage, and a minimum wage of seventy-five centavos a day for agricultural workers. However, they backed down from these reforms when plantation owners argued that any change in the status quo would upset the economy and impoverish the state.[43] These tepid reformers were succeeded by a thorough-going revolutionary from the outside, General Salvador Alvarado of northern Mexico. Venustiano Carranza, leader of the Constitutionalist forces, named Alvarado military governor in early 1915, and the locally supported but frankly counterrevolutionary government of the Yucatecan, Ortíz Argumedo came to an end.[44]

Alvarado had the reputation of being incorruptible, a man totally committed to the ideals of the revolution. As military governor of Yucatán from March 1915, to February 1918, he earned Carranza's trust, for he provided the federal government with at least 30 million pesos (about 15 million dollars) in the form of duties, taxes, and loans from the sale of henequen.[45]

Backed by an army of six thousand men, Alvarado was able to impose his will on the population. Unhampered by a hostile press, a recalcitrant legislature, or an independent judiciary, Alvarado acted as an enlightened despot, bent on reforming both the economy and the culture of Yucatán.

The historian Frank Tannenbaum remarks that Alvarado's "coming to Yucatán was like a cyclone that destroyed a feudalism rooted deep in the soil. . . . He, perhaps more than any other Mexican who took an active part in the revolution, attempted to formulate its program. . . ."[46]

Born in Culiacán, Sinaloa, in northwestern Mexico in 1880, Alvarado moved to the border state of Sonora while young and worked at such jobs as clerk, shopkeeper, railroad contractor, and lumber dealer. While still in his teens he came to feel that Mexican society needed drastic reform, and when the Precursor Movement began, he joined the Mexican Liberal party in 1906. He subscribed to the Flores Magón newspaper *Regeneración* and further demonstrated his revolutionary orientation by becoming involved in the Cananea copper mine strike of 1906.[47] When the strike was crushed, Alvarado fled to Arizona, where "he operated a small business . . . while waiting for a propitious time to return."[48] According to Carlo de Fornaro, an anti-Díaz journalist, Alvarado learned to read and speak English with fluency and, while in the United States, came to greatly admire the "organizing ability and progressive spirit of the Americans."[49]

Alvarado's admiration for the United States was patent in many of the changes he instituted in Yucatán between 1915 and 1918. He introduced the state to everything from the Boy Scouts and Arbor Day ceremonies to parent-teacher associations and home economics courses.[50] In addition, he established a school for monolingual Mayan children patterned on Booker T. Washington's Tuskegee Institute, and he adopted the William George Junior idea of student governance of their own schools in the primary schools of the peninsula.[51] The school of commerce and the agricultural college Alvarado set up were also patterned on American institutions, as were his vocational schools for men and women.[52]

However, what made Alvarado especially unique among Carranza's nationalistic and even xenophobic governors was his pronounced interest in the role, the situation, and the problems of women. Early in his administration, he made it clear that he wanted women to be better educated, to be able to support themselves, and to be treated equally before the law. Around him Alvarado saw mostly passive, self-doubting, and dependent women, still very much under the influence of a traditionalist church. In their place he wanted to see strong, free, and independent women who no longer needed the consolations of religion to give meaning to their lives.[53]

Alvarado may very well have been influenced by the active role he saw women play in North American society. However, he may also have been influenced by contemporary socialist and anarchist ideas in favor of women's liberation. An eclectic, Alvarado borrowed his ideas on social reform from many and sometimes contradictory sources. On the one hand, he believed in the nineteenth-century Victorian values of self-reliance, self-improvement, hard work, and thrift, and on the other, he maintained that the government must protect the weak, unfortunate, and oppressed against the "privileges, the abuses, and the insolence of the powerful."[54]

Alone among his revolutionary colleagues, Alvarado viewed the struggle for woman's emancipation as integral to aiding the weak and the oppressed. As a result, when Alvarado prohibited debt peonage on the plantations, he issued a related decree outlawing another species of slavery, one exploiting female domestic servants who were suffering in the plantation houses and in urban homes. Just as he had done for agricultural and industrial workers, Alvarado decreed minimum wages and maximum hours for domestics, most of whom were women. He also prohibited employers from insisting that maids live in.[55]

Alvarado shared a strong moralistic fervor with his colleagues and his first act upon assuming the governorship was to prohibit gambling in Yucatán. His edict banned lotteries and games of chance, which Alvarado charged were being used for corrupt purposes. He also decreed prohibition, bringing to an end the legal manufacture and sale of alcoholic beverages. There was also a crackdown on drugs, in particular marijuana and opium, because of their degrading effects on their primarily lower-class users and their corrupting influence on public officials. According to Alvarado, before he came to office gambling, alcohol, drugs, and prostitution had not only been permitted but encouraged; they had indeed provided the state government with revenue and public officials with bribes. He sought to change this pattern by having henequen taxes provide all of the state's revenues, a move that was not appreciated by the henequen barons.[56]

In accord with his moralizing campaign, Alvarado next turned his attention to the problem of prostitution. He outlawed brothels, hoping to free prostitutes from exploitation by madames, pimps, and corrupt "vice squad" officers. He established a separate health service, one unconnected with the police or any branch of the government, to provide prostitutes with regular examinations by doctors paid adequately for their services. Alvarado did not try to outlaw prostitution altogether, for he was aware that a long educational program and improved job opportunities were needed first. For now, ending the exploitation of prostitutes and trying to control the high rate of venereal disease was essential. Although quite rigid in his moral standards, Alvarado displayed a good deal more compassion towards prostitutes than most of the *gente decente* ("the respectable element") both in Yucatán and elsewhere in Mexico.[57]

Early in his administration, Alvarado made good his pledge that his administration intended to help women support themselves. He urged qualified women to apply for positions in the state government as office workers, clerks, cashiers, and accountants.[58] He also wanted more women hired in urban commercial establishments. Until his coming to Yucatán, positions were limited. Only library work, teaching, and needlework were considered suitable for middle-class women, while working-class females had little choice but to accept domestic service. Alvarado, however, believed that women should be allowed to work at any position that did not require brute strength.[59]

To emphasize his interest in encouraging women to seek work outside the home, Alvarado changed part of the civil code. Single women could now leave their parental homes before they reached thirty; in fact, they could depart at the same age as single men, twenty-one. Alvarado's Decree no. 167, promulgated on July 14, 1915, came to be called the "Feminist law," and anticipated by eleven years the reform of the national civil code.[60] Now, he hoped, reluctant parents would consent to their daughters seeking outside work.

In explaining his reasons for this reform, Alvarado continually stressed the injustice of treating single women under thirty as minors. Such discrimination violated the individual and collective rights that the revolution symbolized. The old law, he believed, kept women subjected, in an inferior status, and without an opportunity to take advantage of growing employment opportunities. He added that the old law was an unjust restriction on women's freedom of action, helping to keep them in such weakness and dependency that they fell "prey to superstitious ideas and religious preoccupations."[61]

In order to help prepare Yucatecan women and men for an active and full participation in the reconstruction of the country, Alvarado devoted particular attention to education. Education, he stated, was the one department of his administration "to which I have devoted the most lively enthusiasm and the most assiduous and constant dedication."[62] The statistics he provided in his last government report of 1918 bear out his assertion. From late March 1915 to December 25, 1917, Alvarado's administration spent a total of slightly more than eight million pesos (about four million dollars) in running the state. Of this sum, just under three million pesos was spent on education.[63] The maximum that had been spent in any previous government was about 560,000 pesos a year, high by Porfirian standards.[64]

Alvarado wanted all Yucatecans—men and men, Ladinos and Indians, rich and poor, rural and city folk—to be literate. As a result, he concentrated his efforts on those regions previously neglected. He established one thousand rural schools and added some forty new urban schools to towns outside Mérida. He set up the country's first Montessori school in Mérida, appointing Elena Torres of Mexico City, a leading feminist in the early 1920s, as its first director. As mentioned earlier, Alvarado initiated a special school on the Tuskegee pattern for monolingual Maya children and also established a school of agriculture. Despite Yucatán's exclusive dependence on the henequen crop, the peninsula lacked trained agriculturalists.[65]

Alvarado was highly critical of the education imparted to women, in particular, in the existing public schools, and he declared that it was impractical, abstract, and failed to prepare females to earn a living or care for a home.[66] To remedy the situation, he established a model school of domestic arts. As happened in Mexico City when a female vocational school was established there during the Porfiriato, girls and young women flocked to the new Mérida school. At the School of Domestic Arts, females could study subjects ranging from home economics to telegraphy.[67] The school was allocated a large budget, and its female teachers were paid salaries almost as high as those paid the doctors teaching in the newly-formed School of Medicine. Women were now encouraged to study medicine, pharmacy, and dentistry at the latter school.[68]

As part of his effort to create sexual equality, Alvarado introduced coeducation through the fourth grade. His reform, however, met with so much parental opposition that he was soon forced to limit coeducation to the first two grades.[69] He decreed coeducation in the normal schools, to which no opposition was recorded, and in fact he merged the normal schools for men and women into one institution. Alvarado also encouraged all women with intellectual interests to join the Ateneo Peninsular, Mérida's leading cultural center. In the past, only a few outstanding women, such as Rita Cetina Gutiérrez, had belonged as honorary members.[70]

Addressing the Second Pedagogical Congress that he called in September 1916, Alvarado made clear that such educational reforms were intended to liberate women from control by the Catholic church. "The Mexican woman has no will of her own," he lamented, "and she does the bidding of her father, her lover, her husband, and her confessor...." If "the priest continues to be the protector, the counselor, and the guide of women," he said, Mexico "will be in danger and nothing will be done towards its progress and liberation."[71]

For Alvarado, as for Carrancistas in general, the church was the enemy of social justice, enlightenment, and progress. As a result, on September 15, 1915, the governor issued a decree closing all of Yucatán's churches. Then, a week later, notes Nelson Reed in *The Caste War of Yucatan*, "a mob of railroad men and Mexican agitators invaded the cathedral, burning the organ and high altar and destroying many famous images."[72] Although the cathedral was close to the government palace and to the central police station, Alvarado did nothing to stop the destruction.[73] The church had never been as strong in Yucatán as it was in such states as Jalisco and Guanajuato, for example, which may be why the peninsula had been so successful in establishing laical schools. Alvarado failed to appreciate this fact, however, and needlessly antagonized the faithful. He also alienated progressive and secular-oriented Yucatecans, who saw no point in fanning the flames of religious hatred.

One such progressive was Consuelo Zavala y Castillo, in 1916 the director of a private, laical normal school. Her own education had begun at the laical La Siempreviva school. At the same pedagogical congress at which Alvarado attacked the supposed alliance between women and the church, the courageous Zavala wondered aloud why Alvarado—who was seldom criticized to his face—attacked the clergy at every opportunity and particularly at every school festival.[74] Profesora Zavala told Alvarado that such rabid anticlericalism frightened many Mérida parents. As a result, children were flocking to her institution—not because she was teaching religion, which she was not, but because parents did not want to send their children to Alvarado's public schools. Ironically enough, before Alvarado's coming Zavala had had to struggle to get the state to accredit her school, for conservative officials viewed its laical, modern, and national curriculum with suspicion. Alvarado appreciated the irony, remarking that "in the middle of the white conservatism dominating the Yucatecan people, the liberal tone of the intelligent teacher [Zavala] appeared pink. When we arrived, with our red banner, her liberalism appeared white. Thus children flocked to her school."[75]

The forthright Profesora Zavala was not able to dissuade Governor Alvarado from continuing his attacks on the church. Instead he pushed his program for "rationalist education" in the public schools, an idea he adopted from the recently martyred Spanish anarchist and pedagogue, Francisco Ferrer y Guardia. While laical schools simply made no reference to religion, Ferrer's "Escuela moderna" sought to demonstrate that religion was irrational and antiscientific.[76] One important reason why Alvarado called two pedagogical as well as two feminist congresses was to enlist the support of public schoolteachers in his campaign to "defanaticize" the younger generation through the agency of "rationalist" education.[77]

Alvarado's anticlericalism was not, however, the only motive in his decision to call first one and then a second feminist congress in Yucatán. He apparently viewed congresses as vehicles for "raising consciousness," as we would say today, for Alvarado was distressed to find that there was little revolutionary ardor among the people he was trying to help—women, peasants, or workers. The governor had to initiate the revolution from the top, for little impetus came from below. He knew perfectly well that such a procedure was artificial and that, without popular support, his reforms would not last. Periodic congresses would hopefully give Alvarado the popular support he lacked. In addition, these congresses would permit the very people who had been exploited or ignored during the Porfirian era to become familiar with parliamentary procedure. Alvarado was a fervent believer in learning by doing, and he hoped that the feminist and other congresses would be training grounds for Yucatán's future leaders.

On October 28, 1915, Alvarado's decision to call a feminist congress made the headlines of the progovernment newspaper, *La Voz de la Revolución*.[78] According to Artemisa Saénz Royo, a journalist and feminist from Vera Cruz who attended the Second Feminist Congress of November 1916, the idea for calling a feminist congress in Yucatán originated with her friend, Hermila Galindo.[79] However, in 1919 Hermila Galindo wrote frankly about her contributions to the feminist movement and she never claimed the honor of suggesting to Alvarado that he call a women's congress in Yucatán.[80] According to Colonel J. D. Ramírez Garrido, Alvarado's director of public education in 1915 and author of a sympathetic history of world feminism, *Al margen del feminismo*, it was a man, the Yucatecan public schoolteacher, Professor Agustín Franco, who first suggested that a feminist congress be called in Yucatán.[81] Garrido immediately referred Franco's suggestion to Alvarado, and the next day, October 27, 1915, Alvarado approved the idea and communicated his decision without delay to the editor of *La Voz de la Revolución*.[82] In the weeks and months that followed that newspaper gave considerable attention to the coming congress and to the whole question of women's rights in Mexico and the rest of the world. Once the congress met, *La Voz de la Revolución* gave the novel event complete coverage.[83]

The feminist congress called by Alvarado in January 1916 was the first such meeting held in the Republic of Mexico and the second held in all of Latin America. The first had met at Buenos Aires in May 1910. In contrast to the situation in Mexico, the 1910 Argentinian congress was entirely the work of females and was organized by the Association of Argentine University Women.[84] In 1910 Argentina had made the greatest strides towards modernization in Latin America, and with the largest middle class in the southern hemisphere, it is no accident that it was the first country in the region to host a women's congress organized by women themselves.[85]

Governor Alvarado did turn the task of organizing the Yucatecan congress over to women, but at the same time he sought to control the deliberations of the congress by drawing up the agenda.[86] However, it should be noted that Alvarado followed the same procedure in all the congresses he called. In addition, when Constitutionalist governors in other states called pedagogic congresses, they also drew up their agendas.[87]

Alvarado posed four questions for the coming congress, scheduled to meet for four days in Mérida in mid-January 1916. He instructed the organizers of the conference to choose delegates, who in turn would prepare papers on the best means of freeing women from the yoke of tradition and the precise role of the primary school in preparing women for life. Delegates were also asked to ponder what skills and occupations the state should support to prepare Mexican women for "an intense life of progress."[88] Finally, Alvarado wanted the delegates to consider what public offices women could and should fill.[89] Undoubtedly, Alvarado hoped to get a ringing endorsement of "rationalist" education at the congress. He also expected that the delegates would approve female political participation, once, of course, military rule ended and Mexico reestablished constitutional government.[90]

Enemies of Alvarado accused him of doing everything in haste and wanting immediate results, a charge of considerable validity with respect to Yucatán's First Feminist Congress.[91] He chose Profesora Consuelo Zavala to head the organizing committee—a credit to Alvarado—for Zavala was no sycophant. However, he gave her and her committee little more than two months to publicize the congress, select the women who would prepare studies on the themes of the congress, and make travel and lodging arrangements for hundreds of participants.[92]

Zavala and other members of the organizing committee, most of them full-time teachers like herself, worked feverishly. They held a dozen evening meetings from November 13, 1915, to January 9, 1916, laboring on the innumerable details that any large meeting entails.[93] On Alvarado's instructions the organizing committee invited only women of "honest reputation" and with at least a grade school education to attend the congress. It is understandable that prostitutes had to be barred from attending, as in the recent past men hostile to change—including the conservative Yucatecan, Ignacio Gamboa—had linked feminists to "bad women."[94] It is not clear, however, why the delegates had to have at least a grade school education. The restriction obviously kept the attendance at the congress down to manageable proportions, but it effectively excluded all but middle-class Ladino women from participating in the deliberations. For all of Alvarado's talk about equality and the redemption of the Indian, one detects both a racial and a class prejudice in his method of selecting the participants.

In the end approximately 620 delegates from all over Yucatán attended the First Feminist Congress. The large number was certainly a tribute to the hard work of the organizing committee.[95] Alvarado, however, made it possible for so many women to attend by providing the delegates, most of whom were schoolteachers, with free railroad passes, a leave of absence from their teaching posts, and a per diem of eight pesos.[96] Housing posed the biggest problem, and classes in Mérida's schools were suspended from January 13 to January 16, 1916, in order to convert classrooms into temporary dormitories.[97]

On January 9, after the last meeting of the organizing committee of the congress, its president, Consuelo Zavala, was interviewed by *La Voz de la Revolución*. She agreed that she was a feminist and gave the reporter some interesting details concerning her personal struggle for recognition. She had had to fight to gain state accreditation for her *colegio*, which had some four hundred female students enrolled in primary through normal levels. "I think," she told the reporter, "that the modern woman has a right to struggle, to be strong, to learn how to support herself without assistance [from men] in the hard struggles of life."[98] When asked her opinion of the coming congress, Profesora Zavala said that it would be more accurate to call it "talks on feminism." "A congress," she explained, "implies the culmination of an effort, and [these coming meetings] are simply the groundwork for the enormous educational task of making women whole, strong and ready for the struggles of life."[99]

Consuelo Zavala admitted that preparing for the congress had been arduous; what made it worse, however, was the discovery that Yucatán possessed considerably more antifeminist prejudice than she had previously suspected. Men who she thought were intelligent and educated, she lamented, seemed to believe that "feminism is going to come and take away their jobs, their positions," and "that woman wants to set herself above man, to give all the orders and be the absolute mistress...."[100] But for her, feminism meant "educated, strong women, the equals of men in ratiocination, who will form unions in which man and wife will be on the same moral and intellectual level, [and] whose consciences, thoughts, and feelings will run together, parallel.... That is what feminism means, such as few of us seem to understand."[101]

Profesora Zavala revealed that she was not a candidate for the presidency of the congress. She had left a sickbed to head the Junta Directiva, she explained, only because Yucatán had the glory of holding the first feminist congress in the country. No doubt it was this sense of pride and the knowledge that they were participating in both a novel and historic event that accounted for the enthusiasm and euphoria of the delegates at the inaugural session.

The euphoria did not last long, for the reading of Hermila Galindo's paper, "La Mujer en el porvenir" ("Woman in the Future"), at the opening session revealed deep divisions between moderates and extremists. Galindo did not attend the congress; her paper was read by Señor Cesar A. González of the department of education.[102] Galindo's insistence that women have as strong a sex drive as men and that women needed classes in physiology, anatomy, and hygiene in order to understand and control their own bodies absolutely stunned her audience. In addition, Hermila Galindo's approval of divorce, strongly antireligious statements, and attacks on Mexican machismo, shocked the genteel schoolteachers, as did references to foreign pimps who came to Mexico and created a "real industry by exploiting submissive and ignorant Mexican women."[103] One protester, Isolina Pérez, a teacher of astronomy and mathematics at the normal school, thundered from the third row of the Peón Contreras theatre that Galindo's essay should be destroyed.[104] The auditorium erupted in applause, but "there were also some protests among the more radical elements of the congress."[105] After much haggling and confusion, the subject of Galindo's paper was dropped, and the delegates turned their attention to listening to the first papers prepared for the congress.

While Hermila Galindo represented the most radical wing at the First Feminist Congress, Señorita Francisca García Ortiz, identified only as the "granddaughter of the illustrious Don Pablo," represented the small but vocal reactionary wing. This group was patently antifeminist, lamenting that since 1870 more and more Yucatecan women had obtained a secondary education. "Schoolteachers do not marry," insisted García, adding that "encyclopedic knowledge appears to be a barrier to [woman's] happiness...."[106]

The prejudice against educated women that Sor Juana Inés de la Cruz had felt so keenly in the seventeenth century had by no means disappeared in 1916. It had not disappeared by 1966 either, when no more than 26,758 Mexican women out of a total female population of 17,507,809 were studying at the university level.[107] The feminists who published *La Mujer Mexicana* between 1904 and 1908 had often argued that a learned woman did not lose her attractiveness by studying. They thought that men should welcome, not shun, women who were their intellectual equal or superior. For instance, the director of *La Mujer Mexicana*, Profesora Dolores Correa Zapata, writing of Dr. Columba Rivera, stated that

whoever is acquainted with Señorita Rivera will be convinced that knowledge neither kills nor poisons, nor does study cause a woman's youth to wither, nor does it darken her soul, embitter her heart, dress her in mourning or dry up her spirit.[108]

On another occasion Profesora Correa, speaking of Mexico's first woman lawyer, María Sandoval de Zarco, exclaimed:

Don't you see, we have wanted to shout with all our strength, don't you see that knowledge does not rob woman of any of her poetic beauty nor does it incapacitate her for the most humble household tasks?[109]

Neither Hermila Galindo on the left nor Francisca García Ortiz on the right spoke for the majority of the delegates. The pace was set by moderates led by Consuelo Zavala, who, as we saw earlier, had recently made clear her own commitment to feminism. The moderates stressed the opening of schools and teaching careers as the best means of liberating women from the yoke of tradition. They continually maintained that all women, not just 20 percent of the female population, needed access to universal, primary, and laical education. They urged all schools, whether public or private, to foster self-esteem, and declared it was their principal task to help women develop their full potential. Only then could females aspire to positions as doctors, pharmacists, lawyers, and commercial agents, which, in 1916 Yucatán, were careers pursued exclusively by men.[110]

In approaching the sensitive issue of religion, the moderates maintained that the existing system of laical education effectively reduced clerical influence. However, they opposed religious education for those under eighteen, arguing that the young, lacking the full development of their rational faculties, tended to accept all they are taught uncritically. In place of religious education, they stressed that "high principles of morality, humanity, and solidarity" should be inculcated in both men and women.[111] Some delegates wanted to encourage socialist-oriented "pageants" or entertainments to compete with traditional religious festivals.[112] Others suggested that schoolchildren receive special talks by their teachers that would help alleviate fears of an angry and vengeful God.[113] In general, the moderates followed the anticlerical bias of the Liberal party, which had sought to reduce the influence of the church through educational and gradualist means since the 1850s.

The moderates emphatically endorsed the proposal of Señora Porfiria Avila de Rosado, leader of the radicals in attendance, that the Civil Code of 1884 be reformed in every sphere that discriminated against women.[114] The delegates claimed that women would never develop their full potential as free human beings until the legal rights of men and women were equalized. Those articles of the 1884 Civil Code that extinguished the legal and property rights of married women had to be amended. Agreeing with Alvarado, they wanted single women to have the same right as single men to leave the parental home at the age of twenty-one.

The demand for civil code reform was the most important proposal to emerge from the First Feminist Congress and was reflected in President Carranza's Law of Family Relations, dated April 9, 1917. This law guaranteed the rights of married women to (1) draw up contracts, (2) take part in legal suits, (3) act as guardians, and (4) have the same rights as men to the custody of their children. Women were also given equal authority with their husbands to spend family funds. The law also permitted paternity suits and gave parents the right to acknowledge illegitimate children.[115]

The moderates and radicals also agreed on state-sponsored vocational education for women. Coeducational school-farms, they stressed, were needed in the rural areas, and women should be encouraged to develop practical skills in, for example, photography, silver engraving, and henequen fibermaking.[116] Except for a few delegates, the congress agreed that every woman needed to learn how to support herself, for then she could marry out of choice and not out of necessity.

The moderates and radicals parted company, however, in dealing with the questions of "rationalist" education and political rights. In the papers about the second theme of the congress, which was the precise role of the primary school in preparing women for life, some of the delegates supported Alvarado's proposal for "rationalist" schools. The radicals downplayed the antireligious thrust of "rationalist" education, emphasizing that it would replace rote learning and memorization with a freer, more flexible, and more spontaneous method of learning. The moderates, led by Consuelo Zavala, pointed out that few delegates, most of whom were teachers, knew anything about the Spanish anarchist Francisco Ferrer's educational ideas. Teachers first, she argued, had to be trained in the new methods based on Ferrer's "modern school"; then changes could be made.[117] After much heated discussion, the majority of the delegates endorsed Zavala's position.[118]

Ignoring her logic, the radicals accused the moderates of being reactionary and timid. The moderates might well have answered that they, like most women, had been brought up to avoid conflict. Until the general public supported Alvarado's ideas on education, few of the teachers at the First Feminist Congress were willing to endorse changes in the primary schools.

The fourth theme of the congress, centering on leadership roles, revealed Alvarado's assumption that educated Yucatecan women would be eager to participate in political life. Francisca Ascanio spoke for the radicals, arguing that women were intellectually and morally the equals of men, and hence should assume an active role in society. Once constitutional government was reestablished, which Carranza had pledged to do shortly, Señorita Ascanio hoped to see women voting and running for office.[119] At the other extreme, the antifeminists argued that women were not morally and intellectually the equals of men and should *never* participate in public life.[120] Consuelo Zavala, again speaking for the moderates, believed that even educated Mexican women were not psychologically prepared for political participation. For the present, she believed political rights should be reserved for men, and the majority agreed that it was premature to involve women.[121] Women of the future generation would be the ones to receive the vote and fill government positions.[122]

At the very last session of the congress, however, a new petition on suffrage—signed by twenty-eight of the more radical delegates—was hastily submitted. It proposed that Yucatán's constitution be changed so that women over twenty-one could vote in municipal elections and hold local office. It also mandated the state government to initiate an appeal that female suffrage in municipal elections be added to the country's constitution.

The new petition was unanimously approved. Alvarado, who wanted a clearer mandate, announced on June 12, 1916, that a second feminist congress would be held at the end of November. The second meeting, he declared, would be a national feminist congress, and he expressed the hope that women from many Mexican states would be in attendance.[124]

When the second congress met, very few representatives from other states appeared, and from the beginning the conference was named the Second Feminist Congress of Yucatán.[125] The trip to Yucatán from the populous centers of Mexico was long and expensive, and in 1916 even the most liberated women did not usually travel unaccompanied.

The Second Feminist Congress, which took place from November 23 to December 2, 1916, offered an interesting contrast to the first. The novelty had worn off, and only about 234 delegates attended the second congress.[126] While attendance had been voluntary at the first congress, at the second Alvarado made it obligatory for public schoolteachers in

Mérida. Since Consuelo Zavala was absent, the moderates lost their leader; therefore, the radicals dominated the proceedings. After an extremely acrimonious debate, the delegates approved woman suffrage in municipal elections by a vote of 147 to 89. However, when the radicals tried to push for women holding office on the municipal level, their resolution was defeated.[127]

Taking attendance at the congress had wasted at least an hour each day, complained the delegates, so on the last day of the meetings attendance was not taken. As a result, when it came time to vote on the resolution on the election of women to public office, only 90 out of approximately 234 delegates were present and only 30 voted affirmatively.[128] Thus both the first and second feminist congresses of 1916 made clear that few Yucatecan women wanted active political involvement. Only the most radical feminists wanted to vote, and they, only in municipal elections. This was understandable, since until 1910 politics in Yucatán had been the preserve of the henequen kings. Between 1910 and 1915, "politics" consisted of conflict, bribery, electoral fraud, assassination attempts, and finally, military government. It was unreasonable to expect that Yucatecan women, just beginning to claim their rights as full human beings, would want to participate in the dangerous and unsettling game of politics.

In 1915 Profesora María Martínez, a schoolteacher from Mexico City who was observing classroom teaching in the Boston schools, was asked by *The Boston Transcript* about woman suffrage in Mexico. She spoke for most educated, middle-class Mexican women of her day when she said:

Mexican women are not seeking the ballot because at present they are interested in the great rehabilitation of their country. We want the opportunity to study and join every profession open to men. We want all the walks of human society open to us; we believe that by these means we can accomplish as much as by the ballot. However, when the time comes and the women of Mexico feel the need of the franchise we shall demand it, and I am sure we will attain it very easily. At present we are interested in education.[129]

Alvarado was unhappy with the results of the two feminist congresses he had called. He had hoped that women would want to vote in state and national elections and, of course, would vote for him. A man with presidential ambitions, Alvarado saw a possible term as elected governor of Yucatán as a stepping-stone to Mexico's highest office.[130] Despite the recent rebuff at the Second Feminist Congress, when 147 delegates favored women participating in municipal elections only, during 1917 Alvarado encouraged the formation of feminist clubs. The groups, located all over Yucatán, would support his gubernatorial candidacy.[131] Much to his chagrin, he was declared ineligible for election to the governorship because he was not Yucatecan by birth nor had he resided in the state for the required minimum of five years.[132]

Had Alvarado been genuinely popular in Yucatán such constitutional requirements might have been suspended or at least circumvented. This was never the case, despite his earnest efforts to help the state. Because of increased demand during World War I, and because Alvarado broke the power of the International Harvester Company to dictate its price, henequen rose from a low of six cents a pound in 1915 to 19 cents a pound in 1917 and to a maximum of 23 cents a pound in 1918.[133] While Alvarado was governor, the henequen plantation owners received 42 percent of the profits from the sale of henequen; the rest went to supporting Alvarado's educational and social reforms, buying a fleet of eight ships, making harbor and rail improvements, rebuilding a cordage factory, and erecting petroleum storage tanks in Progreso.[134] At the same time, Alvarado was not a bloodthirsty man, he maintained discipline among his troops, and he did not enrich himself at the expense of the public treasury.[135]

His enemies made clear, however, why Alvarado was unpopular. He was a rigid and extremely self-righteous man. As the Mexican historian Fernando Benítez notes, other revolutionary generals could not bear him.[136] Yucatecans, who had an instinctive dislike of "outsiders," accused Alvarado of being despotic, tyrannical, and megalomaniacal.[137] These accusations were not unjustified, for Alvarado stifled contrary public opinion and shut down opposition newspapers.[138] We have already seen how he expected the feminist congresses he called to support *his* views on education and woman suffrage.

In addition, Alvarado's rabid anticlericalism antagonized most Yucatecans, especially when he did nothing to stop the vandalism that destroyed precious works of religious art in the cathedral. Lastly, Alvarado's exemplary and well-intentioned aid to the Maya Indians working in the henequen fields won him the enmity of the Ladino population. Once the Mayas were freed from peonage, they left the plantations in large numbers, and since no Ladino would cut henequen leaves, the peninsula suffered an acute labor shortage.[139]

Although he was not popular in Yucatán, Alvarado was a man of vision. He was the lone revolutionary leader who wanted women to play an equal role in creating a new Mexican society. This explains his concern for female education, insistence that women gain legal equality, and conviction that women were capable of participating in political life. His efforts to help domestic servants and prostitutes were concrete examples of how best to correct some of the most glaring social injustices of the Porfirian era.

The two feminist congresses Alvarado called in January and November 1916 were landmarks in the development of feminist consciousness in modern Mexico. It is true that the radical governor could never have called the two congresses if there had not been a significant number of educated women in Yucatán. Yet it is also true that without his leadership and assistance the two congresses might never have met at all. The resolutions of the delegates impressed both local and national leaders. As we shall see in the next chapter, one of Alvarado's heirs as leader of the Yucatecan Socialist party, Felipe Carrillo Puerto, became an equally determined advocate of female participation in the revolutionary transformation of Mexico. On the national level, President Venustiano Carranza followed the advice of the Yucatecan feminists, for his Law of Family Relations ended the legal inequality of married women. Yucatán was no longer on the periphery, but at the very center of revolutionary change in Mexico.

NOTES

1. Ernest H. Gruening, *Un viaje al estado de Yucatán* (Guanajuato: Talleres Gráficos de *Los Sucesos*, 1924), p. 5.

2. R. B. Brinsmade and M. C. Rolland, *Mexican Problems* (n.p., [1916]), p. 29. In 1923 President Obregón observed that "good work has been done in Yucatán." Gruening, *Un viaje*, p. 3.

3. See, for example, Fernando Benítez, *Ki: El drama de un pueblo y de una planta*, Vida y pensamiento de México (México: Fondo de Cultura Económica, 1956), pp. 95-119; Antonio Bustillos Carrillo, *Yucatán al servicio de la patria y de la revolución* (México: Casa Ramírez Editores, 1959), pp. 105-76; Nelson Reed, *The Caste War of Yucatan* (Stanford: Stanford University Press, 1964), pp. 259-69; and David A. Franz, "Bullets and Bolshevists: A History of the Mexican

Revolution and Reform in Yucatan, 1910-1924'' (Ph.D. diss., University of New Mexico, 1973), pp. 108-275.

4. *The Encyclopedia Americana*, 1976 ed., s.v. "Yucatan," "Yucatan peninsula"; Reed, *The Caste War of Yucatan*, pp. 3-4.

5. Cumberland, *Mexico: The Struggle for Modernity*, pp. 206-7.

6. Howard F. Cline, "The 'Aurora Yucateca' and the Spirit of Enterprise in Yucatan, 1821-1847," *Hispanic American Historical Review*, 27 (February 1947): 48.

7. Ibid., p. 49.

8. *The Encyclopedia Americana*, 1976 ed., s.v. "Henequen."

9. Cline, "The 'Aurora Yucateca'," p. 59. See also Reed, *The Caste War of Yucatan*, p. 8.

10. Mary W. Williams, "Secessionist Diplomacy of Yucatan," *Hispanic American Historical Review* 9 (May 1929): 132.

11. Ibid., pp. 133-43.

12. Cline, "The 'Aurora Yucateca'," p. 31.

13. Benítez, *Ki*, pp. 64-69.

14. Cline, "The 'Aurora Yucateca'," p. 32.

15. Ibid., p. 31. See also Reed, *The Caste War of Yucatan*, p. 26.

16. Quoted by Cline, "The 'Aurora Yucateca'," p. 47.

17. Rodolfo Menéndez, *Rita Cetina Gutiérrez* (Mérida: Yuc.: Imprenta Gamboa Guzmán, 1909), p. 5.

18. Ibid., pp. 14-15.

19. Efrém Leonzo Donde, "Páginas históricas. La educación pública en Yucatán. El Instituto Literario de Niñas (1877-1912)," *La Revista de Yucatán* (Mérida, Yuc.), 13 May 1923, pp. 12-13.

20. Menéndez, *Rita Cetina Gutiérrez*, p. 15.

21. Quoted in ibid.

22. Ibid., p. 20.

23. Ibid., p. 41; and Bustillos Carrillo, *Yucatán al servicio de la patria*, p. 178.

24. *La Voz de la Revolución* (Mérida, Yuc.) 10 January 1916, p. 1; and Bustillos Carrillo, *Yucatán al servicio de la patria*, p. 186.

25. Menéndez, *Rita Cetina Gutiérrez*, p. 31.

26. Ibid., p. 33.

27. Ibid., p. 41.

28. Franz, "Bullets and Bolshevists," p. 18.

29. Ibid.

30. Secretaría de Educación Pública, *La educación pública en México* (México: Talleres Gráficos de la Nación, 1922), p. 73.

31. Ibid.

32. Ibid.

33. Preston E. James, *Latin America* (New York: Odyssey Press, 1942), p. 637.

34. Reed, *The Caste War of Yucatan*, pp. 229-49.

35. Ibid., p. 234.

36. Cline, "The 'Aurora Yucateca'," p. 48, notes that there were 1,515 estates in 1794, 2,413 in 1836, and 3,428 in 1845. Cumberland, *Mexico: The Struggle for Modernity*, pp. 206-7, writes that during the Porfiriato, Yucatecan *hacendados* ("plantation owners") "illegally dispossessed between 60 and 70 Mayan villages of nearly a third of a million acres of land."

37. Cline, "The 'Aurora Yucateca'," p. 53.

38. Franz, "Bullets and Bolshevists," p. 13.

39. Reed, *The Caste War of Yucatan*, p. 22.

40. John Kenneth Turner, *Barbarous Mexico*, The Texas Pan American Series (Austin: University of Texas Press, 1969), p. 15. Turner noted that "men and women are beaten in the fields as well as at the morning roll call," p. 16.

41. Ibid., p. 9.

42. Ibid., pp. 12-13.

43. Reed, *The Caste War of Yucatan*, p. 257.

44. Ibid., p. 258.

45. Franz, "Bullets and Bolshevists," pp. 130-31.

46. Frank Tannenbaum, *Peace by Revolution: An Interpretation of Mexico* (New York: Columbia University Press, 1933), p. 117.

47. Carlo de Fornaro, "General Salvador Alvarado: Fighter and Administrator," *Forum* 55 (January 1916): 74-75.

48. Franz, "Bullets and Bolshevists," p. 108.

49. Fornaro, "General Salvador Alvarado," p. 75.

50. [Salvador Alvarado], *Breves apuntes de la administración del General Salvador Alvarado, como gobernador de Yucatán, con simple expresión de hechos y sus consecuencias* (Mérida, Yuc.: Imprenta del Gobierno Constitucionalista, 1916), pp. 11-15.

51. "La ciudad escolar de los Mayas," *La Voz de la Revolución*, 25 March 1917, pp. 1, 3, and "La obra revolucionaria en Yucatán," *La Voz de la Revolución*, 6 October 1916, p. 4. In 1890 the American philanthropist William R. George founded the George Junior Republic for homeless boys in Freeville, New York. Students ran the school themselves, an idea which appealed to Alvarado as he was trying to train Mexican children in the art of self-government. *La república escolar y su establecimiento en las escuelas yucatecas por decreto del General Salvador Alvarado, gobernador del estado, de 16 de noviembre de 1915* (Mérida, Yuc.: Imprenta y Linotipía, "La Voz de la Revolución," 1916), pp. 1-10.

52. Bustillos Carrillo, *Yucatán al servicio de la patria*, pp. 151-55.

53. [Salvador Alvarado], *Speech of General Alvarado, Governor of the State of Yucatan, at the Closing Session of the Second Pedagogical Congress, held at Mérida* (n.p.: Latin American News Co., [1916]), pp. 11-14.

54. Percy Alvin Martin, "Four Years of Socialistic Government in Yucatan," *The Journal of International Relations* 10 (1919-1920): 210.

55. [Salvador Alvarado], "Ley concediendo libertad a la servidumbre doméstica," Decreto Número 20, 23 April 1915, in Bustillos Carrillo, *Yucatán al servicio de la patria*, p. 159.

56. [Salvador Alvarado], *Informe que el General Salvador Alvarado rinde al primer jefe del Ejército Constitucionalista C. Venustiano Carranza. Comprende su gestión administrativa desde el 19 de marzo de 1915 al 28 de febrero de 1917* (Mérida, Yuc.: Imprenta del Gobierno Constitucionalista, 1917), pp. 26-28; *La Voz de la Revolución*, 26 March 1915, pp. 1, 3.

57. Salvador Alvarado, *La reconstrucción de México*, 2 vols. (México: J. Ballesca y Cía., 1919), 2: 250-54.

58. *La Voz de la Revolución*, 30 April 1915, pp. 1-2.

59. Alvarado, *La reconstrucción de México*, 2: 302.

60. "Reforma a un artículo del código civil," Decreto Número 167, 14 July 1915, in *Diario oficial del Gobierno Constitucionalista del Estado de Yucatán* (Mérida, Yuc.), 5 January 1916, pp. 74-76.

61. Ibid., p. 75.

62. [Salvador Alvarado], *Informe que de su gestión como gobernador provisional del estado de Yucatán, rinde ante el H. Congreso del mismo, el ciudadano General Salvador Alvarado* (Mérida, Yuc.: Imprenta Constitucionalista, 1918), p. 16.

63. Ibid., pp. 14-15.

64. Rafael de Zayas Enríquez, *El estado de Yucatán* (New York: Little and Ives, 1908), p. 292.

65. [Alvarado], *Informe que de su gestión*, pp. 16-30.

66. [Alvarado], *Speech of General Alvarado*, p. 7.

67. [Alvarado], *Informe que de su gestión*, p. 21.

68. Primer Congreso Feminista de Yucatán, *Anales de esa memorable asamblea* (Mérida, Yuc.: Talleres Tipográficos del "Ateneo Peninsular," 1916), p. 96.

69. [Alvarado], *Informe que rinde . . . al C. Venustiano Carranza*, p. 38.

70. Menéndez, *Rita Cetina Gutiérrez*, p. 21.

71. [Alvarado], *Speech of General Alvarado*, p. 14.

72. Reed, *The Caste War of Yucatan*, p. 260.

73. Ibid.

74. [Alvarado], *Speech of General Alvarado*, p. 9.

75. Ibid., pp. 9-10.

76. Bustillos Carrillo, *Yucatán al servicio de la patria*, p. 166; [Alvarado], *Breves apuntes*, p. 9.

77. [Alvarado], *Informe que rinde...al C. Venustiano Carranza*, p. 80.

78. *La Voz de la Revolución* was dubbed *La Voz de la Adulación* by Carlos R. Menéndez, the peninsula's leading journalist and editor, whose modern press was confiscated by Alvarado in order to establish *La Voz de la Revolución*. See Carlos R. Menéndez, *La evolución del periodismo en la península de Yucatán* (Mérida, Yuc., 1931), pp. 24-25. *La Voz de la Revolución* first appeared on March 25, 1915, and ended publication in 1919, just after Menéndez was able to reestablish *La Revista de Yucatán* as the leading newspaper of the peninsula. Ibid., p. 25.

79. Artemisa Saénz Royo, *Historia político-social-cultural del movimiento femenino en México, 1914-1950* (México: M. León Sánchez, 1954), pp. 48-49. Ms. Saénz's account of the feminist congresses in Yucatán is completely erroneous. In the first place, she was unaware that two congresses were called, and she confused the November 1916 congress (which she attended) with the one held in January 1916. She asserts that "hundreds of women sent from different European and Latin American countries" attended the January 1916 conference, a fantastic claim unsupported by the memoir of the congress or the daily accounts of its meetings in *La Voz de la Revolución*. For the only complete and reliable account of the Second Feminist Congress one must turn to the pages of *La Voz de la Revolución* from November 23 to December 2, 1916.

80. Hermila Galindo, *Estudio de la Srita. Hermila Galindo con motivo de los temas que han de absolverse en el Segundo Congreso Feminista de Yucatán.* (Mérida, Yuc.: Imprenta del Gobierno Constitucionalista, 1916), p. 5. See also her *La doctrina Carranza y el acercamiento indolatino* (México: n.p., 1919), pp. 159-61.

81. J. D. Ramírez Garrido, *Al margen del feminismo* (México: Talleres "Pluma y Lapiz," 1918), p. 44.

82. Ibid.; and *La Voz de la Revolución*, 29 October 1915.

83. See *La Voz de la Revolución* from 16 November 1915, to 9 January 1916, for the preparations for the congress and from 11 January to 17 January 1916 for an account of its meetings.

84. Primer Congreso Femenino Internacional de la República Argentina, *Historia, Actas y Trabajos* (Buenos Aires: Imprenta A. Ceppi, 1911), p. 7.

85. Ibid., pp. 25-29.

86. *La Voz de la Revolución*, 17 November 1915, p. 3, and Primer Congreso Feminista de Yucatán, *Anales*, pp. 40-41.

87. *Memoria del Primer Congreso Pedagógico del Estado de Chiapas* (Tuxtla Gutiérrez: Imprenta del Gobierno del Estado, 1916), pp. 4-5; Juan Jiménez Méndez, "Informe sobre su gestión gubernativa en el estado de Oaxaca, 1917-1919," (Oaxaca: n.p., 1920), pp. 26-27.

88. *La Voz de la Revolución*, 17 November 1915, p. 3.

89. Ibid.

90. Primer Congreso Feminista de Yucatán, *Anales*, p. 97.

91. Luis Rosado Vega, *El desastre: Asuntos yucatecos. La obra revolucionaria del General Salvador Alvarado* (Havana: Imprenta "El Siglo XX," 1919), p. 109.

92. Primer Congreso Feminista de Yucatán, *Anales*, pp. 39-52.

93. Ibid.

94. See chapter 1.

95. *La Voz de la Revolución*, 14 January 1916, p. 1.

96. Primer Congreso Feminista de Yucatán, *Anales*, pp. 47, 50-51, 55.

97. Ibid., p. 57.

98. *La Voz de la Revolución*, 10 January 1916, p. 1.

99. Ibid.

100. Ibid.

101. Ibid.

102. Primer Congreso Feminista de Yucatán, *Anales*, p. 69.

103. Hermila Galindo, *La mujer en el porvenir* (Mérida, Yuc.: Imprenta y Litografía de "La Voz de la Revolución"), p. 13.

104. Primer Congreso Feminista de Yucatán, *Anales*, p. 69.

105. Ibid., p. 70.

106. Ibid., p. 72.

107. In 1966 only a third of secondary school graduates and only a sixth of university graduates were women. See United Nations, *Statistical Yearbook, 1969* (New York: United Nations, 1970), p. 734. There has been a significant increase in women graduates in the 1970s. By 1976, 26 percent of the 577,595 students attending Mexican institutions of higher learning were women, and, by 1978, 34.9 percent of the students attending the Universidad Autónoma Nacional de México were females. See *The Chronicle of Higher Education* (Washington, D.C.), 8 September 1980, p. 15.

108. *La Mujer Mexicana*, 1 August 1904, p. 1.

109. Ibid., 1 October 1904, p. 2.

110. Primer Congreso Feminista de Yucatán, *Anales*, pp. 80, 90-92, 93-96.

111. Ibid., pp. 77-78, 111.

112. Ibid., p. 73.

113. Ibid.

114. *La Voz de la Revolución*, 14 January 1916, p. 6.

115. Sofía Villa de Buentello, *La mujer y la ley* (México: Imprenta Franco-Americana, 1921), pp. 137-47; Venustiano Carranza, *Ley sobre relaciones familiares* (México: Imprenta del Gobierno, 1917), pp. 9, 22-24, 38-40. It should be noted, however, that according to Article 215 of Carranza's law, a married woman could not, without her husband's consent, acknowledge a child born of

another father before her marriage. On the other hand, Article 216 permitted a husband to acknowledge an illegitimate child born before or during his present marriage, without regard for his wife's sentiments. Ibid., p. 47.

116. Primer Congreso Feminista de Yucatán, *Anales*, pp. 95-96.

117. Ibid., pp. 90-93.

118. Ibid., p. 93.

119. Ibid., pp. 102-6.

120. Ibid., p. 106.

121. Ibid., pp. 108-9.

122. Ibid., p. 109.

123. Ibid., p. 127.

124. *La Voz de la Revolución*, 16 November 1916, p. 1.

125. Ibid., 24 November 1916, p. 1.

126. Ibid.

127. Ibid., 30 November 1916, p. 5.

128. Ibid.

129. *Carranza and Public Education in Mexico* (New York: n.p., 1915), p. 23.

130. Benítez, *Ki*, p. 108. *La Revista de Yucatán* (Mérida, Yuc.), reported that when the Moderate Socialist party that Alvarado helped form fell apart, he gravitated to the Partido Liberal Constitucionalista, hoping to be named its presidential candidate. *La Revista de Yucatán*, 10 January 1923, p. 1, and 7 March 1923, p. 1.

131. *La Voz de la Revolución*, 11 December 1916, p. 1; 15 December 1916, p. 1; 16 December 1916, p. 1. By December 16, there were eighteen feminist political clubs in Yucatán, ibid., 17 December 1916, p. 1.

132. Ernesto Higuera, ed., *Actuación revolucionaria del General Salvador Alvarado en Yucatán* (México: Costa-Amic, 1965), p. 19.

133. Benítez, *Ki*, p. 107.

134. Ibid., pp. 111-13.

135. Bustillos Carrillo, *Yucatán al servicio de la patria*, p. 162; Benítez, *Ki*, p. 102.

136. Benítez, *Ki*, p. 102.

137. Rosado Vega, *El desastre*, p. 234.

138. Menéndez, *La evolución del periodismo*, pp. 24-25.

139. For a highly critical view of Alvarado's labor and other policies, see [Carlos R. Menéndez], *Las seis coronas del General* (Mérida, Yuc.: Imprenta "La Amadita," 1917), pp. 34-39. See also Martin, "Four Years of Socialistic Government in Yucatan," pp. 216-19.

4

FELIPE CARRILLO PUERTO AS CHAMPION OF WOMEN'S RIGHTS IN YUCATÁN, 1922-1923

The late Frank Tannenbaum, in his *Peace by Revolution*, published in 1933, believed that the upheaval that began in Mexico in 1910 "was essentially an agrarian movement. The other aspects of the Revolution have been incidental by-products and trimmings."[1] This attitude may explain why Felipe Carrillo Puerto (1874-1924), the socialist governor of the state of Yucatán from February 1922 until his execution by political enemies in January 1924, is remembered almost exclusively as a modern, and martyred apostle of the oppressed male peasantry of Yucatán. Very little attention has been paid to Carrillo Puerto's program for Yucatecan women, whom he regarded as a group oppressed by most men, whether the men were rich or poor, strong or weak.[2]

How does one account for Carrillo Puerto's interest in women's liberation? What influence did Carrillo's predecessor, the profeminist Governor Salvador Alvarado have on Carrillo's ideas about the emancipation of women? What did Carrillo seek to do for women in Yucatán and elsewhere? Finally, how did women respond to his ideas on their future liberation? In this chapter we shall provide some answers to these previously unraised questions and try to shed some light on a largely ignored and almost totally forgotten aspect of twentieth-century history.

In the same book cited above, Tannenbaum remarked that the 1910-20 upheaval "has not been a national revolution in the sense that all of the

This chapter originally appeared in Asunción Lavrin, ed., *Latin American Women: Historical Perspectives* (Westport, Conn: Greenwood Press, 1979).

country participated in the same movement and at the same time. It has been local, regional, sometimes by counties."[3] This was also the case with respect to women's liberation in Mexico. Yucatán championed women's rights under the leadership of Salvador Alvarado and Felipe Carrillo Puerto, just as the state of Morelos became the center of the agrarian revolution under the leadership of Emiliano Zapata.

As indicated in the previous chapter, there are a number of reasons why Yucatán became the center for a women's liberation movement in Mexico. In contrast to many of the landlocked, mountainous states of Mexico's interior, Yucatán faced the sea and exported most of her henequen abroad. For at least fifty years before the revolution that region had regular steamship service with Havana, New Orleans, New York, and European ports. As a result, Yucatán was in closer contact with and subject to greater influence by the United States and Western Europe than were most Mexican states. Mérida, the capital, was only twenty-two miles from Yucatán's chief port, Progreso, and at Mérida, as we have seen, an incipient feminist movement began in 1870. By the time the 1910 Revolution broke out, there were also a few distinguished teachers at the Mérida School of Jurisprudence and later at the School of Medicine who favored the cause of feminism in Yucatán. Between 1910 and 1915 eight students at the law school prepared theses on the subject of divorce and the legal rights of women, an extraordinarily large number when one considers the school's size.[4] And later, in the early 1920s, Dr. Eduardo Ursáiz, rector of the University of Yucatán, and author of a profeminist novel, *Eugenia*, was to give the first lectures on birth control to medical students in Mérida.[5]

Encouraged by the progressive ambience he found in Yucatán, General Salvador Alvarado developed more radical programs in every area of life in Yucatán than Carranza did in Mexico City. And, once Mexico's new constitution of early 1917, ended the preconstitutional or military phase of Carranza's revolutionary government, Alvarado sought to consolidate his reforms and launch his candidacy as constitutional governor of Yucatán by founding, by June 1917, the Socialist party of Yucatán.[6] However, when it became clear that legal obstacles against Alvarado's candidacy could not be overcome (he was not a native Yucatecan nor had he resided in the state a minimum of five years), the political ambitions of Alvarado's protégés in the newly formed Socialist party were kindled. It was at this point that Felipe Carrillo Puerto emerged as one of the key leaders of the radical left in Yucatán.

Felipe Carrillo Puerto was born in Motul, Yucatán, in 1874, of a large but not impoverished white, middle-class family. His friend and biographer, Edmundo Bolío Ontiveros, states that from childhood, Carrillo Puerto felt great sympathy and affection for the oppressed masses of Indians and peasants of Motul. Like most whites, however, Carrillo never worked in the henequen fields. Instead, he tried his hand at various occupations and business ventures, all of which failed. His attempt to run a newspaper, *El Heraldo de Motul*, also ended in failure, not necessarily because Carrillo lacked business sense, but more probably because his muckraking irritated powerful landlords. At the start of the revolution he was business agent and correspondent in Motul for the prestigious *La Revista de Mérida*, and his friendship with its owner, Delio Moreno Canton, and its ablest reporter, Carlos R. Menéndez, destined to become Yucatán's greatest journalist and newspaper publisher in the period from 1910 to his death in 1955, helped launch Carrillo Puerto's political career.[7]

A life-long enemy of the *casta divina* ("divine caste") as the *hacendados* of Yucatán were called, Carrillo Puerto also seems to have had differences with whatever government was in power in Mexico, whether Porfirian, Maderista, or Carrancista.[8] Nor did he become a close associate or member of Alvarado's inner circle, although as governor, Carrillo was to carry on many policies and programs first initiated or proposed by Alvarado in 1915-18. In 1916 Carrillo Puerto was president of the Agrarian Committee of Motul, and worked to organize peasants into "Leagues of Resistance" against the landowners. His political influence grew, and in late 1916 and early 1917 he served as alternate delegate to the Querétaro constitutional convention. In 1918, when Alvarado had to step down as governor and the ex-railroad worker Carlos Castro Morales became the Socialist party's candidate for Alvarado's post, Carrillo Puerto succeeded Castro as the head of the Socialist party. Working from the offices of the Central League of Resistance in Mérida, from 1918 to 1921 Carrillo became the most powerful political figure in Yucatán (while also serving in the national Chamber of Deputies). His supporters included some seventy thousand peasants and workers he had organized into militant resistance leagues. In addition to providing muscle against the Yucatecan upper classes, these workers paid monthly dues of at least a peso and a half each, thus providing Carrillo Puerto with campaign funds. On February 1, 1922, at the age of forty-eight, Felipe Carrillo

Puerto became governor of Yucatán, a post he was to hold until his January 3, 1924 execution by enemies who took advantage of the De la Huerta uprising against President Obregón to stage a counterrevolutionary military coup in Yucatán.[9]

Despite the fact that Alvarado and Carrillo Puerto had never been close personal friends, as Socialists they shared similar ideas on social and economic issues, and this was especially true of their ideas on women. In some cases Carrillo continued programs and policies first initiated by Alvarado, while in others he implemented ideas first suggested but never realized by his predecessor. However, Carrillo did not merely plagiarize Alvarado, as his conservative enemies charged,[10] but he took some radical initiatives, especially with respect to "free love," easy divorce, and birth control, which owed little to Alvarado and even less to Mexican feminists.

Both Alvarado and Carrillo Puerto viewed religion as an archenemy of progress, and both sought to free women from church control and convert them into active agents of "defanatization," as they both stated in their campaign against Catholicism in Yucatán. In his campaign against the church, Alvarado won the support of the more radical teachers at the feminist congresses of 1916, who advocated a "rationalistic" approach to religion. Carrillo Puerto went further and tried to enlist women of all classes, not just secular schoolteachers, in his effort to rid Yucatán of religion altogether. However, he seems to have underestimated the depth of religious sentiment among the ordinary people of Yucatán, and his campaign against religion alienated many women as well as men who otherwise agreed with his policies.[11]

Alvarado and Carrillo Puerto deplored the influence of the church over women and sought to diminish its power by interesting women in political affairs. In his *La Reconstrucción de México* (1919), Alvarado advocated that women should first vote in municipal elections and later in state and national elections. Once their civic education had progressed, Alvarado urged that women be permitted to run for office. Carrillo Puerto, who had built up what amounted to a one-party regime in Yucatán and thus controlled elections, accelerated the process. Early in 1922 he proposed a law to the state legislature giving women the right to vote. Then he urged women who agreed with his principles to run for office. In that same year, the schoolteacher Rosa Torres, who participated in the First Feminist Congress of Yucatán in January 1916, became the first woman in Mexican history to hold an elective office when she served as president of the Municipal Council of Mérida.[12]

In elections for the state legislature in 1923, Carrillo's Socialist party picked three women as deputies and one as an alternate out of a total of eighteen deputies and eighteen alternates. His younger sister, Elvia Carrillo Puerto, a close collaborator in all his initiatives on behalf of women, ran in the fifth district and won by an overwhelming majority of 5,115 votes.[13] Beatriz Peniche, a librarian who had also participated in the First Feminist Congress called by Alvarado, won in the second district, while Raquel Dzib and Guadalupe Lara were successful as candidate and alternate in the third and fourth legislative districts respectively.[14]

Their victory was short lived, however, and the November 1923, elections were set aside when Carrillo Puerto's enemies gained control in Yucatán in December. When Socialists regained power in Yucatán by April 1924 they did not reinstate the women candidates. Furthermore, there was no further reference to women in politics in Socialist party platforms for the rest of the decade.[15]

Alvarado and Carrillo Puerto believed that women's liberation meant primarily the liberation of women from exclusive concern with domestic life. They advocated that women join the work force, but the economic opportunities available to women in a one-crop, agricultural economy were severely limited, even when the price of henequen was high, as was the case during World War I. By 1922, however, the price of henequen had plummeted, and worse, Yucatán's chief customer, the United States, was turning to other producers of sisal to satisfy its needs for binder twine. Without economic diversification, growth, and development, none of which occurred under Alvarado or Carrillo Puerto, women could not possibly join the work force without competing with men for the few available jobs in public administration, commercial houses, banks, and the like. Women dominated in primary school education simply because the pay was so wretched, usually less than two pesos a day, and the need for dedication, so complete, that few men sought these positions.[16]

Given this situation, one can understand why Alvarado and Carrillo Puerto after him urged women to devote some of their time to unremunerated educational, charitable, and welfare activities. In his essay, *Mi sueño*, in which Alvarado described his hopes for Yucatán's future, he envisioned the day when Yucatecan women would form organizations to combat alcohol, drugs, and prostitution, and would establish the "Republic of Virtue" that is the dream of modern revolutionaries.[17] He wanted to see educated women help unemployed females, care for abandoned children, and redeem fallen women.[18] No doubt influenced by the important role women played in charitable activities in the United States, he urged Yucatecan women to hold charity bazaars, care for and console the sick, set up *cocinas económicas* (inexpensive restaurants) for working women, administer a free milk program for poor children, organize literacy campaigns for adults, establish children's libraries, and give talks on home economics and hygiene to poor women. These many goals were to be carried out by women themselves, organized into *Ligas Femeniles* ("Feminine Leagues") with financial and moral support from the state.[19]

Carrillo Puerto agreed with Alvarado that women should organize into associations and take an active part in the transformation of Yucatecan society. Helped by his sister Elvia, who shared Carrillo's radical sentiments, *Ligas Feministas* were established throughout Yucatán, beginning in Mérida, with the Rita Cetina Gutiérrez Feminist League. Elvia Carrillo became president of the Mérida league and dominated it and the provincial feminist leagues as Felipe Carrillo dominated the male resistance leagues through his control of the central league in Mérida. The *Ligas Feministas* of 1922-23 addressed themselves to the problems Alvarado mentioned in his writings, and Elvia Carrillo and her associates conducted a moralizing campaign designed to rid Yucatán of drugs, alcohol, and prostitution. In addition, they stimulated the literacy campaign, awarding prizes to those who taught the most women to read and write in a given period of time. And, as urged by Alvarado in his *Mi sueño*, members of the Rita Cetina Gutiérrez League also gave talks on home economics, child care, and hygiene to poor women. However, it was precisely in this area that the Ligas soon scandalized *la gente decente* by advocating birth control in their talks to *la gente humilde* ("the lower classes") of Yucatán.[20]

While governor, Alvarado sought to introduce some modern ideas on sex education in Yucatán, but he met such a wall of resistance that he was forced to retract his suggestions for sexual education in the schools and even had to abandon his program of coeducational classes beyond the first two grades.[21] Carrillo Puerto ignored this resistance, and at the beginning of his administration in February 1922 he had a thirteen-page pamphlet by Margaret Sanger entitled "La regulación de la natalidad, o la brújula del hogar'' (''Birth control, or the compass of the home'') published in Mérida for wide distribution.[22] It was precisely this pamphlet ''on safe and scientific measures for avoiding conception'' that Mrs. Sanger could not distribute in the United States at the time because, as she stated in 1920 in *Women and the New Race,* ''a law dating back to 1873. . . prohibits by criminal statute the distribution and regulation of contraceptive measures.''[23] In mid-1923 Carrillo Puerto, through his friend Dr. Ernest Gruening, who was a member of the National Council of the American Birth Control League, Inc., invited Mrs.Sanger to come to Yucatán to set up birth control clinics. On July 3, 1923, Mrs. Anne Kennedy, executive secretary of the league, wrote Carrillo Puerto that Mrs. Sanger could not come herself but had instructed Mrs. Kennedy to go in her place and report to the governor on the league's clinical work in New York. As a result of Mrs. Kennedy's visit to Yucatán in August 1923, plans were made to establish two birth control clinics in Mérida.[24] Ernest Gruening wrote that the clinics were set up to provide recently married couples with information on contraception.[25] However, *Tierra,* the mouthpiece of Carrillo's Socialist party, specified that one of the clinics was being established at the Women's and Children's Hospital in Mérida, while the other ''would be established in the segregated district for prostitutes,'' thus contradicting Gruening's assertion that the birth control clinics were solely for young proletarian couples seeking to rear only as many children as they could support. In retrospect it appears that in providing prostitutes with contraceptive information Carrillo Puerto was trying to reduce the high rate of venereal disease in Yucatán (he even decreed a law requiring men to present the prostitutes they solicited with a certificate of health), but few of his contemporaries saw matters with such scientific detachment and were outraged at his actions. Carrillo Puerto's measures with respect to prostitutes called into question his claim of moralizing society, and his efforts to help them were viewed as evidence that Carrillo Puerto and his friends were receiving payoffs from prostitutes.[26]

Even if one sympathizes with Carrillo Puerto's desire to help women avoid having unwanted children, it is questionable if his methods were of any real help to most women in that society at that particular time. What good were Mrs. Sanger's methods to women who could not read and write, who lacked a supply of uncontaminated running water, and who could not afford to pay for the syringes, douche bags, douche solutions, suppositories, or pessaries recommended in her pamphlet? Also, Mrs. Sanger's assertion that the methods she advised were safe and sure was misleading and in fact untrue. After considerable experimentation, and beginning only in 1923, a year after the Sanger pamphlet was published in Yucatán, Dr. Dorothy Bocker, the head of the Clinical Research Bureau in New York, found that the most successful contraceptive techniques required the use of a spermicidal jelly in combination with a Mensinga-type diaphragm, which was produced only in Germany.[27] That may have been great news for middle- and upper-class women in New York, but it could hardly help the impoverished women of the world who lacked the means of purchasing such sophisticated items. Lastly, Mrs. Sanger's advice that women take a good laxative four days before the menstrual cycle began was downright dangerous in a region where diarrhea, dysentery, and gastroenteritis were (and still are) endemic. In 1924, Sofía Villa de Buentello summed up the views of moderate feminists on the subject of birth control by stating that "we are not yet ready to advocate it."[28]

Carrillo Puerto's radical views on marriage and divorce also aroused considerable controversy in Yucatán. He supported the idea of "free love," which to radical Socialists meant that "a man and a woman, moved by instinct to preserve the species, united their hearts, minds, and bodies" without the sanction of church or state.[29] As a result, Carrillo believed that marriage was neither a religious rite nor a civil contract, thus departing from both age-old tradition as well as from more recent secular liberal legislation. This legislation and Carranza's divorce law of 1914 and Law of Domestic Relations of 1917 defined marriage as a civil contract that could be dissolved only by mutual consent or at the instance of the guiltless spouse.[30] Carrillo Puerto's March 1923 divorce law, on the other hand, defined marriage as "a voluntary union based on love, for the purpose of founding a home, and dissoluble at the wish of either party."[31]

Socialists insisted that Carrillo Puerto's ideas on free love and divorce would have a moralizing effect.[32] However, on March 5, 1923, Carrillo Puerto's old and once intimate friend, Carlos R. Menéndez, published an article in his *La Revista de Yucatán*, the most widely read newspaper in the peninsula, which did not support the socialist thesis that Carrillo Puerto's divorce law was intended as a moralizing factor. The article revealed that Carrillo had sent a note to all the Mexican consuls in the

United States informing them that Americans could get a divorce with ease after thirty-days' residence in Yucatán. Divorces by mutual consent would cost 15 dollars while those at the request of only one of the spouses would cost 125 dollars. All divorce cases were to be handled exclusively by lawyers who were members of Carrillo's Leagues of Resistance, which was another way of saying that Carrillo Puerto would personally profit from each divorce case, for every member of the Resistance Leagues paid dues commensurate with his income.[33]

Carrillo Puerto's image was further tarnished when he took advantage of the very divorce law he promulgated and left his wife of thirty years, Isabel Palma, to court a much younger woman, the American writer Alma Reed.[34] His behavior gave credence to the charge that in Mexico, where male supremacy was the rule, divorce would be an advantage only to "the blackguards who, avid for pleasure, will increase the number of repudiated women."[35]

For all its radical features, Carrillo Puerto's divorce law kept intact the sexual double standard so conspicuous in Mexican legislation and so galling to feminists. Under the new law, adultery by men was viewed with indulgence, and any divorced man could remarry immediately. A divorced woman, on the other hand, had to wait three hundred days before she could remarry, which was obviously intended to assure the second husband that she was not pregnant by the first.

The reaction of most legally married Yucatecans to Carrillo Puerto's divorce law was to ignore it. From March 1923 until Carrillo Puerto's death ten months later, many Americans sought a divorce in Yucatán, but fewer than a dozen Yucatecan couples resorted to the new law.[36] Until very recent times, divorce has been fairly uncommon in Mexico. The 1930 census noted that only 40,534 persons, or slightly more than 1 percent of the legally married population, were divorced.[37] This confirms the American lawyer R. B. Gaither's observation in 1923 that laws like the recent Yucatecan divorce decree were "not really the basic laws of the people of Mexico. They are merely the nightmare of the respectable element."[38]

Carrillo Puerto had an opportunity to publicize his ideas on women's liberation and feminists had their chance to react to them when the Mexican branch of the Pan American League for the Elevation of Women decided to hold its first congress in Mexico City from May 20 to May 30, 1923. The congress was the brainchild of Profesora Elena Torres, a remarkable woman who, possibly because of her radical ideas, has received very little attention from the more conventional feminists who have compiled the few books available on notable Mexican women.[39] Profesora Torres was a pioneer in progressive education in Mexico and a close collaborator of both Salvador Alvarado and Felipe Carrillo Puerto. She was also a friend of Hermila Galindo, Mexico's most radical feminist from 1915 to 1919, and went to Yucatán to represent her at the Second Feminist Congress of Mérida, convoked by Alvarado in November, 1916.[40] Impressed with her abilities and her advanced views on education, Alvarado asked Profesora Torres to establish a Montessori school in Mérida, the first in the republic. After Alvarado left Yucatán, Profesora Torres remained, and in 1918 she and Felipe Carrillo Puerto were among the original organizers of the Latin American Bureau of the Third International, a socialist organization that sought to create solidarity between the Mexican and Russian working classes.[41]

In April 1922, at the first Pan American Conference of Women, held in Baltimore, Maryland, Profesora Torres was elected vice-president for North America (comprising the United States, Mexico, and the Caribbean) of the newly formed Pan American League for the Elevation of Women.[42] In this capacity, she issued invitations to all the state governors of Mexico and to feminist organizations in the United States, Cuba, and Mexico to send representatives to a congress on women to be held in Mexico from May 20 to May 30, 1923. The congress was attended by delegates from at least twenty Mexican states, some appointed by the governors and others representing the various feminist organizations that were springing up in Mexico City and the larger provincial cities.[43] Most of the delegates were professional women, and among the distinguished representatives were Mexico's first women doctors, Matilda P. Montoya and Columba Rivera, and Julia Nava de Ruisánchez, one of the founders of La Sociedad Protectora de la Mujer (the Women's Protective Society), the oldest feminist society in Mexico City, in 1904. In addition, from the United States the National League of Women Voters, the Women's International League for Peace and Freedom, the Parent Teachers Association, the YWCA, the Los Angeles Council of Catholic Women, and the American Birth Control League, also sent one or more delegates.[44] With such divergent organizations represented, the historic congress promised to be most interesting.

It was. Not because the American delegates ever had a chance to air their differences, but because the three delegates from Yucatán, led by Elvia Carrillo Puerto, had the congress in an uproar from the beginning. Undaunted by their total lack of experience as delegates to an international congress, the Yucatecan delegation sought to impose their views and dominate the meetings, much to the distress of President Elena Torres, who privately shared many of their radical ideas. However, Profesora Torres was an experienced parliamentarian who had worked long and hard to bring the congress to fruition, and although decidedly anticapitalist and antiimperialist in her views, she found herself in the ironic position of conspiring with the American delegates to keep such controversial issues as female sexuality, birth control, "free love," and sex education in the schools from dominating, and possibly wrecking the congress.[45]

On the second day of the congress, President Torres had a secret meeting with the American delegates. Backed by the majority of the feminists at the congress who feared the Yucatecan delegates would discredit the women's movement in Mexico, they passed a resolution limiting debate on each matter under discussion. However, the Yucatecans countered by boycotting the sessions and threatened to leave the congress altogether. The Yucatecan delegation won out, and articles in the leading newspapers of Mexico City reveal that the debate on birth control and sexual problems, for example, dominated two of the six days of meetings.[46] In addition, the Yucatecan delegates gave a number of other papers on controversial issues. They denounced conventional marriage as "legal slavery," offered remedies for the white slave traffic, advocated coeducation and sex education in the schools, and said easy divorce would force women to seek work outside the home. They also propagandized in favor of socialist leagues of resistance as the only means of bringing social reform to Mexico.[47] By the end of the conference, the delegates had been fully apprised of Felipe Carrillo Puerto's ideas on women's liberation in Yucatán.

The Yucatecan delegation stole most of the headlines and monopolized most of the sessions, but the published resolutions of the congress reveal that their more controversial suggestions were either rejected or considerably watered down. For example, their proposal for birth control was rejected overwhelmingly in favor of a resolution calling on the Superior

Council of Health to establish pre- and post-natal clinics throughout
Mexico to combat the very high infant mortality rate in the country.[48] The
delegates reasoned that birth control was not the answer for a country that
had experienced a severe population decline during the Mexican Revolution,
which every day continued to lose Mexican workers to the United States,
and where as many as 80 percent of all infants born died within weeks.
One delegate noted that "first it is necessary to teach people to read
before you can teach them not to have children,"[49] an observation that
experience has confirmed. In an article published in 1973, Nora Scott
Kinzer observed that in Latin America "birth rates are low where there is
a high literacy rate . . . and lowered drastically where literacy campaigns
are combined with governmental birth control efforts."[50]

The delegates also rejected the Yucatecan proposal that the congress
endorse the idea of "free love" on the grounds that such a doctrine only
encouraged licentiousness. Instead they passed a resolution calling on
feminist organizations to use their influence to change the marriage
ceremony from an expensive, theatrical display to a simple one that
emphasized the nobility of the act.[51] Another resolution asked that the
law providing that no fees be charged for the civil marriage ceremony be
strictly enforced.[52]

The delegates rejected the use of the term "sexual education," but did
recommend that biology, hygiene, prenatal and infant care, eugenics,
and euthenics be part of the school curriculum. The Yucatecan recommendation for coeducational schools was not mentioned in the resolutions. Lastly, the Yucatecan recommendation that militant leagues of
resistance be established in Mexico was diluted into a resolution calling
for the formation of women's associations to be active in social reform.

Susana Betancourt of Yucatán made one recommendation that was
heartily endorsed by the congress, as it had been a persistent demand of
feminists for some time. The Mexican branch of the Pan American
League of Women went on record "emphatically in favor of a single
sexual standard for men and women." In this connection, the president of
the congress, Elena Torres, presented a paper at the last working session
of the meetings calling on the Mexican Congress to remove the inequita-
ble features in the Law of Family Relations of 1917. Specifically, Torres
wanted Articles 77, 93, 97, and 101 to apply the same criterion to men
and women, and she recommended that two other articles be suppressed,
one which did not permit an "innocent" wife to remarry for 300 days or a

"guilty" one for two years.[54] Articles 77 and 93 severely punished a wife's infraction of the moral code, both before and after a divorce, and Article 97 specified that a guiltless wife could lose custody of her children if she did not live "honestly." At the same time, Article 101 made it possible for the ex-spouse to pay an amount equivalent to five years of support and be free of any further obligation.[55] In a country where honest labor by unskilled women is paid a pittance, and where divorced women, like unwed mothers, are considered "unowned goods of easy access," as María Elvira Bermúdez observed in 1955 in *La vida familiar del mexicano*,[56] it is easy to see why Torres and other feminists objected to the stern dictates of the Law of Family Relations insofar as women were concerned.

At the May 24, 1923, meetings, when the assembly voted down birth control, Elvia Carrillo Puerto accused the majority of being "bourgeoise," reactionary, and ignorant of the misery in which the masses lived.[57] The charge was inaccurate, for while most Mexican feminists rejected the very ideas that had gained Carrillo Puerto notoriety in the country, they supported other proposals which reveal that they were acquainted with Mexico's most pressing social problems and wanted to participate in their solution. For example, the delegates petitioned the Mexican Congress to pass the labor legislation provided for in Article 123 of the 1917 constitution, a reform not enacted until 1931. They asked that domestic servants be protected by that same legislation; today they are still virtually unprotected. Only since 1975 have domestic servants been eligible for national health services, *but* only at the discretion of the employer. The delegates also urged that juvenile courts be established in Mexico, an urgent need that began to be attended to only in 1929 when the first juvenile court was established in Mexico City.[58]

Unlike their more timid predecessors at the feminist congresses of Yucatán of 1916 who asked for political rights at some future time, the majority of the delegates at the First Feminist Congress of the Pan American League agreed that the only way women would see the laws they proposed enacted was to vote and run for office. They therefore resolved to petition the Mexican Congress to establish equal political rights for men and women. No doubt the extension of the vote to women in England and the United States a few years earlier accelerated the demand for political rights in Mexico, but it took the feminists another thirty years to convince the men in power to end the political inferiority of women.[59]

The 1923 Pan American Women's Congress provides the historian with evidence that Carrillo Puerto's espousal of women's liberation during 1922-23 did not win the endorsement of the country's leading feminists. They rejected his ideas on "free love" and birth control, not because they were religious bigots, as was suggested, but because they saw social problems in another light. To the feminists, Mexico's big problem was "paid love," not "free love," and prostitution was as much in evidence in Yucatán as elsewhere, despite all the revolutionary rhetoric.[60] Also, advocating "free love" in a country where at least seven hundred thousand couples lived in free union and an unspecified number of mothers had no mate at all must have struck feminists as superfluous, if not perverse.[61] As for birth control, in 1923 feminists rejected it as inapplicable and premature. Only when Mexico's population growth, which was minus 0.5 percent in 1921, rose dramatically, would birth control begin to get serious attention.[62]

What feminists had most consistently demanded since 1904, a single sexual standard, was not found in Carrillo Puerto's divorce law, nor was it conspicuous in his own behavior. On close scrutiny, the claim by his North American admirers that Carrillo Puerto was a champion of women's rights in Mexico needs to be qualified.[63] On the one hand, Carrillo Puerto did further the right of women to participate in activities outside the home, but on the other his controversial ideas merely convinced conservatives that feminism was dangerous.[64]

In 1923, Mexican feminists had their work cut out for them. In their efforts to end their seclusion from the world, to terminate their legal, social, and political inferiority, and to achieve greater personal freedom, they had to contend with powerful conservative enemies while at the same time disassociating themselves from male champions like Felipe Carrillo Puerto, whose radical ideas had discredited their cause.

NOTES

1. Frank Tannenbaum, *Peace by Revolution: An Interpretation of Mexico* (New York: Columbia University Press, 1933), p. 127.

2. Of all the writers who praised or damned Carrillo in the 1920s, only one, the North American Ernest Gruening, noticed that Mayan Indian women were sexually exploited by the henequen plantation owners. See Ernest Gruening, *Un viaje al estado de Yucatán* (Guanajuato: Talleres Gráficos de *Los Sucesos*, 1924), p. 8.

3. Tannenbaum, *Peace by Revolution*, p. 121.

4. A list of these works is found in the section on social structure in volume one of Luis González y González, et al., eds., *Fuentes de la historia contemporánea de México*, 3 vols. (México: El Colegio de México, 1961-62).

5. Antonio Bustillos Carrillo, *Yucatán al servicio de la patria y de la revolución* (México: Casa Ramírez Editores, 1959), p. 182.

6. Luis Rosado Vega, *El desastre: Asuntos yucatecos. La obra revolucionaria del General Alvarado* (Havana: Imprenta, 'El Siglo XX,' 1919), p. 202.

7. Edmundo Bolío Ontiveros, *De la cuna al paredón: Anecdotario histórico de la vida, muerte y gloria de Felipe Carrillo Puerto* (Mérida, Yuc.: Talleres de La Compañía Periodista del Sureste, n.d.), pp. 14-17, 51-52.

8. Ibid., p. 55.

9. See the chapter on Carrillo Puerto and the *Ligas de Resistencia* in John W. F. Dulles, *Yesterday in Mexico: A Chronicle of the Revolution, 1919-1936* (Austin: University of Texas Press, 1961), pp. 136-144.

10. Bernardino Mena Brito, *Bolshevismo y democracia en México*, 2d ed. (México, n.p., 1933), p. xxv.

11. By his own account, Carrillo Puerto was meeting considerable resistance in his antireligious campaign. See *Tierra* (Organo de la Liga Central de Resistencia, Mérida, Yuc.), 8 July 1923, p. 9.

12. Bustillos Carrillo, *Yucatán al servicio de la patria*, pp. 180, 273.

13. *Tierra*, 2 December 1923, p. 7.

14. Ibid., 18 November 1923, p. 27.

15. Bartolomé García Correa, *Cómo se hizo su campaña política* (Mérida, Yuc.: Imprenta y Litografía Gamboa Guzmán, 1930), pp. 46-48.

16. Ernest H. Gruening, *Mexico and its Heritage* (New York: D. Appleton-Century Co., 1928), p. 630n.

17. *La Voz de la Revolución*, 7 January 1917, p. 4.

18. The 1921 census reported that 102,969 women were unemployed, as opposed to 55,471 men out of work. *Resumen del censo general de habitantes de 30 de noviembre de 1921* (México: Talleres Gráficos de la Nación, 1928), p. 99.

19. *La Voz de la Revolución*, 7 January 1917, p. 4.

20. "Propaganda feminista," in *Tierra*, 19 August 1923, pp. 4-13.

21. [Salvador Alvarado], *Informe que el Gral. Salvador Alvarado...rinde al primer jefe del Ejército Constitucionalista...C. Venustiano Carranza. Comprende su gestión administrativa desde el 19 de marzo de 1915 al 28 de febrero de 1917* (Mérida, Yuc.: Imprenta del Gobierno Constitucionalista, 1917), p. 38.

22. A copy of this now rare pamphlet is found in the Basave Collection of the Biblioteca de México in Mexico City. According to Adolfo Ferrer in *El archivo de Felipe Carrillo: El callismo. La corrupción del régimen obregonista* (New

York: Carlos López Press, 1924), p. 55, "pamphlets on birth control were distributed even to minors in the schools."

23. Margaret Sanger, *Woman and the New Race* (New York: Brentano's Publishers, 1920), p. 130.

24. The letter of Mrs. Kennedy to Governor Carrillo was stolen by the latter's executioners and reproduced in Adolfo Ferrer, *El archivo de Felipe Carrillo*, p. 57, to discredit his memory. Evidence of Mrs. Kennedy's visit is found in *Tierra*, 30 September 1923, p. 9.

25. Ernest H. Gruening, "Felipe Carrillo Puerto," *La Reforma Social* (Havana), February 1924, p. 222. The original version of this article appeared in *The Nation* on 16 January 1924.

26. Gardner Hunting in an article highly critical of Carrillo Puerto in *Collier's Weekly*, 26 April 1924, as quoted by Ferrer, *El archivo de Felipe Carrillo*, p. 58.

27. David M. Kennedy, *Birth Control in America: The Career of Margaret Sanger* (New Haven: Yale University Press, 1970), p. 183.

28. Sofía Villa de Buentello in an interview published in the *New York Times*, 2 March 1924, section 9, p. 13.

29. Rosendo Salazar and José G. Escobedo, *Las pugnas de la gleba, 1907-1922*, 2 vols. (México: Editorial Avante, 1923), 1:259.

30. Venustiano Carranza, *Ley sobre relaciones familiares* (México: Imprenta del Gobierno, 1917), Article 13, p. 17.

31. Ernest H. Gruening, "The Assassination of Mexico's Ablest Statesman," *Current History* 19 (October 1923-March 1924):738.

32. *Tierra*, 15 July 1923, p. 20.

33. Ferrer, *El archivo de Felipe Carrillo*, p. 13.

34. For details of the Reed-Carrillo relationship, see Erna Fergusson, *Mexico Revisited* (New York: Alfred A. Knopf, 1955), pp. 116-17.

35. Quoted in Moisés González Navarro, *El porfiriato: La vida social*, vol. 5 of *Historia moderna de México*, ed. Daniel Cosío Villegas, (México: Editorial Hermes, 1957), p. 411.

36. Gruening, "Felipe Carrillo," *La Reforma Social*, p. 222.

37. Estados Unidos Mexicanos, Secretaría de la Economía Nacional, Dirección General de Estadística, *Quinto censo de población; 15 de mayo de 1930. Resumen general* (México: Dirección General de Estadística, 1930), p. 51.

38. R. B. Gaither, "The Marriage and Divorce Laws of Mexico," *American Law Review* 57 (1923):412.

39. See, for example, Consuelo Colón R., *Mujeres de México* (México: Imprenta Gallarda, 1944); Artemisa Saénz Royo, *Historia política-social-cultural del movimiento femenino en México, 1914-1950* (México: M. León Sánchez, 1954); and Rosalía d'Chumacero, *Perfil y pensamiento de la mujer mexicana*, 2 vols. (México, n.p., 1961).

40. Hermila Galindo, *Estudio de la Srita. Hermila Galindo con motivo de los*

temas que han de absolverse en el segundo congreso feminista de Yucatán (Mérida, Yuc.: Imprenta del Gobierno Constitucionalista, 1916), p. 4.

41. Salazar and Escobedo, *Las pugnas de la gleba*, 2:64.

42. *Sección Mexicana de la Liga Pan-Americana para la elevación de la mujer* (México: Talleres Linotipográficos "El Modelo," 1923), p. 7.

43. *El Universal* (México), 17 May 1923, p. 1.

44. Ibid.

45. Ibid., 23 May 1923, p. 1.

46. Ibid., 17-30 May 1923, and *El Demócrata*, 21-30 May 1923. *Excelsior* refused to cover the congress in its news columns and published two long editorials on May 24 and May 29, 1923, denouncing the congress as "scandalous."

47. *La Revista de Yucatán*, 23 May 1923, p. 1.

48. *Primer Congreso Feminista de la Liga Pan-Americana de Mujeres* (México: Talleres Linotipográficos "El Modelo," 1923), p. 5.

49. *El Demócrata*, 25 May 1923, p. 1.

50. Nora Scott Kinzer, "Priests, Machos and Babies: or Latin American Women and the Manichean Heresy," *Journal of Marriage and the Family* 35 (May 1973): 306.

51. *Primer Congreso Feminista de la Liga Pan-Americana de Mujeres*, p. 4.

52. Ibid., p. 5.

53. Ibid., p. 6.

54. *El Universal* 27 May 1923, p. 8; and *El Demócrata*, 30 May 1923, p. 8.

55. Carranza, *Ley sobre relaciones familiares*, pp. 31-32.

56. María Elvira Bermúdez, *La vida familiar del mexicano*, México y lo mexicano, vol. 20 (México: Antigua Librería Robredo, 1955), p. 77.

57. *El Universal*, 25 May 1923, section 2, p. 8.

58. Salvador M. Luna, *Los niños moralmente abandonados y la función social del tribunal para menores de la ciudad de México* (México: Herrero Hermanos Sucesores, 1929), p. 33.

59. Ward M. Morton, *Woman Suffrage in Mexico* (Gainesville: University of Florida Press, 1962), p. 84.

60. Anastasio Manzanilla, *El bolchevismo criminal de Yucatán* (México: Ediciones de "El Hombre Libre," 1921), p. 188.

61. The 1921 census did not provide figures on free unions, but by 1930, when the number of legal marriages had increased and the number of free unions had declined, the census still reported 695,619 women living in free union. *Quinto censo... de 1930*, p. 51.

62. *Resumen del censo general... de 1921*, p. 59.

63. Ernest H. Gruening and Erna Fergusson are unqualified in their praise of Carrillo Puerto as a champion of feminism.

64. See especially the editorials in *Excelsior*, 24 May 1923, p. 3; and 28 May 1923, p. 3.

5

MEXICAN WOMEN ON THEIR OWN, 1924-1930

INTRODUCTION

Contrary to the persistent belief that Mexico has never sustained a feminist movement, in the 1920s and 1930s Mexican women organized so effectively and worked so diligently for equal civil and political rights for their sex that, beginning with the reform of the civil code in 1927, nineteenth-century discriminatory restrictions against single and married women were progressively erased. In addition, during the 1930s Mexican women mounted so impressive a mass campaign for the right to vote and hold office that by the end of 1939 it appeared that Mexico would be the first major Spanish-American country to grant women suffrage.[1] In this chapter we will examine the activities of Mexican women in the 1920s that, among other things, culminated in their attainment of greater legal equality. The succeeding chapter will detail how and why Mexican women almost won the right to vote in the presidential elections of 1940.

With the death of the radical revolutionary leaders Salvador Alvarado and Felipe Carrillo Puerto in 1924, the center of feminist activity shifted from Yucatán to Mexico City. Aware that the Revolution of 1910-20 had exposed and exacerbated deep divisions between the traditional and modernizing sectors of Mexican society, most of the largely middle-class feminists of the 1920s studiously avoided association with the more radical tendencies of the revolution that Alvarado and Carrillo Puerto had represented. Instead they sought to identify their cause with the nationalistic reform impulse and the cultural renaissance that was so conspicuous a part of the "eager, postrevolutionary days" of the 1920s which attracted worldwide attention.[2] Despite meager financial resources, limited official support, an often hostile press, and an indifferent public, between 1924 and 1930 Mexican feminists established a number of organizations, held an international congress of Spanish-speaking feminists, and supported a feminist journal for three years. In addition, in their work as educators, social workers, bureaucrats, and writers, feminists participated in the task of national reconstruction, while they also worked for the emancipation of all Mexican women.

The 1921 census reveals the sources of feminist recruitment and strength and also indicates why Mexican feminism of the 1920s was elitist in composition. Modern feminism is largely an urban phenomenon whose leaders have been women with an above average education, and feminism in Mexico is no exception. In 1921 Mexico was an overwhelmingly rural country, with only 4,465,504 out of its 14,334,780 inhabitants living in an urban environment. Illiteracy was the general rule, especially in the rural areas, and only about 24 percent of the population, 1,878,434 men and 1,686,333 women, could read and write.[3] That three and a half million Mexicans were literate was due largely to the efforts of over sixteen-thousand women primary schoolteachers, who outnumbered male teachers by almost three to one.[4] As in the past, Mexican feminism in the 1920s drew the bulk of its recruits from these same women: the overworked and underpaid primary schoolteachers.

In 1921 an additional 10,000 Mexican women were listed as exercising a skill or a profession, including 602 secondary schoolteachers, 1,962 trained midwives, 276 druggists, 170 doctors, 74 dentists, 11 lawyers, 32 accountants, 19 real estate agents, and several thousand typists, stenographers, and telegraphists.[5] Most of these women lived and worked in Mexico City and the larger provincial capitals. In 1924, Sofía Villa de Buentello observed that "it is from these professional women and office workers that the feminists are recruiting their forces."[6]

A much larger group of women, close to half a million out of an adult female population of over four million, also worked for a living outside their homes. Some 207,971 were domestic servants, 49,026 were involved in commerce, 28,568 worked in agriculture, and 1,503 worked in the mines. In addition, 193,453 women (as opposed to 439,226 men) worked in industry. Women were largely concentrated in the making of apparel, with 73,421 employed in the hat and clothing industries, 70,563 working as seamstresses, and 22,961 women working in textile mills.[7] A few of these working-class and peasant women formed feminine organizations in the 1920s that sometimes cooperated with feminist groups when the latter addressed themselves to economic issues. For the most part, however, Mexico remained a class-conscious society in the decade after the revolution, and the feminist movement never succeeded in either losing its largely middle- or upper middle-class orientation or in recruiting large numbers of working-class or peasant women to its ranks.[8]

The 1921 census also revealed that there were 102,969 unemployed women in need of jobs, which meant that one out of six of the female work force was idle.[9] The same census listed an additional 150,440 females whose occupation could not be ascertained. It is impossible to determine how many of these women were in fact prostitutes; we only know that the dramatic rise in prostitution as a result of the misery engendered by the revolution remained a constant problem in the 1920s and during the depression years as well. Feminists and social reformers were deeply concerned with the problem, and in 1934 a national congress on prostitution met in Mexico City.[10]

FEMINIST ORGANIZATIONS AND ACTIVITIES, 1920-1930

Mexican women began to form organizations on their own while the revolution was still in progress. In 1918, for example, Elena Torres and a group of progressive women founded the National Council of Mexican Women in Mexico City. Torres was assisted by Elisa Acuña y Rossetti, the politically aware schoolteacher and journalist who helped Juana B. Gutiérrez de Mendoza edit *Vesper*.[11] Another of its founders and general secretary was Luz Vera, a teacher and writer who, along with Torres, represented the council at the 1922 Baltimore meeting of the League of Women Voters. At Baltimore Luz Vera and Elena Torres were actively involved in the founding of the Pan American League for the Elevation of Women and the latter was elected the league's vice-president for North America.[12] Until 1920 the National Council of Mexican Women was too poor to rent office space, but in that year the group reorganized under the name of the Feminist Council of Mexico (Consejo Feminista de Mexico) to emphasize that it was not simply a feminine but also a feminist organization.[13]

Elena Torres, it will be recalled, was the friend of the radical feminist Hermila Galindo and represented Galindo at the Second Feminist Congress in Yucatán in 1916. Torres also established the first Montessori School in the Republic of Yucatán when Alvarado was governor. In the early 1920s, in addition to her feminist activities, Elena Torres directed several government welfare programs. In 1923, for example, while working under the dynamic and innovative minister of education, José Vasconcelos, she administered a school breakfast program which provided some ten-thousand undernourished children in Mexico City with a morning meal.[14] The *Women of 1924 International* also reported that in cooperation with the Ministries of Education, Agriculture and Health, ''Señorita Torres is now undertaking a promising experiment in general welfare among the peasants of the isolated regions of the country.''[15]

The ever-active Elena Torres also participated in the January 1923 Second Mexican Congress on the Child, an important but now forgotten meeting at which the Chilean poet, Gabriela Mistral, was guest of honor and at which Mexico's most distinguished professional women and creative writers read papers on their areas of interest and specialization.[16] Torres expressed her concern over the political dilemma of Mexico by giving a paper on how civics needed to be taught in the primary schools so that such training would be really useful. Alluding to the still unsettled political status of Mexico, she asserted that the politics of one group of caudillos against another group of caudillos, which kept the country in constant turmoil, had to disappear. She concluded that the only long-term solution to the problem was an awakening of public opinion through mass education.[17]

The desire to see an end to periodic revolutions and gratuitous slaughter in Mexico led María Casas y Miramon, a ''self-educated liberal'' and office worker, to form a group called Las Mujeres Libres (The Free Women) early in 1924, when Mexico was convulsed by the de la Huerta rebellion against President Obregón's government.[18] The *New York Times* reported that ''the ranks of the Free Women are filling with stenographers and other office workers and many teachers of the grade schools, whose work outside the home has given them a broader view of life.''[19] In addition to calling for a halt to the fighting, Las Mujeres Libres stressed ''equality in all things for women'' and in particular advocated that the divorce laws be modified so that it would be as easy for a wife to obtain a divorce as for a husband.

The problem of divorce in Mexico, which President Carranza first decreed in early 1915, in particular preoccupied Profesora Sofía Villa de

Buentello, the upper-middle-class wife of a lawyer. By 1923 Profesora Buentello had established a third feminist society, the Cooperative Women's Union (Union Cooperativa 'Mujeres de la Raza'). Earlier, in 1921, Señora Buentello published *La mujer y la ley (Woman and the Law)*, one of the few books by a woman to examine the civil status of Mexican females and to treat the problem of divorce in Mexico.

In the 1920s leading feminists disagreed sharply on the question of divorce. The more radical ones, like the Socialist schoolteacher, Inés Malváez of Puebla, who was actively involved in the revolution against Díaz and who was the only woman to sign the Socialist Party Platform of 1921,[20] agreed with Felipe Carrillo Puerto that Carranza's 1917 Law of Domestic Relations should be amended to permit divorce at the will of only one spouse in a marriage. A similar position was taken even earlier by another Socialist, Evelyn Roy of the Centro Radical Femenino of Guadalajara, who was a delegate to the National Socialist Congress held in Mexico City on September 25, 1919.[21] As indicated in the previous chapter, Elena Torres took a second position on divorce, arguing at the May 1923 Pan American Women's Congress that the discriminatory features against women in Carranza's divorce law needed to be eliminated. In effect, Elena Torres agreed with María Casas y Miramon that divorce should be as uncomplicated for the wife as for the husband.

Sofía Villa de Buentello, although a fervent feminist and advocate of equality of civil rights for men and women, was totally against divorce in Mexico. She did not oppose divorce on religious grounds; like most moderate feminists of liberal persuasion of her day she avoided any reference to religion. Rather, she argued that given the dependent state of most Mexican wives, divorce would only hurt them by creating an unstable situation. She believed that in Mexico most divorces were sought by men who had tired of their spouses and who wanted either younger wives or their freedom. She also believed that because of the traditional concepts of honor and shame in Mexico, no matter what the cause of divorce, or who was guilty, "the divorced woman is viewed with contempt."[22] She asserted that an innocent woman who could not endure an unfaithful husband got no sympathy. Instead, people would say that "nobody can put up with her, not even her husband."[23] She also believed that Mexican women generally did not seek divorce for fear that they would remain alone and helpless or would simply acquire another master. Buentello, herself the mother of two children, argued that indissoluble marriage was the only means of obtaining happiness for the children and future security for the wife. She did allow that in rare cases where both spouses were miserably unhappy and the marriage a prison for both, divorce might be permitted so long as the economic well-being of the wife and children were assured.[24]

Although divorce was one of its major concerns, *La mujer y la ley* was primarily an appeal to end the legal inequality of single and married women in Mexico, and Buentello quoted approvingly the lawyer and historian Genaro García, "our great writer and jurisconsult" who, in 1891, had denounced the legal inferiority of women in Mexico.[25] Señora Buentello's book states that one major revolution and thirty years after Genaro García wrote in defense of the equality of the sexes, Mexican women were as weak, dependent, and defenseless before the law as ever. She believed that most Mexican men, and especially lawyers, viewed women as inferior. There were many more educated women in Mexico in 1921 than in 1891, but Buentello argued that they were as intellectually isolated as ever. Even in upper-class society, she observed, women formed a group apart from men because on every level of society there was a profound moral, political, and social separation between men and women.[26] She believed that

the Mexican woman, single or married, young or old, and even in old age, never ceases to be a child, even if she speaks several languages, paints, writes, or teaches; though she may be dressed in silk and go covered with jewels, she is insignificant.[27]

Buentello argued that married women had a right to remain close to their relations, that they needed to have friendships, and that they needed to enjoy intellectual independence and liberty of thought and conscience like every citizen. Everywhere in the world, she found, tyrants and despots abound. "Kings, princes and presidents oppress nations; masters their servants, and men their wives and children." Señora Buentello conceded that "in reality we are none of us free, but, if a man enjoys a fictitious liberty, a woman enjoys none at all."[28] She asked why it was that a single woman in Mexico was not allowed to leave her parents' home until she was thirty, why she could not go to the theatre by herself, go for a walk alone, or travel unaccompanied in her own country. The answer Mrs. Buentello was given was always the same: a woman alone is in danger because of the infamy and immorality of men. "Well then," Buentello retorted, "why not punish the men instead of imprisoning the women?"[29] In this connection, Buentello remarked that in Mexico rape was common but seldom punished, a situation that Mexican feminists consistently deplored. They believed that the only remedy for the problem, which was especially prevalent among the lower classes, was to appoint qualified women as judges in the criminal courts.

Sofía Villa de Buentello took an active role in the May 1923 Pan American Women's Congress where, as *El Universal* reported on May 27, 1923, she "declared herself a very vigorous enemy of matrimonial divorce." Buentello then went on to organize an international congress of Iberian and Hispanic-American women, which was to meet in Mexico City for two weeks in July of 1925. However, after a week's session the congress was abruptly terminated by Buentello because of irreconcilable divisions between right-wing and left-wing factions.[30] Despite this failure, most feminists of her generation remembered her for her eloquent and impassioned appeal for the legal equality of the sexes in *La mujer y la ley*. She was credited with being one of the leaders behind the reform of the civil code in 1927.[31]

Sofía Villa de Buentello argued in favor of woman suffrage in Mexico, asserting that without the vote the stigma of female inferiority would never be erased. By the time she published *La mujer y la ley* in 1921, most Mexican women who considered themselves feminists had come around to her position; at the 1923 Pan American Congress feminists from at least two-thirds of the Mexican states voted in favor of female suffrage in the republic. While more and more Mexican women, whether conscious feminists or not, became interested in female political rights after 1920, no such change in attitude occurred among the men in power. All through the 1920s women were to find little official support for female suffrage or for the right of women to run for office. Elvia Carrillo Puerto discovered this to be the case when her martyred brother's Socialist followers regained political control in Yucatán in 1924. They proved unwilling to reinstate her and three other women who the previous November had been elected as delegates or alternates to the state legislature. While most male revolutionaries argued that it was not "convenient" to grant women the vote, meaning that they feared women would vote for conservative, Catholic enemies of the revolution, the situation in Yucatán makes it clear that there was a prejudice against *all* women in politics, not just Catholic women.

When Elvia Carrillo Puerto was rejected by her brother's followers in Yucatán, she decided to take her fight for the political rights of women elsewhere. In 1923 the state of San Luis Potosi under the leadership of the distinguished Socialist intellectual, Rafael Nieto, adopted such progressive measures as an income tax, proportional representation, the recall and the initiative, and female suffrage, albeit with restrictions.[32] The state's legislature approved a bill that permitted literate women, who were not members of religious associations or under the care of such associations, to vote in municipal elections in 1924 and to vote for deputies and governor in 1925. Rafael Nieto left the governorship in late 1923, but his successor, Aurelio Manrique, made it known that he favored the woman suffrage law.

In late 1924 Elvia Carrillo Puerto won the support of Governor Manrique and the Jefe de Operaciones (head of military operations) in San Luis Potosi, General Saturnino Cedillo, to run for the national Chamber of Deputies from the fourth district of the state. It was the first challenge to the exclusion of women from political office since Hermila Galindo tried to run for deputy in Mexico City in 1917. Since the Constitution of 1917 did not specifically bar women from voting and since San Luis Potosí permitted women to vote and run for office in the elections of 1925, Elvia Carrillo Puerto requested and received a favorable opinion on her candidacy for that year from the secretary of the interior (Gobernación), Adalberto Tejeda. Tejeda, one of the few profeminist revolutionaries in a powerful position during the Calles presidency (1924-28), also contributed financially to Elvia Carrillo Puerto's campaign in San Luis Potosí.[33]

Near the end of the campaign, Ernest Gruening noted that

Governor Manrique was ousted and replaced by Governor Abel Cano who let it be known that no woman would represent the state if he could prevent it. At the last minute another candidate named Florencio Galván was entered. He made no attempt to campaign, the only evidence of competition being that in the village of Guadalcazar, eight shots were fired at Señora Carrillo by her opponent's substitute, one Cesareo Vásquez.[34]

Despite Abel Cano's violent opposition, Elvia Carrillo Puerto and her substitute Hermila Zamarrón, received 4,576 votes against Galván's 56. This did not impress the Permanent Commission of the Chamber of Deputies, which refused to seat Carrillo Puerto on the grounds that the national election law of June 1918 limited suffrage and the right to hold office to males.[35]

The following year on October 4, 1926 San Luis Potosi rescinded Governor Nieto's 1923 law, and the brief experiment in even restricted woman suffrage came to an end.[36] As in Yucatán, it was clear that there was blatant hostility to any woman running for office, even if she were the sister of the idolized martyr of the revolution, Felipe Carrillo Puerto. It appears that the fear of ''reactionary and Catholic women'' in politics was more the excuse than the reason for the total exclusion of women from the electoral process in the 1920s.

Elvia Carrillo Puerto was forced to give up her attempts at directly challenging the constitutionality of the 1918 electoral law, but on her return to Yucatán she organized the Liga Orientadora de Acción Femenina (Orienting League of Feminine Action), which actively lobbied in favor of woman suffrage for the remainder of the decade and all through the 1930s.[37]

The pressure to grant women the right to vote increased once women were granted equal civil rights in 1927. In March 1929 the government acknowledged this pressure when the National Revolutionary Party (the PNR-Partido Nacional Revolucionario) was founded by Plutarco Elías Calles to bring to an end the endemic political violence that still plagued the country. The new party's platform promised that the PNR would ''aid and stimulate the full right of participation of Mexican women in the activities of the political life of Mexico.''[38] However, at the Women's International League for Peace and Freedom meetings held in Mexico City in July 1930 the head of the Political Action Section of the PNR, García Tellez, stated that in Mexico women were ''politically unprepared'' for suffrage.[39] This position was challenged by feminists at three congresses of women workers held in 1931, 1933, and 1934. But it was not until General Lázaro Cárdenas became the PNR's candidate for the presidency that anything was done to meet the growing demand for political rights for women.

In addition to the national and regional feminist organizations founded between 1918 and 1925 by Elena Torres, María Casas y Miramon, Sofía Villa de Buentello, Elvia Carrillo Puerto, and others, women actively concerned with the reconstruction of Mexico but who were not primarily or necessarily feminists formed organizations to promote their social concerns or professional interests. For example, the highly respected teacher María Rosaura Zapata became president of the Mexican Pestalozzi-Froebel Society, established sometime before August 1923. Profesora Zapata and her colleagues were primarily interested in promoting child welfare. They worked to establish a training school for kindergarten teachers, they urged that kindergartens be established throughout the republic, they promoted the organization of Parent-Teacher Associations, they advocated the scientific study of the child, and they also worked for the legal protection of minors.[40]

By 1923 the Asociación Femenina de Temperancia (the Feminine Temperance Association) was also established with Ernestina Alvarado (no relation to Governor Salvador Alvarado) as president.[41] Without a doubt alcoholism was one of the most pressing problems in Mexico, and alcohol abuse, like prostitution, increased alarmingly during the revolution. Charles Cumberland points out that in 1864 Mexico City had 51 *cantinas* or saloons; by 1900 the capital had 1,300 *cantinas* but only 34 bakeries. "At any given moment," Cumberland relates, "it would have been possible to crowd about one-fifth of the total population [of Mexico City] into its drinking parlors."[42]

On May 22, 1923, Berthe Westrup de Velasco, a normal school professor, gave a paper at the Pan American Conference of Women which indicated that the situation had worsened considerably since the days of Don Porfirio. She counted 3,170 *cantinas* in Mexico City, in a total population of 251,250, of whom approximately half were men. At the same time, Profesora Westrup de Velasco said that there were only 521 public and private schools in the capital, which led the newspaper *El Universal* to blazon in headlines on the next day that "for every forty men there is a *cantina* and for every 800 children there is one school."[43]

Profesora Westrup de Velasco appealed to the government of President Alvaro Obregón for total prohibition in Mexico as the only means of dealing with the problem of alcoholism. The more energetic and idealistic revolutionary governors, including Alvarado, Carrillo Puerto, Calles, and Cárdenas tried prohibition at one time or another. However, powerful agricultural interests, who cultivated millions of acres of maguey plants that produced the intoxicant pulque consumed by the masses, thwarted the efforts of reform-minded men and women who advocated temperance. And, when prohibition was tried in Yucatán, for example, a thriving black market immediately emerged.[44] Also, in Mexico a liter of pulque was less expensive than a liter of milk, for maguey grows in the semiarid soil that abounds in Mexico, while pasture for dairy cattle has always been at a premium. The children of the poor were even given pulque to forget that they were hungry and cold.[45]

It is not surprising why determined revolutionaries encouraged Protestant missionaries to labor in Mexico, for without exception the Protestants working in the republic advocated total abstinence. In this connection, the Asociación de Mujeres Cristianas, the Young Women's Christian Association of Mexico City, led by Señorita Elena Landázuri, often referred to as the "Jane Addams of Mexico," was established in August 1923.[46] Landázuri and her associates, who were also in favor of women's liberation, established a Mothercraft Center on the edge of the famous Thieves Market in Mexico City where *cantinas* abound, to help women of the lower classes cope with the problems of raising a family in the most discouraging ambience. The Mexican "Y" invited the Union of Catholic Women to join them in their work of social redemption, but the latter declined on the grounds that they could not work with any organization not under the aegis of the Catholic church.[47]

However, Catholic women were not idle in the work of reconstruction in the years immediately after the revolution. The North American Helen Bowyer, who worked with the Mexican Ministries of Health and Agriculture to improve the health of children and rural families reported in 1924 that "the *Damas Católicas* are centering their efforts largely on the relief of destitute children and of working women. Closely allied with the Damas is the [Catholic] Army in Defense of Women, which under Concepción D. de Galindo is working out a National program for safeguarding girls against sexual exploitation."[48]

During the 1920s two of the oldest professional organizations of women still in existence were established, the Association of Mexican University Women in 1925, and the Association of Mexican Women Doctors in 1929. The latter's major objective was to extend the role of Mexican women in modern medicine, while the former wished to promote cultural exchange and joint scientific investigation between Mexican university graduates and their foreign counterparts.[49]

A willingness, in fact an eagerness, to affiliate with foreign women's groups characterized the organizing efforts of feminists and their friends during the 1920s. This trend began in 1922, when Elena Torres, Eulalia Guzmán, Luz Vera, Aurora Herrera de Nobregas, Julia Nava de Ruisánchez, and other leading Mexican feminists accepted an invitation to attend the

League of Women Voters' annual meeting in Baltimore, which resulted in the formation of the Pan American League for the Elevation of Women. Then, in 1923, Mexican women who were Protestants affiliated with the YWCA. In this same period, Elena Arizmendi, who worked hard for the reform of the civil code, became secretary-general of the International League of Iberian and Latin American Women. The League sponsored a congress of Spanish-speaking women in Mexico City in July 1925, chaired by Sofía Villa de Buentello. The Pan American Round Table of Mexico, which promoted better relations among the nations of the Western Hemisphere, dates from 1928, while the Mexican branch of the Women's International League for Peace and Freedom was established in 1929.[50]

On the other hand, some Mexican feminists were wary of associating with North American feminists, and this was especially true of more left-wing Mexican feminists, who resented what they considered North American imperialism. However, other feminists who were political moderates, as the obstetrician Doctora Antonia de Ursúa, also believed that Mexico had many legitimate grievances against the United States. At the Pan American Congress of Women in May 1923 when one North American delegate, Mrs. Baker, spoke effusively of the friendship existing between Mexicans and North Americans, a Señorita Garces, representing a women's group in Orizaba, objected and stated that

daily events demonstrate to us that across the Rio Bravo (the Rio Grande) they are very far from loving us. This is demonstrated by active campaigns against Mexico, the deprecatory names that, generally, are used in the neighboring country to insult us, the wide dissemination of denigratory films and the little attention that the North American government has paid to the many remonstrances of our government, protesting this conduct.[51]

Señorita Garces was roundly applauded by the Mexican delegates, all of whom resented the fact that the United States had refused to recognize the Obregón government for three years despite its ability to effectively govern Mexico since 1920.

Later, and in 1926 and 1927, Mexican feminists also resented North American accusations that the Calles regime was "Bolshevik" because of its anticlericalism, its support of the Sandino revolution in Nicaragua, its establishment of diplomatic ties with the Soviet Union, and its determination to enforce those articles of the 1917 constitution that affected American economic interests in Mexico. When relations between Mexico and the United States reached a crisis stage in February 1927, a group of twenty-seven Mexican women, many of them prominent feminists, organized a Liga Nacional de Mujeres (National League of Women). They urged all Mexican women to rally around President Calles in his defense of the sovereignty and freedom of the republic. The president of the National League of Women was María A. Sandoval de Zarco, Mexico's first woman lawyer and an active feminist since the days of Don Porfirio. The secretary of the organization was Doctora Antonia L. Ursúa, Mexico's best-known woman doctor, head of the Sociedad Obstétrica Mexicana, and a participant at the 1923 Pan American Congress. Elvia Carrillo Puerto was also active in the league, which appears to have disbanded once the tactful diplomacy of Ambassador Dwight Morrow succeeded in reducing the strains between the two neighboring countries.[52]

THE FEMINIST JOURNAL, *MUJER* (1926-1929)

By late 1926 a young and aspiring journalist, María Ríos Cárdenas, decided that the time had come to launch a new woman's journal in Mexico City. Although the women's rights movement had been making more and more converts between 1919 and 1926, no one had attempted to publish a frankly feminist journal since Hermila Galindo published *La Mujer Moderna* in Mexico City from 1917 to 1919. The first issue of Ríos Cárdenas's new monthly, *Mujer*, appeared on December 12, 1926, and sold for ten centavos, less than the cost of the daily *El Universal* or the cost of a lottery ticket. Señorita Ríos, herself an upper-middle-class woman who apparently used her own funds to establish *Mujer*, hoped to reach a large enough audience of literate women to keep the new enterprise solvent. "There is not one single publication in the Republic," María Ríos Cárdenas declared in her first editorial, "that has taken on the task of enlightening women through varied, didactic, and interesting articles affording mental nourishment, for the moderate price of ten centavos."[53]

María Ríos Cárdenas believed that Mexican women had to carry out their own liberation, and *Mujer* was intended to aid them in this endeavor. She declared that women first of all had to get over their own low self-esteem and not be their own worst enemies. "I wish to destroy the anathema," she wrote, "that the worst enemy of woman is woman herself."[54] She emphasized that "it is up to women to work to consolidate their rights, developing always a constant and gentle labor of rapprochement among themselves and between themselves and men, in order to form a sound society."[55] Hence, *Mujer* publicized the achievements of Mexican women in photography, journalism, the law, and economics. In addition, *Mujer* publicized the efforts of individuals and feminist organizations in Mexico in the campaign to reform the civil code, to achieve world peace through arbitration of international disputes, and to promote child welfare through day-care centers (*salas cunas*) and juvenile courts.

It is impossible to determine how wide a readership *Mujer* achieved in the three years of its existence. We do know that in a contest sponsored by *Mujer* on the "most intelligent woman in Mexico" some 1,320 readers of the journal took the trouble to mail in their ballots by June 1, 1927.[56] As *Mujer* was frankly though not aggressively feminist, a readership of at least 1,320 and more likely twice that figure was not an inconsiderable achievement at the time. Ríos Cárdenas was able to publish thirty-five issues of *Mujer*. It folded in December 1929, one of the casualties of the Great Depression. It will be remembered that earlier the panic of 1907 and the economic dislocations that followed brought to an end the publication of *La Mujer Mexicana* in 1908.

The aforementioned contest on the most intelligent woman in Mexico is of interest, for it provides some qualitative data on the activities and achievements of individual women not readily available elsewhere. For instance, the winner of the contest was Señora María Elena de García Sánchez Facio, a voice teacher and composer who achieved international acclaim at the Paris opera. By 1927 she had given up an active career as an opera singer, *Mujer* informed its readers, because of her devotion to her husband and her son. At the same time, however, Sra. García was an active feminist who had represented the National Council of Mexican Women at the 1923 Pan American Women's Conference and was, in 1927, the secretary-general of the Peace and Arbitration Committee of that council.

Catalina d'Erzell, the drama critic and author of popular plays that were to become the favorites of Spanish-speaking audiences from as far away as Los Angeles and Buenos Aires, was a close runner-up in the contest.[57] Other women who received many votes included Soledad González, President Calles's private secretary and secretary to three of his predecessors; María Luisa Ocampo, a government personnel director and poet, dramatist, and novelist as well; and María Suárez, a worker who represented the Casa del Obrero Mundial (affiliated with the International Workers of the World) at the 1923 Pan American Women's Conference.[58] Also among the contestants was Eulalia Guzmán, the future archeologist who was also a delegate at the 1923 congress and who was active in the campaign against illiteracy as a high official in the Ministry of Education. The economist Refugio Román, who wrote clear and informative articles for the financial pages of leading newspapers in Mexico City, also received a number of votes. Another choice was Adela Hernández, a lawyer whose detailed study of the legal disabilities of women was of decisive influence in the revision of the civil code in 1927. Lastly, María Santibáñez, an artist and self-trained photographer whose work appeared in Mexico City's widely read illustrated weekly, *El Universal Ilustrado*, won a number of votes.[59]

Mujer also provides us with interesting data concerning the problems that confronted urban Mexican women in a period of rapid social change. Articles in the journal make it clear that in Mexico City, at least, traditional patterns of social behavior were breaking down in the face of North American influence. Dancing salons, short skirts, and bobbed hair were all the rage in Mexico City and were roundly condemned by Catholic women's groups alarmed by the changing mores.[60] María Ríos Cárdenas believed that wearing comfortable modern clothes and bobbing one's hair was not incompatible with womanly modesty. However, she agreed with conservative women that mothers ought not to permit their daughters to attend the dancing salons in the capital. It was no place to find a husband, Ríos Cárdenas warned, for the men who frequented these dance halls measured all the women there by the same low standard.[61]

María Ríos Cárdenas complained that Mexico was indiscriminately adopting North American customs except for the most important custom of all: the habit of respecting women, which she attributed to North American men. In article after article Ríos Cárdenas expressed the view that Mexican machismo was a constant source of concern and grief to women. *Mujer* emphasized that in the streets of the capital women of all ranks and ages, including schoolgirls, working women, and female shoppers, had to endure obscene and offensive remarks directed at them by men of all ages. Much more serious than verbal assault was the problem of physical assault, including the rape of minors. The crime of rape was supposed to be punished by twelve to fifteen years of jail, but

Ríos Cárdenas pointed out that rarely did a rapist serve a long sentence. She found that the fault was not so much with the male judges as with the all male juries (*jurados populares*), which refused to view rape as a serious crime.[62]

María Ríos Cárdenas also gave special attention to the plight of the unmarried mother in Mexico City. In far too many cases these women were abandoned before the birth of their children and had to find work to support themselves and their babies. She appealed to her readers to become actively involved in the establishment of day-care centers to ease the burden of these unfortunate women.[63]

By late 1928 Ríos Cárdenas was urging her readers to unite their efforts for the feminist goals of full political rights and for socioeconomic reforms by establishing, in the place of a myriad of small feminist organizations, one national federation of women. In order that none of the problems of the country be slighted, she urged that the proposed federation include women of all social ranks, of all occupations, and of all political and religious creeds. The succeeding decade, a time of economic crisis and dislocation, was to test the ability of Mexican women to organize a mass movement in their pursuit of the twin goals of equality and socioeconomic reform.

THE 1927 REFORM OF THE CIVIL CODE

The crowning achievement of *Mujer* and of individuals and groups urging legal equality for Mexican women was the revision, in March 1927, of the civil code in effect in the Federal District and in the federal territories. The changes had two purposes: to equalize the legal status of men and women and at the same time to offer certain protection to married women. The second article of the revised code stated that "men and women have the same legal capacity." This article implemented those features of the Law of Family Relations of 1917 that gave married women the right to take part in civil suits, to draw up legal contracts, and to act as guardians. Article 2 also made it possible for Mexican women to practice law without any restrictions, which meant that women lawyers could now act as *procuradoras en juicio* (attorneys-at-law) and represent third parties before all courts of justice.[64] Single women could now leave the parental home at the same age as men, although few women probably availed themselves of this choice for economic and other reasons. From

1954 to the present this writer has met few single women in Mexico who live away from their parents' home if they both happen to live in the same city. In March 1974 a male friend explained why a mutual acquaintance, a successful medical librarian in her forties, while sharing an apartment with a female friend in Mexico City, still went home to her parents' house over the weekend. "It is not socially acceptable," he explained, "for an unmarried woman to live away from her parents' home." In this case, as in so many others, changing the law has not led to changing the custom. Be that as it may, after 1927 a single woman who lived in the Federal District or the federal territories could not be legally prevented from leaving her parental home.

In Article 98, Section 4, the new Civil Code of 1927 also sought to protect women, in particular, by declaring that "those who suffer a chronic and incurable disease which moreover is contagious and hereditary, will not be permitted to marry."[65] While the word syphilis was not mentioned in the article, it was probably this disease that preoccupied the legal reformers of 1927. The previous year, Doctor Bernardo J. Castelum, head of the Department of Health in the Calles administration, told the first Pan American Congress of Public Health Officers that "in Mexico... 60 percent of the inhabitants suffer from syphilis; in the capital more than 50 percent....In the population between 15 and 25 years of age, 35 percent are afflicted with it."[66]

The Law of Family Relations of 1917 had provided that married couples were to have exclusive control over their own property and wealth, which was intended to permit a wife to keep her own earnings and administer her own property. However, this arrangement, called *separación de bienes* ("separation of property"), was of no help, and, in fact, a disadvantage to married women who had no property or income of their own. Under *separación de bienes* a housewife or economically dependent wife had no legal claim on her husband's earnings or wealth if he chose to withhold financial support. As a result, Article 98, Section 5 of the revised civil code provided that when the marriage contract was drawn up prior to the civil wedding ceremony, the two parties had to specify if they were to administer their property jointly (*sociedad conyugal*) or separately.[67] This was to safeguard the interests of both married women who worked and wives who were economically dependent on their husbands.

The new Civil Code of 1927 was hailed as a great vindication for all Mexican women by the newspapers in Mexico City and by feminists who worked for the reforms.[68] However, the new provisions had little relevance for the masses of impoverished Mexican women for whom each day was a struggle for physical survival. The new code benefited primarily middle- and upper-class women for whom juridical equality and property guarantees were important.

At the same time the new code fell short of the demands of Elena Torres and other critics who insisted that sections of the divorce law of 1917, which accepted a double standard, also be amended. A married woman still needed her husband's permission to work outside the home, while a husband did not need his wife's consent to change their residence or leave the country altogether. Even for middle- and upper-class women, the reform of the Civil Code in 1927 was a limited victory. However, this did not discourage Mexican feminists who, having gained greater legal equality, now turned their energies to other goals, including the right to vote and to hold office.

NOTES

1. By the end of 1939 Cuba, Ecuador, El Salvador, and Uruguay had granted women the right to vote in national elections. Portuguese-speaking Brazil granted women the right to vote in 1932. See United States Department of Labor, Women's Bureau, *Political Status of Women in the Other American Republics. February 1958. Notes for Reference* (Washington, D.C.: Government Printing Office, 1958).

2. Ida Clyde Clarke and Lillian Ballance Sheridan, eds., *Women of 1924 International* (New York: Women's News Service, 1924), p. 254.

3. Estados Unidos Mexicanos, Departamento de la Estadística Nacional, *Resumen del censo general de habitantes de 30 de noviembre de 1921* (México: Talleres Gráficos de la Nación, 1928), p. 100.

4. Ibid., p. 97.

5. Ibid.

6. Sofía de Buentello in an interview published in the *New York Times*, 2 March 1924, Section 9, p. 13.

7. Estados Unidos Mexicanos, *Resumen del censo...de 1921*, pp. 84-94.

8. One exception in the 1930s was the *Frente Unico Pro-Derechos de la Mujer*, which organized some fifty thousand women, many of them indigenous. Verna Carleton Millan, *Mexico Reborn* (Boston: Houghton Mifflin Co., 1939), pp. 164-65. See chapter 6 for more details on the *Frente*.

9. Estados Unidos Mexicanos, *Resumen del censo...de 1921*, p. 99.

10. See *El Universal* (México), 11 June 1934 to 24 June 1934 for a day-by-day account of the Congress on Prostitution.

11. Clarke and Sheridan, eds., *Women of 1924 International*, p. 253.

12. "The Recent Pan American Conference of Women: Proceedings; Their Significance and Promise," *Bulletin of the Pan American Union* 55 (July 1922):10; *Sección Mexicana de la Liga Pan Americana para la Elevación de la Mujer* (México: Talleres Linotipográficos "El Modelo," 1923), p. 7.

13. Clarke and Sheridan, eds., *Women of 1924 International*, p. 253.

14. Ibid.

15. Ibid.

16. Secretaría de Educación Pública, *Memorias del segundo congreso del niño*, Publicaciones de la Secretaría de Educación Pública, vol. 2, no. 1 (México: Secretaría de Educación Pública, 1925).

17. Ibid., p. 17.

18. The *New York Times*, 2 March 1924, Section 9, p. 13.

19. Ibid.

20. Partido Socialista Mexicano, *Manifiesto del Partido Socialista Mexicano* (México: Imprenta "Naco," 1921), p. 24.

21. Rosendo Salazar and José G. Escobedo, *Las pugnas de la gleba, 1907-1922*, 2 vols. (México: Editorial Avanti, 1923), 2:63-64.

22. G. Sofía Villa de Buentello, *La mujer y la ley* (México: Imprenta Franco-Americana, 1921), p. 98.

23. Ibid.

24. Ibid., p. 62.

25. Ibid., p. 19. See Genaro García, *La desigualdad de la mujer* (Tesis presentada por el alumno...en su examen profesional de abogado; México, 1891).

26. Villa de Buentello, *La mujer y la ley*, p. 23.

27. Ibid., p. 24.

28. Ibid., p. 45.

29. Ibid., p. 47.

30. For details of the Congress, see *Excelsior* (México) 2-16 July 1925.

31. "Abogadas en el foro público" (Women lawyers in the public forum) *Mujer: Revista Quincenal Ilustrada. Para la Elevación Moral e Intelectual de la Mujer* 1, no. 4 (1 April 1927), p. 9; *Excelsior* (México) 24 March 1927, section 2, p. 1.

32. Rafael Nieto, *Mas allá de la patria* (México: Andrés Botas e Hijo, 1922), p. 97; *La Revista de Yucatán*, 5 January 1923, p. 1; and Ward M. Morton, *Woman Suffrage in Mexico* (Gainesville: University of Florida Press, 1962), p. 10.

33. Gruening, *Mexico and Its Heritage* (New York: D. Appleton-Century Company, 1928), p. 629.

34. Ibid.

35. Morton, *Woman Suffrage in Mexico*, p. 10.

36. Ibid. All of Nieto's progressive legislation was rescinded after he left office. See Antonio Enríquez Filio, *Problemas sociales mexicanos* (México: Talleres Gráficos de la Nación, 1929), p. 279.

37. *Vesper*, 15 April 1932, p. 6, and 30 April 1932, p. 4; *El Universal* 28 January 1932, p. 8, and 28 February 1932, pp. 1, 6.

38. Morton, *Woman Suffrage in Mexico*, p. 14.

39. Ibid.

40. "Social Progress—Mexico," *Bulletin of the Pan American Union* 57 (August 1923), p. 211.

41. Clarke and Sheridan, eds., *Women of 1924 International*, p. 254.

42. Charles C. Cumberland, *Mexico: The Struggle for Modernity* (New York: Oxford University Press, 1968), p. 205.

43. *El Universal*, 23 May 1923, p. 1.

44. Adolfo Ferrer, *El archivo de Felipe Carrillo* (New York: Carlos López Press, 1924), p. 58.

45. *El Universal*, 23 May 1923, p. 1; *El Demócrata*, 23 May 1923, p. 3.

46. Clarke and Sheridan, eds., *Women of 1924 International*, p. 253; "Social Progress—Mexico," *Bulletin of the Pan American Union* 57 (August 1923), p. 211.

47. Clarke and Sheridan, eds., *Women of 1924 International*, p. 254.

48. Ibid.

49. Ifigenia M. de Navarrete, *La mujer y los derechos sociales* (México: Ediciones Oasis, 1969), pp. 188-89.

50. Ibid., p. 201; *Mujer*, 1 June 1929, p. 12.

51. *El Universal*, 29 May 1923, Section 2, p. 1.

52. *Excelsior*, 9 February 1927, Section 1, p. 3.

53. *Mujer*, 12 December 1926, p. 3. See also Lola Anderson, "Mexican Woman Journalists," in *Bulletin of the Pan American Union* 68 (May 1934), p. 318.

54. *Mujer*, 12 December 1926, p. 3.

55. Ibid.

56. Ibid., 1 June 1927, p. 11.

57. Ibid. See also Lillian E. Fisher, "The Influence of the Present Mexican Revolution Upon the Status of Mexican Women," *Hispanic American Historical Review* 22 (February 1942), pp. 223-24.

58. *Mujer*, 1 June 1927, p. 11.

59. Ibid.

60. See *Excelsior*, 7-8 November 1922, for details of a congress of Catholic women held in Mexico City, which particularly deplored the appearance of dancing halls, bobbed hair, and short skirts in Mexico.

61. *Mujer*, 12 December 1926, p. 5.
62. Ibid., 1 June 1929, p. 5.
63. Ibid., 1 February 1929, p. 5.
64. Ibid., 1 August 1928, p. 5.
65. Ibid.
66. Quoted in Gruening, *Mexico and Its Heritage*, p. 544.
67. *Mujer*, 1 August 1928, p. 5.
68. Ibid.; *Excelsior*, 24 March 1927, pp. 1, 8, and 27 March 1927, pp. 1, 6.

6

THE FEMINIST MOVEMENT IN THE 1930s

MEXICAN WOMEN AND THE GREAT DEPRESSION

The Great Depression cast a long shadow over Mexico in the 1930s, and the effects of the economic paralysis were felt immediately by Mexican women. The 1930 census reported a drastic drop since the previous census of 1921 in the number of women working outside the home for wages or a salary in every category of employment. For example, although the female population in Mexico increased by one million from 1921 to 1930, the number of women textile workers dropped from 22,961 in 1921 to 8,722 in 1930. In industry as a whole, ninety thousand fewer women were working in 1930 than in 1921.[1] The number of skilled and professional women in the work force dropped by about eight thousand in 1930, while the middle- and upper-classes made do with eighty thousand fewer female domestic servants in 1930 than in 1921.[2]

The only category of employment in which women registered a gain from 1921 to 1930 was in public administration. The 1921 census reported only 614 females employed as bureaucrats, but the 1930 census listed 10,122 women in public administration.[3] This increase did not escape the notice of the influential Mexico City daily, *Excelsior*, which was very conservative and markedly antifeminist in the 1920s and 1930s. In editorials on November 29 and 30, 1933, the newspaper suggested that Mexico's leaders follow the example of Mussolini, who had recently ordered that no more than 5 percent of government positions were to be held by women. The rest were to be dismissed. Had the Mexican government followed the advice of *Excelsior*, some 3,000 women, or 30 percent of the total number of females employed by the government would have joined the ever-growing ranks of the unemployed.[4]

Although the 1931 labor code provided elaborate protection for working mothers, that law, like most advanced social legislation in Mexico, reflected an ideal rather than the reality. A November 1933 statement to the press by the secretary of public education, Narciso Bassols, denied that his ministry was in accord with the suggestion of a male teacher that pregnant teachers be dismissed from their posts. But the statement also revealed that the Mexican government made no budgetary provision whatsoever for substitutes to take over for teachers who were granted pregnancy leaves.[5]

In the United States the Great Depression put a damper on the feminist movement, but in Mexico, paradoxically enough, the peak of feminist activity in the first half of the twentieth century was reached between 1930 and 1940, precisely at a time when fewer women could find work outside the home and when the prejudice against working women was extremely intense. How is one to explain this paradox? Why was there an enormous increase in feminist activity in the 1930s? Why did women concentrate their attention on the question of suffrage between 1934 and 1940? And why, after relentless pressure by women, did the Mexican government accede to the demand for female suffrage, only to renege on the promise in the elections of 1940?

To explain the paradox of increased feminist activity at a time of profound economic crisis, one must take into account the special conditions that prevailed in Mexico in the 1930s. From 1910 to 1920, the country had undergone a long and costly revolution, which up to 1930 had failed to realize its basic goals of agrarian reform, universal literacy, and national economic development. Despite a decade of revolutionary rhetoric, real equality, whether between classes or sexes, was as elusive as ever, and the Great Depression only sharpened the awareness of the profound inequalities and injustices in Mexican society. The awareness that the revolution had not yet lived up to its promise impelled many Mexican men and women, both intellectuals and peasants, to increase their activism in the 1930s. Peasants demanded land, laborers sought better working conditions, economic nationalists called for expropriation of foreign enterprises, and women appealed for the full rights of citizenship, especially the right to vote and be elected to office.

All of these demands received the sympathetic attention of General Lázaro Cárdenas, president of Mexico from 1934 to 1940. During his presidency over 40 million acres of arable land were distributed to peasants, workers struck in record numbers to achieve their demands, the railroads were nationalized, and the foreign oil companies were expropriated. And once Cárdenas made known his interest in women's rights early in his presidency, feminists responded by forming a Frente Unico Pro-Derechos de la Mujer (Sole Front for Women's Rights), which at its height counted fifty thousand members representing eight hundred feminist organizations in the republic.[6]

ATTEMPTS AT UNIFYING THE FEMINIST MOVEMENT, 1930-1934

Feminist activity also increased in the 1930s because of the very real threat of the loss of livelihood many women faced. Before Cárdenas. came to office and in the period from 1930 to 1934, working women and women who defended the right of their sex to work outside the home turned to the feminist movement as their only support in the face of increasing male hostility and resentment. To impress upon the government and the general public the situation of working women in urban and rural areas, between 1931 and 1934 three congresses of women workers and peasants met, the first two in Mexico City and the last in Guadalajara. What especially distinguished these congresses from earlier ones is that unlike the two feminist congresses of Yucatán of 1916, which were convened by Governor Salvador Alvarado, or the 1923 Pan American Congress of Women, which met, in part, because of North American influence, the 1931, 1933, and 1934 congresses of women were entirely the work of Mexican women.

One of the chief architects of the congresses was María Ríos Cárdenas, (no relation to the president) who published the feminist journal *Mujer* from 1926 to 1929. She joined forces with the leaders of two Mexico-City-based feminist organizations that appeared in the late 1920s, the Partido Feminista Revolucionario (the Feminist Revolutionary Party) and the Bloque Nacional de Mujeres Revolucionarias (National Bloc of Revolutionary Women). These organizations issued invitations in early 1931 to all local, state, and national women's groups to send delegates to the first congress. The primary aim of Ríos Cárdenas and her associates was to bring together Mexican women of every class, every ideological tendency, and every race to form one unified organization that would pressure the government to recognize and meet the special needs and the special demands of Mexican women.[7]

The First Congress of Women Workers and Peasants was held from October 2 to October 5, 1931, at the Alvaro Obregón Civic Center in the old Ayuntamiento (Town Hall) building facing the cathedral in Mexico City. Some six hundred delegates attended the session, most of whom seem to have been professional women with only a sprinkling of peasants and workers present.[8] However, the delegates were clearly concerned with the plight of working women, and a large majority of the delegates approved resolutions calling for minimum wages and an eight-hour work day for white and blue collar workers and for domestic servants. Other resolutions demanded that peasant women be given the same opportunity as men to acquire land through the agrarian reform program and that the government step up its program of social services and primary education in the rural areas of the country.[9] The delegates also approved a resolution calling on the government to ensure that its female employees be granted a paid leave of absence a month before and two months after childbirth as the 1917 constitution stipulated.[10]

An overwhelming majority of the delegates also approved a resolution calling on the government to amend Article 34 of the constitution to permit women to exercise the full rights of citizenship. On the very day that the congress opened, *El Universal*, which had favored woman suffrage since it began publication in 1916, announced in large headlines on page one that "Spain sets the example for the New World: Women are to vote."[11] The implication was clear: the new Spanish Republic was more progressive than Mexico's supposedly revolutionary regime.

At the second day's sessions of the congress, which was briefly attended by President Pascual Ortíz Rubio (the first Mexican executive to attend a feminist congress), María Ríos Cárdenas read an essay on "The organization of women in the social struggle."[12] Ríos Cárdenas argued, as she had argued in her feminist journal, *Mujer*, that unless and until Mexican women formed a nationwide feminist organization seated in Mexico City and with branches in every state and locality, their efforts to improve the status and condition of all Mexican females would come to naught. She suggested that once all existing feminist organizations merged into a single confederation, through its officers such an organization would establish formal relations with the government, with labor unions, and with peasant groups. Ríos Cárdenas insisted that such a feminist confederation was absolutely necessary since "only woman recognizes her problems and, consequently, only she has the ability to resolve them."[13]

There was a vocal contingent of Marxist delegates at the congress and their leaders, Concepción Michel, a well-known writer of revolutionary *corridos* ("ballads"), and Profesora María del Refugio García, a regular contributor to *Machete*, the organ of the Mexican Communist party, objected to Ríos Cárdenas's plan and insisted that the only way Mexican women could improve their status and condition was to work through existing peasant organizations and labor unions.[14] At that time the small Communist party in Mexico viewed feminism as a bourgeois tactic that diverted women workers and peasants from the struggle to liberate the dispossessed masses of Mexico. Ironically enough, beginning in 1935, María del Refugio García was to become the secretary general of the largest feminist organization ever to be organized in Mexico, while in 1938 Concepción Michel was to publish a powerfully cogent critique of the Marxist view of women.

The Marxists created an uproar at the 1931 congress similar to the one that had been created by the radical Yucatecan delegation at the 1923 Pan American Conference of Women eight years before. On October 4, the Marxists walked out of one session in protest, while at the closing session fourteen young women identified as "extreme Communists" by the press, including Concepción Michel, were arrested by government security officers as they loudly denounced high officials in President Ortíz Rubio's administration. Once the outspoken women had made a declaration at police headquarters, they were released by order of the president.[15] However, it was clear from this incident that women who publicly denounced members of the government for betrayal of the revolution suffered harassment.

Despite the unwillingness of extreme left-wing women to cooperate in the creation of a single, unified feminist organization in Mexico, the moderates, led by María Ríos Cárdenas, went ahead with their plans to establish a nationwide feminist organization that would unify the hundreds of existing women's groups in the country. In late October 1931, at the offices of the Partido Feminista Revolucionario, a small party that had come into existence after the creation in 1929 of the official government party, the Partido Nacional Revolucionario (PNR), a group of delegates from the recent Congress of Women Workers and Peasants formed an executive committee for the projected Mexican Women's Confederation. The committee then wrote a letter to the head of the PNR, General Manuel Pérez Treviño, asking for formal recognition and a small subsidy, both of which were granted by a government anxious to demonstrate that it had meant what it said when it invited women in 1929 to take part in the political life of the nation.[16]

The same group of women also formed a permanent commission for a future Second Congress of Women Workers and Peasants, which was to be held in 1933.[17] Although the members of the permanent commission were unhappy over the division between themselves and more left-wing women, which had led to many shouting matches at the recent congress, the moderates believed that the advantages of holding a second congress far outweighed the disadvantages. For one, holding a congress gave women visibility and gave the press, in particular, the opportunity to air the problems of Mexican women. For another, the brief appearance of President Ortíz Rubio at the October 1931 congress had been an indication of how seriously the government took the efforts of organized groups of women to make known their needs and demands.

Having achieved visibility and recognition by the government, the moderates pressed their advantage and on November 20, 1931, the twenty-first anniversary of the commencement of the Mexican Revolution, a group of women presented a petition to the Chamber of Deputies.[18] The petitioners represented the Bloque Nacional de Mujeres Revolucionarias, ("National Bloc of Revolutionary Women") a group of largely progovernment professional women who, like the members of the Partido Feminista Revolucionario, had organized after the PNR was created in 1929. The petitioners, many of whom had attended the recent Congress of Women Workers and Peasants, did not mince words when they stated that

a government which denies the majority (and women form a majority [in Mexico]) the right of citizenship lacks morality, lacks justice and fails in its political task; yet [that government] obliges us to carry out the obligations [of citizenship], as to be judged by the same penal laws that govern males, to pay taxes determined by the national treasury, to contribute financially to the support of political parties, and to march in public demonstrations.[19]

The petitioners went on to argue that

it is not proper for revolutionary governments to withhold rights from woman because she is [said to be] fanatical, for nothing practical has been done to defanaticize her. We can point out the large number of Catholic representatives who are in the Chamber [of Deputies] and in other public posts, which does not scandalize the other individuals [in the government] who call themselves revolutionaries.[20]

In Mexico a spade is seldom called a spade in public life, and there is a refreshing frankness about the feminists' November 1931 petition. But their request that women be permitted to exercise political rights fell on deaf ears. The Chamber of Deputies made no response to the petition at the time it was presented or in the succeeding weeks and months.[21]

Approximately two months later, on January 27, 1932, Elvia Carrillo Puerto, speaking for the Liga Orientadora de Acción Femenina of Yucatán, made another attempt to persuade the Chamber of Deputies to grant women full political rights. She argued that when permitted to vote and be elected to office, women in Yucatán had acquitted themselves well.[22] It should be noted in passing that Elvia Carrillo Puerto was one of the few feminists prominent in the 1920s who continued the struggle through the succeeding decade. In Mexico, one of the weaknesses of the feminist movement was the lack of continuity in leadership and in organizations from one decade to the next. Of the women who were prominent feminists in the 1920s, for example, only Elvia Carrillo Puerto and María Ríos Cárdenas continued to be active in the 1930s. And of all the feminists active in the 1930s, only normal school professor and writer Julia Nava de Ruisánchez had participated in the movement since the establishment of the Women's Protective Society in 1904.[23] Apparently, the discouraging milieu and the lack of financial support led women like Hermila Galindo and Sofía Villa de Buentello to abandon the struggle for women's rights and retreat into obscure domesticity or, as in the case of Elena Torres, to devote themselves entirely to professional activities.[24]

As the 1932 congressional elections approached, Margarita Robles de Mendoza, who maintained a home in New York while serving as Mexico's delegate to the Pan American Union's Inter-American Commission on Women, wrote an open letter to Mexican feminists on February 2, 1932, urging them to appear at the polls in the coming elections and to insist on casting ballots. From the safe distance of New York, Robles counseled Mexican women to insist on voting, even if it meant arrest and imprisonment. "Remember," she advised her distant audience, "that the women who have won the vote in some parts of the world have had to suffer hunger, mockery, and imprisonment before reaching their goal."[25] Robles evidently fancied herself as the Mexican Emmeline Pankhurst or the Latin American Alice Paul, but with one difference: she lacked their willingness to suffer imprisonment to achieve female suffrage.

Margarita Robles de Mendoza is a good example of a select group of upper-class women in Latin American society who, in the 1930s, made a profession out of feminism and who concentrated exclusively on the issue of woman suffrage.[26] Robles spent most of her time abroad, and she was out of touch with all but a few members of her own class in Mexico. As a consequence, her brand of feminism was but a poor imitation of the English or North American variety. Without reflecting on the fact that Mexican jails were *not* English or American jails, she cheerfully counseled her countrywomen to submit to the horrors of confinement while she continued to draw a handsome salary as a representative to the Inter-American Commission on Women. As it happened, no one followed her advice in 1932.[27]

Later, in 1935, when Emilio Portes Gil recommended that Margarita Robles de Mendoza be named president of the Feminine Section of the PNR, scores of prominent feminists in Mexico placed paid notices in Mexico City's dailies denouncing her selection.[28] It was then revealed that Robles had no knowledge of or association with any feminist organization in Mexico.[29] Juana B. Gutiérrez, the authentic revolutionary and radical journalist who knew what Mexican jails were like, discovered in an interview she had with Robles that the latter had no sympathy with the egalitarian goals of the Mexican Revolution. Robles had even scornfully referred to impoverished Mexican women, that is, to about 90 percent of the country's female population, as *peladas* ("penniless nobodies").[30] Robles's selection by Portes Gil was vetoed by President Cárdenas, and eventually she was replaced as Mexico's representative to the Inter-American Commission by the distinguished writer, educator, and social reformer, Amalia Castillo Ledon.[31]

While Margarita Robles de Mendoza made empty gestures from abroad, Elvia Carrillo Puerto followed up her January 27 appeal for female suffrage with a demonstration by herself and members of her Liga

Orientadora de Acción Femenina at the opening of congress on February 28, 1932.[32] Neither this demonstration, nor the petitions of November 1931 and January 1932, nor the recent attainment of woman suffrage in Spain made any impression on the Mexican government. The only answer to the increased feminist activity was absolute silence on the part of government officials.

On November 25, 1933, the Second Congress of Women Workers and Peasants began its meetings in the same Alvaro Obregón Civic Center facing the Zócalo (main plaza) in Mexico City where the first congress had met two years before. Very little had happened in two years, except that more women than ever who needed to work were unemployed. The government continued to write off women as "lacking a revolutionary conscience" and at the same time did nothing to ensure that working mothers received paid leaves of absence during and after pregnancy as stipulated in the 1931 labor law. The moderates who organized the 1933 congress were well aware that the Marxist contingent, which had grown in strength and organization as the depression deepened and the revolutionary ardor of the regime lessened, would at best be disruptive and at worst seek to assume leadership of the women's movement. However, in the face of public apathy and governmental indifference, the feminists saw no other means than a congress to dramatize their cause. If it served no other purpose, a national congress of women affirmed that a feminist movement really did exist in Mexico.

El Universal's daily accounts of the meetings of the Second Congress of Women Workers and Peasants from November 25 to November 30, 1933, reveal that the delegates devoted most of their attention to the worsening effects of the economic depression on Mexican women. The papers read at the congress and the debates that followed make clear that more women had been reduced to mendicity and to prostitution than ever before and that peasant women lacked land, tools, seed, extension services, and marketing facilities.[33] In addition, the sessions revealed that the government was making no attempt to establish minimum wages for domestic servants and for employees in the private sector and that those lucky enough to find work in the garment industry, for example, were being paid three pesos a week at a time when newspapers advertised shoes at twelve pesos a pair and a meal in an inexpensive restaurant at over one peso.[34] The sessions also made clear that women and children were not being protected against night work, that minimum health and safety standards were being ignored by employers, and that pregnant workers were being fired.[35] In short, the 1933 Congress of Women Workers and Peasants spelled out the misery in which the vast majority of Mexican men, women, and children lived and of the inability of the government to live up to its own legislation on behalf of peasants and workers. Given this situation, it is no wonder that more and more Mexicans became Marxists in the 1930s.

The government of President Abelardo Rodríguez demonstrated its hostility and contempt for the delegates by refusing to give women government workers time off to attend the sessions and by sending to the congress not the secretary of labor, as it had promised, but a lower-level official.[36] And, as the government had done at the 1931 congress, it sent police agents to monitor the meetings.[37] When Consuelo Uranga, a normal school professor from Chihuahua[38] and a Communist delegate at the congress, demanded that the police agents present be asked to leave, one of them, an agent by the name of Sotomayor, shouted, ''You are the one who will leave these premises shortly.''[39] Sotomayor announced to an undoubtedly stunned audience that the goverment had instructed him to observe the labors of the congress, especially because a group of Communists were at the congress. No one thought to ask Sotomayor if it was against the law to be a Communist in Mexico. (It was not.) Instead, María Ríos Cárdenas, the leader of the moderates at the congress, stated that since the assembly was meeting in a government building, no one had a right to expel anyone. Irritated, however, with what she viewed as a Communist attempt to sabotage the congress, Ríos Cárdenas went on to say that ''women ought to construct rather than destroy, because for the latter there are millions of men [available], and what needed to be done was to study the problems facing women with all the attention they deserve.''[40]

Consuelo Uranga ignored both the police agent and Ríos Cárdenas and spoke up time and again during the debates. When one reformist-minded delegate suggested that the state intervene to see that jobs were made available, Uranga countered that the ''state is one of the weapons of the bourgeosie and the large landowners to oppress the proletarian masses.''[41] She argued that reforming laws would not get them anywhere. The laws, she insisted, were merely a deceitful means the capitalists used to lull to sleep the workers, ''but,'' she affirmed, ''these are no longer willing to be deceived and they will obtain their conquests by means of [armed] struggle.''[42] At another point Uranga interrupted another reformist speaker to say that the only way women and men could be emancipated was through social revolution.[43]

The congress was almost evenly divided between reformists and Communists, and Ríos Cárdenas admitted that she won the presidency of the permanent commission of the second congress, which was charged with carrying out its resolutions and planning a future congress, by only four votes.[44] Her opponent, Luz Encina, a garment worker and union representative, was supported by the Communist faction and refused to concede the election to Ríos Cárdenas. On December 2, 1933, a week after the stormy second congress ended, the officers of the Bloque Nacional de Mujeres Revolucionarias, which had convoked the recent congress, found it necessary to declare to the press that it disavowed and declared null those accords reached by the ''minority Communist faction'' that had set itself up as the permanent commission.[45] So far, the two attempts to unify all the country's feminists had been futile. And, while the reformists and Communists were at loggerheads in 1933 and 1934, women on the right were united against the government. On September 10, 1934, at least thirty thousand Catholic women protested in Mexico City against the closing of churches and against the plan for ''socialist education'' outlined in the ruling PNR's ''Six Year Plan'' to be carried out during the 1934-40 presidential term.

The rift between the reformists and Communists intensified in 1934, when two more feminist congresses met. The Liga Internacional de Mujeres Ibéricas e Hispanoamericanas (''The International League of Iberian and Spanish-American Women'') convoked the first Mexican congress of intellectuals and professionals to study the problem of prostitution in the republic.[47] It began its meetings at the Bolívar amphitheatre of the National Preparatory School in Mexico City on June 10, 1934. Then, from September 13 to 15, the Third National Congress of Women Workers and Peasants held its sessions in Guadalajara, the third largest city in Mexico and capital of the important state of Jalisco.[48] Both congresses were stormy affairs, and the divisions were so serious at the June congress on prostitution that the Communist group was physically barred from the Bolivar amphitheatre on June 14 and set up another congress at the national university.[49]

Before that occurred, however, the congress on prostitution came to grips with one of the country's most devastating social problems. One doctor reported that in one month no less than forty-one thousand persons sought medical attention for venereal disease in Mexico City alone.[50] While the Communists and non-Communists disagreed violently as to the causes of prostitution in Mexico, all agreed that the first step in combating the problem was for the state to end its policy of regulating brothels. The delegates passed a resolution urging the government to cancel all permits issued to bordellos on the grounds that rather than "regulate" prostitution, the issuance of permits encouraged its growth by public officials eager for bribes.[51] It was no secret that more than one Mexican politician owed his wealth to the traffic in women.

At their last meeting on June 18, 1934, the Marxist dissidents, led by the educator and journalist Profesora María del Refugio García, the surgeon Doctora Esther Chapa, and the lawyer Licenciada Elisa Zapata Vela declared that poverty was the principle cause of prostitution and that prostitution would never disappear so long as capitalism survived. In their view, until Mexico underwent a Marxist revolution, the best that could be done was to reduce its incidence. They passed resolutions calling for the termination of government regulation of prostitution and urged that cabarets and other "centers of vice" be closed down.[52] They also believed that certain positive measures could be taken by the coming regime of General Lázaro Cárdenas, who was regarded as an honest man and sincere revolutionary, to attack the basic causes of prostitution: poverty and ignorance. They called for enforcement of the laws guaranteeing equal pay for equal work and minimum wages, and they urged that the cost of food and housing for the working classes be reduced. In addition, they called for the setting up of day-care centers in working-class neighborhoods and the provision of free textbooks and one free meal a day to poor school children. The delegates urged that the military budget be drastically reduced to provide funds for the social and educational reforms they proposed.[53]

The moderates placed less emphasis on remedial social action and more on censorship, urging the government to prohibit the sale of obscene books and magazines and to bar young people from attending films unacompanied by adults. They urged that all dance salons as well as cabarets be closed, and they also suggested that the campaign against alcohol be intensified.[54] One cannot help but conclude that the moderates attacked the symptoms of the malaise while the Communists had a better perception of the economic causes of prostitution in Mexico.

In the end the Communists had better organization too. After the moderates at the third and last national congress of women workers under the leadership of María Ríos Cárdenas failed to create a single, unified feminist organization at its September 13-15, 1934, meetings in Guadalajara, María del Refugio García and other Marxist women took over the task of establishing a mass feminist organization in Mexico.[55]

The failure of the delegates at the Third National Congress of Women Workers and Peasants to agree on anything of substance brought to an end the experiment in periodic national congresses as a way of furthering the movement for women's rights in Mexico. Yet the congresses of 1931-34, however divisive they may have been, had positive results. They gave the lie to the supposed passivity of Mexican women and their presumed lack of interest in matters outside the home. The congresses of 1931-34 also indicated that there was one issue on which all feminists agreed regardless of ideological persuasion, and that was the issue of woman suffrage. As chief organizer and strategist of what was to be the Frente Unico Pro-Derechos de la Mujer (Sole Front for Women's Rights), henceforth referred to as the Frente Unico, María del Refugio García concentrated her organization's efforts on gaining suffrage for women, in part because this tactic would draw the support of every feminist in Mexico and in part because the 1934 election to the presidency of Lázaro Cárdenas, the "immaculate revolutionary" as one feminist called him,[56] gave promise that a determined campaign to achieve woman suffrage might meet with success.

LÁZARO CÁRDENAS AND THE WOMEN'S RIGHTS MOVEMENT, 1934-1940

The predecessors to Lázaro Cárdenas in the presidency—Emilio Portes Gil, Pascual Ortíz Rubio, and Abelardo Rodríguez—who each served as chief executive for no more than two years from 1928 to 1934, found that it was perilous to cross General Plutarco Elías Calles, the "maximum chief" or undisputed leader of the revolution. Although the reform of the legal code in 1927 came during Calles's presidency (1924-1928) and although he had approved in principle the idea that Mexican women should participate in "the activities of the political life in Mexico," Calles seems to have believed that all but a few Mexican women were reactionaries and traditionalists.[57] His extreme anticlericalism alienated millions of Mexican women, and many of them participated in demonstrations and economic boycotts in support of the church and actively supported the devout Catholics who rebelled against the government in the late 1920s.[58] Nor could Calles forget that it was a woman, the underground nun La Madre Conchita, who had counselled the young man who assassinated president-elect Alvaro Obregón in 1928. The puppets of Calles, as Portes Gil, Ortíz Rubio and Rodríguez were often called, shared the maximum chief's prejudice against women and pretty much ignored the increased activity by feminists from 1928 to 1934. In that period the consensus of the regime was that women were not "ready" to vote. What was meant was that large numbers of Mexican women could not be counted on to vote for PNR candidates.

The lack of interest by Calles and his associates in any of the social, economic, or political issues that women had raised at the congresses of 1931-33 is seen in the Six Year Plan adopted at the PNR convention at Querétaro in December 1933 when Lázaro Cárdenas was chosen as the candidate for the presidency. There was only one reference to women in that detailed blueprint; one of its provisions called for improving female prisons.[59] The plan ignored the feminists' call for the protection of working mothers, for equal rights to own land by peasant women, and for measures to curb prostitution.

Up to the time of his selection for the presidency, Lázaro Cárdenas had not demonstrated any special interest in women.[60] He had remained loyal to Calles and had been rewarded for his loyalty by high political posts, including a term as governor of his native state of Michoacán, head of the National Executive Committee of the PNR, and minister of war in the cabinet of first Ortíz Rubio and then Abelardo Rodríguez.[61] Cárdenas campaigned vigorously for the presidency everyone knew he would win, but his campaign statements on women were unexceptional. He exhorted women to do more for the revolution, to aid in antialcohol campaigns, and, in his words, "que sean dignas compañeras del hombre" ("to strive to be worthy companions of men").[62] The emphasis was clearly on what Mexican women needed to do to find favor with the government, not on what the government should do or proposed to do for women.

However, in his acceptance speech at Querétaro on December 6, 1933, Cárdenas raised the hope of feminists when he stated that

[We] need to invigorate and expand the effort Mexican women are making to participate in the nation's public life. [This must be done] in a balanced and progressive manner in order to employ their great wealth of energies and virtues for the general welfare. For women are beings eminently aware of human problems and sufficiently generous to seek the general interest.[63]

Nothing more was said about political rights for women, however, until just after the election of Cárdenas was made official. On September 15, 1934, the PNR issued a statement to the press announcing that it would begin a campaign to organize Mexican women "under the banners of the PNR."[64] The announcement added that "the State Committees of the PNR are proceeding to organize Mexican women so that they will collaborate with the Party in the development of the social axioms that the Six Year Plan contains." *Excelsior*'s source believed that this was the first step the PNR was taking to incorporate Mexican women into the political, social, and economic movement initiated by the revolution. The article in *Excelsior* continued:

With time, once the women of Mexico are duly prepared by their social and educative effort to participate in the country's politics [the Party] will study the convenience of beginning to constitutionally concede [to women] the political rights that the Fundamental Charter grants to men. That is to say, within some years Mexican women will be able to vote and be elected for popular elected offices. It is believed that the first political right that will be granted to women is the right to take part in municipal governments in the country, for on the local level women can perform work beneficial to the community. After this step, our sources state, women will be duly prepared to serve in the State legislatures and in the national congress.[65]

This statement is of interest because the gradualist approach outlined in this editorial of September 15, 1934, was later adhered to by the governing party in extending the vote to Mexican women from 1946 to 1958.

Both the December 6, 1933, statement of Cárdenas and the September 15, 1934, announcement of the PNR (which spoke for Cárdenas) emphasized that political rights for women would be granted only gradually and over an unspecified period of time. Clearly, at the start of his term Cárdenas was as wary of women as were his predecessors, and the mass demonstration in Mexico City on September 10, 1934, by over thirty thousand Catholic women against Cárdenas's plan for "Socialist education" merely confirmed the president's fears that more women opposed the government than supported it.[66]

Feminists, however, could take heart from two actions of Cárdenas at the start of his term that indicated his interest in improving the status of women and their employment opportunities. First, on December 29, 1934, he announced that Mexico would adhere to the Convention on the Nationality of Women signed at the Seventh International Conference of American States in Montevideo the previous year.[67] Then, in January 1935, Cárdenas appointed the gifted teacher and literary critic, Palma Guillén, as Mexico's minister to Colombia.[68] It was entirely appropriate that Mexico should be the first Latin American country to appoint a woman ambassador. Nine years before, in 1926, Mexico had accepted the credentials of Alexandra Kollontay as the Soviet Union's second ambassador to Mexico, becoming the first country in the New World to receive a woman ambassador.[69] Although ill health forced Madame Kollontay to quit her post in Mexico after six months, her brief stay favorably impressed the government, the press, and that part of the public which viewed the Russian revolution with sympathy.[70]

Feminists applauded Cárdenas's initiatives in favor of women, but they were clearly disappointed with his cautious approach to the question of women's political rights. While the government insisted that women needed to be prepared to exercise the vote, feminists held that without the vote all Mexican women were being stigmatized and singled out as inferior and untrustworthy. It should be emphasized here that in a country like Mexico, where elections were controlled, the ballot was viewed not as an end in itself but as an indispensable means for attaining full equality before the law. Feminists asked if it was just to deny the vote to women who had favored the revolution, while no man who had been an enemy of the revolution because of his religious convictions was denied the right to vote.

Cárdenas began to see the justice of the feminists' arguments after his dramatic break with Calles in mid-1935. In June Cárdenas replaced the Callistas in his cabinet with friends like Francisco J. Múgica of Michoacán, a leftist who had helped draft the most radical articles of the 1917 constitution.[71] Múgica had long been attuned to the feminists' cause. He was not a feudal Marxist as one observer found was true of too many Mexican men in the 1930s, that is, a Marxist outside and a feudalist within the home.[72] Múgica took great pains to see that his daughters received an excellent education that would prepare them for serious careers.[73] And his wife, Matilde Cabo Rodríguez, was one of the outstanding feminists of her time. She participated in the 1931 and 1933 Congresses of Women Workers and Peasants and became active with other left-wing women, including María del Refugio García, Doctora Balmaceda, and Doctora Esther Chapa in establishing the Frente Unico in 1935.[74]

On September 1, 1935, Cárdenas read his first presidential message to the nation at the opening of congress. In that message he recognized the "right of Mexican working women to vote and enjoy other privileges of citizenship."[75] The *New York Times* reported that,

Although the Constitution is not specific on that point, the President asserted the laws of the land granted women workers equal rights and that their temperament "equips them to embrace sincerely and enthusiastically a generous struggle, placing aside all selfish interest."[76]

Emilio Portes Gil, whom Cárdenas had recently appointed to head the PNR, was asked by Margarita Robles de Mendoza how he defined "working women." Portes Gil replied that anyone who "contributes to the development of the country may be called a 'worker,' " and he identified housewives, teachers, clerks, and others in this category.[77] As a result, Mrs. Robles de Mendoza reported to the *New York Times*, some eighty thousand women voted in the municipal elections in Vera Cruz after Portes Gil's clarifying statement.[78]

In the spring of 1936, Cárdenas, who wanted to create a genuine workers' and peasants' state in Mexico in place of an age-old authoritarianism, encouraged both men and women to vote in primaries, called "elecciones internas" in Mexico. In the April 5, 1936, primaries for congressional and state offices, some 2,753 women and 44,000 men cast their votes in the Federal District.[79] As Ward M. Morton points out in *Women Suffrage in Mexico*, "the women voted as members of labor unions, peasant organizations and women's sections into which they were incorporated."[80] The outcome of this primary indicated that women organized by the PNR or affiliated with government organized labor and peasant groups posed no danger to the government. On the contrary, recognizing the civic equality of women removed a glaring contradiction between revolutionary ideology and actual practice.

Heartened by Cárdenas's support for woman suffrage, the Frente Unico mounted an effective campaign to win full political rights immediately and not over an unspecified period of time. María del Refugio García forged a genuinely popular union embracing some eight hundred feminine organizations with fifty thousand members, many of them native women. The Frente Unico placed the right of women to vote and be elected to office at the head of its list of goals. But of equal importance to the Frente's left-wing leaders was their insistence on changing the federal labor law to make female labor compatible with maternity and on making sure that agrarian reform (which Cárdenas was pushing vigorously) benefited women as much as men.[81] The Frente also called for further reforms in the civil code to ensure the complete equality of men and women before the law. In addition, the Frente wanted to see Indian women integrated into the sociopolitical life of the country.[82] The Frente expressed its concern for the continuing problem of unemployment among women by asking that the state set up employment centers for females in need of a job. Lastly the Frente concerned itself with the problems of children, asking that a children's bureau be established to protect infants and children from neglect, abuse, and exploitation.[83]

The Frente Unico steadfastly maintained its independence from the government and its party apparatus, the PNR, especially as the head of the PNR, Emilio Portes Gil had, in October 1935, appointed Margarita Robles de Mendoza to serve as director of the committee that was to reorganize the women's sector of the ruling party.[84] When Mexico's most well-known feminists protested that Mrs. Robles de Mendoza was totally unacquainted with the work of feminist centers or women-worker and peasant organizations in Mexico, her appointment was withdrawn. In August 1936, Portes Gil, a Callista and inveterate enemy of leftists like Múgica and the leaders of the Frente, resigned as president of the PNR and lost his influence in the Cárdenas administration.[85]

In July 1937, the Frente pursued its aim of immediate political equality for women by having its secretary, María del Refugio García, run for a seat in the Chamber of Deputies from her native district of Uruápan, Michoacán.[86] Like Hermila Galindo and Elvia Carrillo Puerto before her, María del Refugio García, known as ''Cuca'' to her friends, decided to run for office since the constitution did not specify that women were excluded from citizenship.[87] ''Cuca,'' whom Verna Carleton Millan in 1939 characterized as ''one of the most genuinely popular women in Mexico,'' was the apparent winner of the chamber seat, but in mid-August 1937 the Electoral Committee of the Chamber of Deputies refused to seat her and chose a male opponent instead.[88] Earlier, at the time of "Cuca's" victory in Uruápan, the National Executive Committee of the PNR insisted that it would be necessary to amend the constitution before women could vote or hold office on the national level.[89] Between August 15 and 26 "Cuca" and her followers in the Frente staged a hunger strike outside the president's residence of Los Pinos in Mexico City, protesting the decisions of the PNR and the Congressional Electoral Committee.[90] Cárdenas, who was in Vera Cruz at the time, decided that it was no longer possible to ignore the demands of the Frente and all the other feminist organizations in the republic. Speaking to the Mexican Feminine Confederation of Vera Cruz, Cárdenas stated that he would submit a bill to change Article 34 of the constitution at the next congressional session opening in September.[91]

True to his word, on September 1, 1937, Cárdenas told the nation that awarding Mexican women full political rights was an act of "intrinsic justice" that could no longer be delayed. He argued that those who insisted that Mexican women were conservative, fanatical, and reactionary were forgetting the efforts of those Mexican women who, over the years, had "taken part in the most perilous activities. . . in defense of the most advanced ideas."[92] This was a reminder to the legislature that a number of women schoolteachers had been murdered by religious fanatics who opposed the government's policy of socialist education.[93] On November 23, 1937, the minister of the interior (Gobernación) sent to the Mexican Senate Cárdenas's proposed amendment of Article 34 of the constitution which, by merely adding the three words "men and women" to that article would make women eligible for all the rights of citizenship, including the right to vote and hold political office.[94]

The Senate acted with unusual speed and on December 22, 1937, passed the amendment to Article 34. In that same month, Aurora Mesa was elected municipal president of Chilpancingo, capital of the State of Guerrero. She was credited with instituting an efficient and honest government in that locality.[95] By July 6, 1938, when the Chamber of Deputies meeting in special session finally voted in favor of the amendment to Article 34, some sixteen of the twenty-eight Mexican states had already accorded women the franchise.[96]

In his September 1, 1938, annual message to the nation, Cárdenas urged the states to quickly ratify the woman suffrage amendment. Two weeks later, at a giant rally by Mexican feminists for the Spanish parliamentarian, Margarita Nelken, homage to the embattled Spanish Republic mingled with joy at the victory for women that seemed within sight in Mexico. But 1939 brought defeat to the Spanish Republic, which surrendered to the Francoists on March 31, 1939, and betrayal to the Mexican feminists. By May 1939 all the Mexican states had ratified the amendment to Article 34, and all that remained to be done was for Congress to formally declare that, the states having ratified the amendment, it was now in force. Pressed by the feminists to act, members of Congress assured the women, who anxiously crowded the visitors' gallery, that they would not adjourn until they had declared the amended Article 34 the law of the land.

The members of Congress broke their word and pigeonholed the amendment. Despite mass demonstrations and repeated petitions by the Frente Unico and other organizations from June 1939 to July 1940 and despite Cárdenas's plea in his last annual message of September 1, 1939, that the Chamber of Deputies complete the ratification process, nothing was done. What had gone wrong?

The few feminists who have written about this period are either vague about or profess ignorance of the motives of Congress in killing the woman suffrage amendment in 1939, possibly because they did not wish to admit that many Mexican women were, indeed, enemies of the revolution. It is impossible to verify just how many women were involved, but the establishment in early 1939 of a well-financed Feminine Idealist party, which supported the right-wing candidate for the presidency, General Juan Andreu Almazán, appears to have been the decisive factor in the defeat of the woman suffrage amendment.[97] While vigorously carrying out many radical reforms and urging workers and peasants to unite against the propertied classes, Cárdenas had alienated large sectors of the population, both men and women. Almazán capitalized on the growing polarization of Mexican society between left and right and undertook an effective campaign that badly frightened the official party (now reorganized as the Party of the Mexican Revolution, or PRM). Cárdenas, fearful that his hard-won reforms would be undone, agreed to pick a middle-of-the-road candidate, General Manuel Ávila Camacho, rather than his friend, Francisco Múgica, to succeed him. Múgica, the choice of the left and of most of the feminists in Mexico because of his vigorous espousal of their cause, had to be sacrificed. At the same time, the reform of the constitution to permit women to vote had to be undone, for while the Frente Unico and all feminist and left-wing women could be counted on to support the government candidate, it was feared that an overwhelming majority of adult Mexican women would vote for Almazán. This fear was never tested.

The presidential election of July 7, 1940, at which a handful of women attempted to vote, was marked by violence at the polls, and a number of bystanders, including women and children, lost their lives during the balloting. Although Ávila Camacho was declared the victor by a wide margin, it is possible that Almazán received more votes than were recorded in his favor. Almazán was convinced that he had been defrauded of the election and for a time threatened insurrection, but the lack of enthusiasm for his cause leads one to suspect that even if all the votes had been counted correctly, and even if women had been permitted to vote in 1940, Almazán would probably have lost the election to Ávila Camacho.[98] Unlike Almazán, the mild-mannered Ávila Camacho had made few enemies and was a nonthreatening figure. And to allay the fears of religious Mexicans, the government candidate declared that he was a believer.[99]

That statement marked a turning point in the Mexican Revolution. After 1940, most political observers agree, the Mexican Revolution moved to the right.[100] Part of that process included, if not a reconciliation between church and state, at least a cessation of hostilities. And once the religious conflict that had wracked the nation from 1910 to 1940 was defused, it was possible to bring to a successful conclusion the quest for civic equality for Mexican women. In 1946, the year after France finally overcame its fears concerning the supposed conservatism of its female population and granted them suffrage, Mexico granted women the right to vote and hold office on the municipal level.[101] In 1954 Mexican women voted in congressional elections, and in 1958 Mexico carried out that act of intrinsic justice that Cárdenas had asked for twenty-one years before and granted Mexican women full political rights.[102] By then some seventeen Latin American countries, none of which had undergone the upheaval of a major social revolution, had already granted suffrage to women.[103]

By the time women were granted the right to vote in presidential elections in 1958 the memory of the Frente Unico and of its petitions, meetings, demonstrations, marches, and hunger strikes had dimmed, and the names of its leaders, "Cuca" García, Concha Michel, Doctora

Esther Chapa and others were all but forgotten. However, with the growth of a new feminist involvement in the 1970s there has been a revival of interest in the Frente Unico and the feminist movement of forty years ago.[104] The attainment of full political rights by Mexican women in the 1950s was a belated victory for the 1930s' feminists. Against all odds their plea for simple justice was finally heard.

NOTES

1. Estados Unidos Mexicanos, Departamento de la Estadística Nacional, *Resumen del censo general de habitantes de 30 de noviembre de 1921* (México: Talleres Gráficos de la Nación, 1928), p. 92. Estados Unidos Mexicanos, Secretaría de Economía Nacional, Dirección General de Estadística, *Quinto censo de población; 15 de mayo de 1930. Resumen general* (México: Talleres Gráficos de la Nación, 1930), p. 73.

2. Estados Unidos Mexicanos, *Quinto censo de población* (1930), p. 75.

3. Ibid., p. 73; Estados Unidos Mexicanos, *Resumen del censo general . . . de 1921*, p. 95. It should be noted that the number of men employed by the government rose from 8,155 in 1921 to 142,579 in 1930.

4. *Excelsior*, 29 November 1933, p. 5, and 30 November 1933, p. 7. With 142,579 men employed as bureaucrats, 5 percent of that number is 7,128. Since 10,122 women were employed by the government, 3,000 would have had to be dismissed to achieve Mussolini's quota.

5. Ibid., 29 November 1933, pp. 1, 7.

6. There are no primary sources on the Frente Unico available. Secondary sources include Verna Carleton Millan, *Mexico Reborn* (Boston: Houghton Mifflin Co., 1939), pp. 164-68; Lillian E. Fisher, "Influence of the Present Mexican Revolution Upon the Status of Mexican Women," *Hispanic American Historical Review* 22 (February 1942), pp. 220-22; Ward M. Morton, *Woman Suffrage in Mexico* (Gainesville: University of Florida Press, 1962), p. 21; María Antonieta Rascón, "La mujer y la lucha social," in *Imagen y realidad de la mujer*, ed. Elena Urrutia, SEP-SETENTAS no. 172 (México: Secretaría de Educación Pública, 1975), pp. 160-63.

7. María Ríos Cárdenas, *La mujer mexicana es ciudadana. Historia, con fisonomía de una novela de costumbres, 1930-1940* (México: Epoca, 1940), pp. 29-45.

8. *El Universal*, 2 October 1931, pp. 1-2.

9. Ibid., 3 October 1931, pp. 2, 7.

10. Ríos Cárdenas, *La mujer mexicana*, p. 45.

11. *El Universal*, 2 October 1931, p. 1.

12. Ríos Cárdenas, *La mujer mexicana*, pp. 34-37.

13. Ibid., p. 37.

14. *El Universal*, 4 October 1931, Section 2, p. 1.

15. Ibid., 7 October 1931, Section 2, p. 1.

16. Ríos Cárdenas, *La mujer mexicana*, pp. 49-51.

17. Ibid., p. 49.

18. Ibid., p. 54.

19. Ibid.

20. Ibid.

21. Ibid., p. 55.

22. Ibid., p. 63.

23. A normal school professor and writer, Julia Nava de Ruisánchez, attended the women's congresses of 1923 and 1931 and remained active in the feminist movement through the 1940s.

24. In contrast to Profesora Nava de Ruisánchez, Elena Torres dropped out of the movement after the 1923 congress and devoted herself primarily to fomenting progressive education in Mexico. In 1933, for example, she attended a pedagogical conference in the United States sponsored by The New Education Fellowship and translated one of the conference papers, "Education and Social Ideals," for *México Pedagógico* (Publicación dirigida por la Organización Científica y Técnica de Trabajo Escolar), vol. 1 (November 1933).

25. Ríos Cárdenas, *La mujer mexicana*, pp. 71-72.

26. See Margarita Robles de Mendoza, *La evolución de la mujer en México* (México: n.p., 1931), and her *Silabario de la ciudadanía de la mujer mexicana* (Jalapa: Talleres Gráficos del Gobierno, 1932). A favorable biographical sketch of Margarita Robles de Mendoza is found in María Efraína Rocha, *Semblanzas biográficas de algunas luchadoras mexicanas contemporáneas* (México: Ediciones del Comité Coordinador Femenino, 1947), p. 16.

27. Ríos Cárdenas, *La mujer mexicana*, p. 72.

28. See, for example, *La Prensa* (México), 31 October 1935, p. 2.

29. Ibid.

30. Juana B. Gutiérrez wrote a blistering article on Margarita Robles de Mendoza called "Las mujeres sin patria" ("Women without a country") in her biweekly journal, *Alma Mexicana: Por la Tierra y Por la Raza*, 15 November 1935, pp. 7-8.

31. Consuelo Colon R., *Mujeres de México* (México: Imprenta Gallarda, 1944), p. 53. See also Ríos Cárdenas, *La mujer mexicana*, pp. 134-35.

32. "La Liga Orientadora de Acción Femenina organizarán una manifestación al abrirse las Cámaras," *El Universal*, 28 February 1932, pp. 1, 6.

33. Ríos Cárdenas, *La mujer mexicana*, pp. 77-83. The conference received full coverage in *El Universal* from November 25 through November 30, 1933.

34. *El Universal*, 28 November 1933, p. 8.

35. Ibid., 27 November 1933, p. 7.

36. Ibid., 26 November 1933, p. 1, and 27 November 1933, p. 7.

37. Ibid., 28 November 1933, p. 1; Ríos Cárdenas, *La mujer mexicana*, p. 81.

38. The only source of information on Consuelo Uranga is Rocha, *Semblanzas biográficas*, who notes that Consuelo Uranga taught literature in Chihuahua and that she was persecuted for her radical left-wing beliefs.

39. *El Universal*, 28 November 1933, p. 1.

40. Ibid.

41. Ibid., p. 8.

42. Ibid.

43. Ibid., 29 November 1933, p. 8

44. Ríos Cárdenas, *La mujer mexicana*, pp. 82-83.

45. *El Universal*, 2 December 1933, p. 1.

46. *El Informador: Diario Independiente* (Guadalajara, Jalisco), 10 September 1934, p. 1.

47. *El Universal*, 11 June 1934, p. 1.

48. Ríos Cárdenas, *La mujer mexicana*, pp. 107-15.

49. *El Universal*, 15 June 1934, p. 2.

50. Ibid., 12 June 1934, p. 8.

51. Ibid., p. 1.

52. Ibid., 19 June 1934, p. 8.

53. Ibid.

54. Ibid., 23 June 1934, p. 5.

55. Newspapers in Mexico City ignored this congress and only *El Informador*, the leading newspaper in Guadalajara, gave the Third Congress of Women Workers and Peasants good coverage from September 12 through 16, 1934.

56. *El Universal*, 29 January 1932, p. 2.

57. In Calles's most important speeches and press interviews from 1923 through 1926 there were no references to women's rights. See Esperanza Velázquez Bringas, comp., *Méjico ante el mundo: Ideología del Presidente Plutarco Elías Calles* (Barcelona: Editorial Cervantes, 1927).

58. Mexican women were so conspicuous in defense of the church in 1926-27 that on August 14, 1928, Dwight Morrow insisted that "much of the trouble in Mexico" had been caused by a "disorganized lot of women." Cited in Robert E. Quirk, *The Mexican Revolution and the Catholic Church, 1910-1929* (Bloomington, Ind.: Indiana University Press, 1973), p. 236.

59. Morton, *Woman Suffrage in Mexico*, p. 16.

60. Ibid.

61. Ibid.

62. México. Secretaría de Prensa y Propaganda del CEN del PNR, *La gira del General Lázaro Cárdenas: Sintesis ideológica* (México: n.p., 1934), pp. 136-37.

63. Ibid., pp. 144-45.

64. *Excelsior*, 16 September 1934, p. 1.

65. Ibid., pp. 1, 11.

66. Over thirty thousand women, many of whom belonged to "la mejor sociedad metropolitana" ("the capital's highest society") braved tear gas and water hoses to reach the national palace with a petition calling for religious freedom and protesting the implementation of socialist education in the schools. *El Informador* (Guadalajara), 10 September 1934, p. 1.

67. Morton, *Woman Suffrage in Mexico*, p. 17.

68. Colon, *Mujeres de México*, p. 125.

69. Isabel de Palencia, *Alexandra Kollontay, Ambassadress from Russia* (New York: Longmans, Green and Co., 1947), p. 184; México, *Boletín Oficial de la Secretaría de Relaciones Exteriores*, 49 (January 1927), pp. 28-31.

70. See, for example, "El orígen de nuestra simpatía hacia la Señora Kollontay," *Mujer*, 12 December 1926, p. 9.

71. For an account by Múgica of what the Querétaro congress of 1916-17 had accomplished see Armando de María y Campos, *Múgica: Crónica biográfica* (México: Compañía de Ediciones Populares, S.A., 1939), p. 121.

72. Millan, *Mexico Reborn*, p. 161.

73. María y Campos, *Múgica*, pp. 207-8.

74. See Rocha, *Semblanzas biográficas* for brief sketches of the leading Marxist feminists of the 1930s.

75. The *New York Times*, 2 September 1935, p. 9.

76. Ibid.

77. Ibid., 8 September 1935, p. 7.

78. Ibid.

79. Ríos Cárdenas, *La mujer mexicana*, pp. 131-32.

80. Morton, *Woman Suffrage in Mexico*, p. 22.

81. For a cogent defense of the rights of urban and rural working mothers, see Concepción Michel, *Dos antagonismos fundamentales* (México: Editorial de Izquierda de la Cámara de Diputados, 1938).

82. Millan, *Mexico Reborn*, pp. 165-66.

83. *El Universal*, 22 March 1937, p. 1.

84. *La Prensa*, 31 October 1935, p. 2.

85. Morton, *Woman Suffrage in Mexico*, p. 27.

86. Millan, *Mexico Reborn*, p. 167.

87. Morton, *Woman Suffrage in Mexico*, pp. 28-29.

88. Ibid., p. 29.

89. Ibid.

90. Ibid.

91. Ríos Cárdenas, *La mujer mexicana*, p. 145.

92. Ibid., pp. 148-49.

93. The *New York Times*, 2 September 1935, p. 9.

94. Morton, *Woman Suffrage in Mexico*, pp. 30-31.

95. Ríos Cárdenas, *La mujer mexicana*, p. 165.

96. Morton, *Woman Suffrage in Mexico*, p. 37.

97. Contemporary foreign observers agreed that the church's support for Almazán, who entered the presidential race on July 25, 1939, doomed the effort to grant Mexican women full political rights. Betty Kirk, *Covering the Mexican Front* (Norman: University of Oklahoma Press, 1942) remarks, on page 37, that in 1936 "Cárdenas was strongly in favor of the emancipation of women, as he proved both publicly and privately, but the age-old Church question defeated women's rights in Mexico three years later." Later she notes that "Church organizations . . . were throwing their influence behind Almazán, which accounted in part for the success he had as he swept the country." (p. 237) Another American observer, Virginia Prewett, emphasized the active role women played in supporting Almazán. Quoting Prewett, Fisher writes in "Influence of the Present Mexican Revolution," that "on many occasions members of the Partido Femenino Idealista rose long before daybreak to go out and distribute propaganda for. . . [Almazán's] Revolutionary Party of National Unification." (p. 222) Morton, *Woman Suffrage in Mexico*, writes that "the Feminine Idealists, with much show of proclerical support and what appeared to be an affluent political treasury, began to establish feminine groups in all parts of the country and threatened to control most of the feminine vote if women gained the right to participate in the coming election." (p. 39) Gustavo Casasola, *Historia gráfica de la revolución mexicana*, 8 vols., 2d ed. (México: Editorial Trillas, 1973), pp. vii, x, writes: "Cuando empezó a sonar el nombre del divisionario guerrerense Juan Andreu Almazán, como candidato presidencial, espontaneamente surgieron simpatizadores y partidarios, especialmente, en su mayoría, elemento femenino." ("When the Division General of Guerrero, Juan Andreu Almazán, began to be mentioned as a presidential candidate, sympathizers and followers spontaneously appeared, especially, in the majority, the feminine element.")

98. Morton, *Woman Suffrage in Mexico*, pp. 44-45.

99. Ibid., p. 40.

100. See, for example, Stanley Ross, ed., *Is the Mexican Revolution Dead?* (New York: Alfred A. Knopf, 1966) for evidence that after Cárdenas left office sweeping socioeconomic reforms came to an end.

101. Morton, *Woman Suffrage in Mexico*, p. 57. Ana María Flores, "La

mujer en la sociedad,'' in *México, Cincuenta Años de Revolución* (México: Fondo de Cultura Económica, 1963), p. 217.

102. Morton, *Woman Suffrage in Mexico*, pp. 83-84.

103. Women's Bureau, *Political Status of Women in the Other American Republics*, pp. 14 ff.

104. See, for example, Rascón, ''La mujer y la lucha social,'' pp. 160-74.

CONCLUSION

Feminism, as it developed in Mexico from approximately 1870 to 1940, had a character all its own and bore only a faint resemblance to the feminist movement in the United States or northern Europe. This is especially true with respect to the question of political rights. While the quest for the vote preoccupied North American and northern European women for almost a hundred years, in Mexico up to 1910 there was little interest by men or women in female enfranchisement. The reason for this lack of interest is obvious: effective suffrage, as envisioned in Mexico's 1857 constitution, did not exist during the long rule of Porfirio Díaz. Moreover, if one protested against rigged elections, corruption in office, or political repression, the consequences, as the woman journalist Juana Belén Gutiérrez de Mendoza discovered, were often loss of one's livelihood and a jail sentence.

Given the political realities of late-nineteenth- and early-twentieth-century Mexico, it is no wonder that a member of Díaz's cabinet, Justo Sierra, a man who vigorously championed female education, advised women to form souls rather than laws. Similarly, in the 1890s, Genaro García, the impassioned advocate of legal equality for women, did not advise females to seek the vote. Given the lack of male support, it is no surprise that the question of suffrage was not raised by the editors of the woman's journal, *La Siempreviva* in Yucatán in the 1870s nor by the consciously feminist editors of *La Mujer Mexicana* in Mexico City between 1904 and 1908. Woman suffrage was unthinkable to all but a few visionary socialists at a time when the vast majority of Mexican men were excluded from the political process.

In 1910, when Francisco I. Madero challenged Díaz for the presidency under the slogan of "effective suffrage and no reelection," the ideal of political democracy was rekindled in Mexico. But it took bullets rather than ballots to unseat Díaz, and between 1910 and 1917, during the chaotic years of revolution, counterrevolution, and military rule, the idea of woman suffrage made little headway among the men and women who supported Madero's democratic ideals. In the unsettled conditions of the times, female enfranchisement was as unthinkable as ever. Not, however, to General Salvador Alvarado and a few other revolutionary leaders imbued with the socialist ideas of a just and equitable society.

Alvarado was convinced that women had to be weaned away from the church and incorporated into the political life of Mexico. In 1916 his calling of two feminist congresses at Mérida, Yucatán was largely to convince the delegates at the Querétaro 1916-17 constitutional convention to extend the vote to women, at least on the municipal and state level. However, to Alvarado's chagrin, he discovered that only a few Yucatecan women wanted to vote. Furthermore, after a long debate the delegates at Querétaro decided to extend the vote only to illiterate men. They never seriously considered woman suffrage at all. The 1917 constitution did not exclude women from citizenship, but the 1918 electoral law restricted the vote to men.

By 1918 the electoral process had been restored, the worst of the violence was over, and President Carranza's government was more or less in effective control of the country. Many women, including Carranza's personal secretary, Hermila Galindo, had made significant contributions to the revolutionary cause. Moreover, the president was pledged to observe a new constitution that provided for truly representative government. The political climate had changed, but why had attitudes about woman suffrage not changed?

When forced to come up with an answer, the opponents of woman suffrage in Mexico used arguments made familiar in the United States, Great Britain, and elsewhere. Politics had always been a man's business, and taking part in the political process would taint and corrupt women, would interfere with their duties as wives and mothers, would agitate females unnecessarily, and would introduce discord into the home. Besides, the male opponents of woman suffrage argued, females were too emotional, too illogical, and too capricious to vote sensibly.

From 1917 to 1934, when asked why illiterate men were given the vote while literate women were denied it, government spokesmen repeatedly asserted that Mexicanas were not yet "prepared" to vote. What they meant was that the government feared that, if enfranchised, the majority of women would vote *differently* than men; that is, most females would follow the advice of the clergy and vote for antigovernment candidates. The active role of Catholic women in support of the church when it was under attack by anticlericals during the revolution and during the 1920s was proof enough that women were more susceptible than men to the church's influence.

Meanwhile, by the early 1920s mainstream feminists, unlike their predecessors, agreed that woman suffrage was essential, if only to remove the stigma of civil inferiority. Moreover, many progovernment feminists argued that woman suffrage would improve the political climate in Mexico. They felt sure that the appearance of women at the polling places would reduce the incidence of fraud and violence, and that electing women to office would purify and stabilize the country's still disordered political life. However, despite the holding of five feminist congresses between 1923 and 1934, the movement was fragmented. In those years the feminists were divided over class issues and were unable to organize a united front or develop the tactics necessary to force the government to take women into account.

It should also be emphasized that until 1929 the revolutionary leaders of Mexico had not established a political party structure that could match the superb organizational structure of the church. In 1929, ex-President Calles, to end the cycles of rebellion that plagued postrevolutionary Mexico, established the Partido Nacional Revolucionario (PNR), the predecessor of today's ruling Party of the Institutionalized Revolution. During President Cárdenas's term of office, great strides were made by this government party in mobilizing the organized support of peasants, workers, soldiers, and bureaucrats. No doubt the success in building a strong party structure—one which included women—convinced Cárdenas, by 1937, that extension of the vote to women would vindicate rather than endanger the nationalistic and egalitarian goals of the revolution. At the same time, after 1935 Mexican feminists were more united in their demand for suffrage than they had been previously and were more willing to take drastic action to gain the vote. In 1937 and 1938 the street demonstrations, the picketing, the marches, and the threat of hunger strikes by hundreds of women finally convinced not only President

Cárdenas, but the Congress, the media, and much of the general public as well, that the issue of woman suffrage could no longer be ignored or postponed.

Unfortunately, the deep-seated conviction that most Mexican women were politically unreliable resurfaced just before the process of ratifying the woman suffrage amendment was completed. In 1939, when well-dressed, well-financed, and well-organized conservative women rallied around the charismatic right-wing candidate, Juan Andreu Almazán, the woman suffrage amendment was quietly dropped by the Congress. The 1940 "Call to the National Conscience" and other petitions by Marxist and middle-class feminists pleading for ratification was met by an embarrassing silence. It was a bitter defeat. We shall never know how Mexican women would have voted in 1940. It was to take another generation to demonstrate that in Mexico's one-party state the voting patterns of women were not to differ significantly from those of men.

From approximately 1870 to 1940 male support for feminism was not widespread in Mexico, nor was it generally disinterested. In the United States and Great Britain, feminists could count on support from mainstream liberal and progressive men.[1] In Mexico, however, feminists usually found male allies only among a select group of liberals and from fringe groups made up of socialists and anarchists. In the late-nineteenth and early-twentieth centuries these men wanted to see women educated in secular public schools to achieve equality, but also to lessen the influence of the conservative-backed Catholic church over females. The mission of women, these advocates of female education agreed, was to be supportive wives, efficient homemakers, and intelligent teachers of their children. In time, liberals accepted the idea of secondary education for women so that they might fill ill-paid positions shunned by men, especially in the primary schools. They also agreed that vocational education for working-class females was essential for the economic development of the country. However, only a few socialists pointed out the need for female doctors and other professionally trained women in Mexico. In the late-n ineteenth century, the entry of a few middle-class women into professional schools was due primarily to their own efforts and to the support of their families.

In general, liberal advocates of female education, such as President Benito Juárez, the writer Guillermo Prieto, the educator José María

Vigil, and the historian Justo Sierra did not wish to fundamentally change patriarchal society. Rather, they wished to secularize Mexico and change the country's economic and political structure to conform to that of the more advanced nations of the world. In this period, only a few men, including the lawyer and later historian, Genaro García, agreed with the early feminists that the legal code needed to be reformed. The feminists' plea for a single sexual standard, however, received even less attention than the call for legal equality and property rights for married women.

With so little and so limited male support, it is not surprising that the early feminists tried not to alienate men. The editors of *La Mujer Mexicana* frequently assured the public that Mexican feminists were not radical or extremist. They insisted that education did not harm a woman nor divert her from her role as wife and mother. They claimed that in advocating female education, legal equality, and a single sexual standard, they were trying to strengthen the home and moralize society. These reassurances were not convincing to influential men, such as the educator Felix Palavicini, the anthropologist Manuel Gamio, and a number of both conservative and liberal journalists, who believed that feminists were either disreputable, or unfeminine, or aberrant.

While most nineteenth-century men who called themselves liberals and socialists were essentially conservative in their views concerning women and gave support chiefly to improved educational opportunities for females, some men who advocated women's rights during the Revolution, such as Salvador Alvarado and Felipe Carrillo Puerto, proved to be far too radical for most feminists. In addition, neither Alvarado nor Carrillo Puerto were able to convince their revolutionary associates that women needed to be incorporated into the political life of the country as rapidly as possible. Indeed, between 1914 and 1935 the unprecedented activism of Catholic women in defense of the church hardened and reinforced the prejudice of many male revolutionaries against female participation in public life.

At the first feminist congress of January 1916, Salvador Alvarado gave Yucatecan women a forum and a chance to debate such matters as better educational and employment opportunities for women and legal equality, but when he tried to pressure them into attacking religion or demanding equal political rights, he found that a majority of educated Yucatecan women were not prepared to follow him. Then, when Alvarado called for a national feminist congress to meet at Mérida in December 1916, few delegates from other states attended. Apparently, neither Carranza nor other revolutionary leaders outside Yucatán made efforts to encourage women to attend the congress.

Felipe Carrillo Puerto was even more radical in his ideas than Alvarado and found little support for his programs on divorce, birth control and "free love" among the feminists at the May 1923 feminist congress in Mexico City. At those meetings the majority of the delegates concluded that women needed to win the vote, but they rejected most of Carrillo Puerto's other ideas as either impolitic or inappropriate. Even Elena Torres, who shared Carrillo Puerto's faith in socialism, believed that he and his sister Elvia were hindering the feminist cause by debating taboo subjects.

After Carrillo Puerto's assassination, it became clear that even in Yucatán there was no support for women's liberation or woman suffrage among the leaders of the party he helped to found, the Socialist Party of the Southeast. And, from 1924 to 1934, it was rare to meet high government officials who sympathized with the efforts of women to participate in public life. President Calles favored greater legal equality for women, but his enmity towards the church made it impossible for him to countenance the idea of female suffrage. His secretary of the interior, Adalberto Tejeda, was one of the few revolutionary leaders to come to the aid of Elvia Carrillo Puerto in 1925 in her unsuccessful effort to win a seat in the Chamber of Deputies.

It appears that the socialist principles of Alvarado and Carrillo Puerto were so strong that anticlericalism did not distract them from their efforts to enlist the aid of women in the modernization of Mexico. This was not the case with most of their colleagues, who were oftentimes "revolutionary" only in their enmity towards the church and towards foreign capital.

Lázaro Cárdenas is a good example of a revolutionary leader who did not permit the church-state conflict to distract him from his efforts to achieve revolutionary goals. He carried out agrarian reform, came to the aid of industrial workers, and sought to curb the influence of foreign capital in Mexico. Although his support of socialist education in the schools alarmed many Catholic parents, he avoided conflict with the church whenever possible. Unlike Alvarado and Carrillo Puerto before him, he did not adopt radical positions on women's issues. Instead, he went only as far as the most moderate feminists were prepared to go: he supported the right of women to vote and hold office. What is most notable about Cárdenas is that his motives for espousing woman suffrage were largely disinterested. Before Cárdenas took office in 1934, one feminist called him an "immaculate revolutionary." She was not mistaken.

In general, Mexican men view women as "others," not as equals. To be female is to be reticent, subordinate, and self-sacrificing. To be male is to be decisive, dominant, and courageous. The *soldadera* of the Mexican Revolution fits perfectly the traditional view of womanhood, which may help to explain her popularity in novels, films, and folk music. But what of the woman who takes on heroic qualities—who becomes an outspoken journalist or who takes up arms during the fighting?

The male admirers of Juana Belén Gutiérrez hailed her newspaper as "virile" and claimed that she had "trousers in [her] style." That is, because she demonstrates qualities not expected of a female—courage and forthrightness—she is divested of her womanliness. Interestingly enough, the same phenomenon occurred in the remote past. In Aztec records, for example, there are several allusions to courageous and successful women as being manly.[2] To achieve equality in the eyes of men, a Mexican woman must act like a man.

Small wonder, then, that the woman soldier of the revolution, such as La Coronela, divested herself of her femaleness. She not only dressed like a man, she also cursed like a man, and thought like a man. Only then did men accept her as an equal. As Asunción Lavrin says of La Coronela, "She does not represent womanhood; she is an imitation of manhood." As a result, the heroines' exploits during the revolution did not bring immediate changes in the status of women, since these heroines were acting like men rather than women. The heroine was the exception; the uncomplaining, stoical *soldadera* was the norm. The experience of women in the revolution shows how rigid sexual stereotyping was but one more obstacle Mexican feminists faced in their struggle for equality.

NOTES

1. Richard J. Evans, *The Feminists: Women's Emancipation Movements in Europe, America and Australasia 1840-1920* (New York: Barnes and Noble Books, 1979), p. 234.

2. Anna-Britta Hellblom, *La participación cultural de las mujeres indias y mestizas en el México precortesiano y postrevolucionario*, Monograph Series, no. 10 (Stockholm: The Ethnographical Museum, 1967), p. 299.

BIBLIOGRAPHICAL ESSAY

The purpose of this critical essay on sources is to evaluate the materials used in the preparation of this monograph and to provide a guide for further study on feminism in Mexico. Since the historical literature on Mexican women before the twentieth century is scarce, the first part of this essay includes a number of books and articles that are not specifically about feminism but that provide useful background for the study of modern and contemporary Mexican women. As a result, a number of works cited here do not appear in the footnotes. On the other hand, some works sufficiently identified and evaluated in the footnotes are not scrutinized in this essay.

BIBLIOGRAPHICAL GUIDES AND GENERAL WORKS ON MEXICAN WOMEN

Bibliographical Guides

The student interested in any aspect of women in Mexican history will find a unique and superlative reference guide to the literature in Meri Knaster's work, *Women in Spanish America: An Annotated Bibliography from Pre-Conquest to Contemporary Times* (Boston: G. K. Hall and Co., 1977). For primarily modern and contemporary Latin American women, Ann Pescatello's essay on "The Female in Ibero-America: An Essay on Research Bibliography and Research Directions," *Latin American Research Review*, 7 (1972): 125-141 is useful, as is Jane S. Jaquette's "Women in Revolutionary Movements," in *Journal of Marriage and the Family*, 35 (May 1973): 344-54. Scattered references to women in modern Mexico (approximately 1900 to 1960) are to be found in the monumental reference work of Luis González y González, Guadalupe Monroy, and Susana Uribe, comps., *Fuentes de la historia contemporánea de México: Libros y folletos*, 3 vols. (México: El Colegio de México 1961-62). Under social structure, for example, González and his associates have a section on "los sexos," which includes twenty-eight important references about women and about feminism in Mexico from 1900 to 1940. Less useful to the researcher is the sequel edited by Stanley R. Ross, *Fuentes de la historia contemporánea de México: Periódicos y revistas*, 2 vols. (México: El Colegio de México, 1965-67), which contains few references to Mexican women. For a complete list of bibliographical guides to Latin American women see pp. xlv to xlviii in the aforementioned work of Knaster. Knaster's article on "Women in Latin America: The State of Research, 1975," *Latin American Research Review* 11 (1976): 3-74, also has helpful bibliographical information.

General Works on Mexican Women

A work basic for a study of Mexican women from the past to the present is María Elvira Bermúdez, *La vida familiar del mexicano* (México: Antigua Librería Robredo, 1955). Long out of print, *La vida familiar del mexicano* is a work of incisive and beautiful prose. Ms. Bermúdez makes imaginative use of Octavio Paz's classic work, *The Labyrinth of Solitude*, trans. Lysander Kemp (New York: Grove Press, Inc. 1961). A reading of chapter 2 of Paz's interpretative work, "Mexican Masks," is fundamental for an understanding of the obstacles Mexican women have usually faced in their search for a measure of autonomy and individuality.

While Paz and Bermúdez present a justifiably pessimistic view of the role and situation of women in Mexico, H. M. Loreto, *Personalidad(?) de la mujer mexicana* (México: Impresora Galve, 1961), presents an extremely negative view of Mexican women that is undocumented and that sheds little light but a considerable amount of heat on the subject. The work has been attacked by María del Carmen Elu de Leñero, in *¿Hacia dónde va la mujer mexicana?* (México: Instituto Mexicano de Estudios Sociales, 1969), a study based on nationwide interviews with several thousand married women under the age of forty-five. Elu's work, however, is permeated by what can only be characterized as official optimism, and much of the data negates her thesis that Mexican women live stable, secure, and hopeful lives. The Elu de Leñero study ignores single, widowed, aging, divorced, and abandoned women, who easily make up at least half of the adult female population of Mexico. One need only consult María Luisa Rodríguez Sala de Gómez Gil's work, *El suicidio en México* (México: Instituto de Investigaciones Sociales, Universidad Nacional Autónoma de México, 1963), to dispel the notion that Mexican women live in the best of all possible worlds. The statistics cited by the author indicate that between 1934 and 1959 Mexico City had the highest percentage of suicides by women in the world. In that twenty-five-year period, of 5,698 successful suicides committed in Mexico City, 56 percent were committed by women. In the country as a whole between 1934 and 1959, 63 percent of the attempted suicides were by women and only 37 percent were by men.

A more recent work, written from an explicitly feminist point of view, is Juana Armanda Alegría's *Psicología de las mexicanas* (México: Editorial Samo, 1974). Alegría sees no fundamental changes in the role and situation of Mexican women since Paz and Bermúdez published their studies twenty years ago. Another writer who has studied machismo as it relates to the psychology of Mexican women is Jorge Segura Millán, *Diorama de los mexicanos* (México: Costa-Amic, Editor, 1964). He exhorts women to combat the destructive aspects of machismo by overcoming their feelings of inferiority and self-disdain.

Anthropologists and sociologists provide well-documented studies of the inferior position of females within the family structure and of women's lack of power and influence in their communities. See, for example, the excellent monograph by May N. Díaz, *Tonalá* (Berkeley: University of California Press, 1966), and the four monographs of Oscar Lewis, *Life in a Mexican Village: Tepoztlán Restudied* (Urbana, Ill.: University of Illinois Press, 1951); *Five Families* (New York: Basic Books, 1959); *The Children of Sánchez* (New York: Random House, 1961); and *Pedro Martínez* (New York: Random House, 1964). In addition, Lewis's essays, "Husbands and Wives in a Mexican Village: A Study of Role Conflict," *American Anthropologist* 52 (October-December 1949):602-10; "An Anthropological Approach to Family Studies," *American Journal of Sociology* 55 (1950):468-75; and "Family Dynamics in a Mexican Village," *Marriage and Family Living* 21 (August 1959):218-26 are all enlightening studies of family relations in village Mexico. While submissiveness and passivity on the part of the wife are viewed as the ideal in the communities Lewis studied, he observed that in practice only those households were prosperous where the wife was energetic, enterprising, and imaginative. In "Husbands and Wives in a Mexican Village" Lewis concludes that "without exception, every man [in Tepoztlán, Morelos] who was able to improve his economic situation since the Mexican Revolution of 1910-1920 did so with the active help of his wife," and that "in all the more prosperous homes the wives are known to be unusually capable and industrious."

Other articles on marriage and family life in Mexico that are important for understanding the bases of male supremacy in Mexico are Noel F. McGinn, "Marriage and Family in Middle-Class Mexico," *Journal of Marriage and the Family* 28 (August 1966):305-13; Fernando Peñalosa, "Mexican Family Roles," *Journal of Marriage and the Family* 30 (November 1968):680-89; Santiago Ramírez and Ramón Parres, "Some Dynamic Patterns in the Organization of the Mexican Family," *International Journal of Social Psychiatry* 3 (1957):18-21; and Frank W. and Ruth C. Young, "Differentiation of Family Structure in Rural Mexico," *Journal of Marriage and the Family* 30 (February 1968):154-61. For a perceptive study of machismo see Evelyn Stevens's "Mexican Machismo: Politics and Value Orientations," *The Western Political Quarterly* 17 (December 1965):848-57 and "Marianismo: The Other Face of Machismo in Latin America," in *Female and Male in Latin America*, ed. Ann Pescatello (Pittsburgh: University of Pittsburgh Press, 1972):89-101.

While most writers on machismo, marriage, and family life in Mexico argue that women perpetuate male dominance by the way they bring up their children, Arturo and Genevieve de Hoyos in "The Amigo System and the Alienation of the Wife in the Conjugal Mexican Family," in *Kinship and Family Organization*, ed. Bernard Farber (New York: John Wiley & Sons, Inc., 1966) believe that it is the "amigo system," the Mexican variety of male bonding, which is responsible for the continuing endurance of machismo in Mexico, particularly among the lower classes.

THE ROOTS OF FEMINISM IN MEXICO

Pre-Columbian Mexican Women and Indigenous Women Today

A fundamental source for the role and situation of women in Aztec society and in indigenous Mexican communities today is the thoroughly researched dissertation of the Swedish anthropologist Anna-Britta Hellblom, *La participación cultural de las mujeres indias y mestizas en el México precortesiano y postrevolucionario* (Stockholm: The Ethnographical Museum, 1967). It is clear from Hellblom's study that Mexican machismo derives from the indigenous past as well as from the Spanish conquest and the colonial period. Earlier, Rosa María Lombardo Otero in her pioneer study, *La mujer tzeltal* (México: n.p., 1944), confirmed Ms. Hellblom's thesis that indigenous women lack power and prestige in their communities. Both Lombardo Otero and William Madsen, in his study of a contemporary Aztec community, *The Virgin's Children* (Austin: University of Texas Press, 1960), point out that indigenous women who are sterile are reduced to utter misery. Mary L. Elmendorf, in her study *La mujer maya y el cambio* (México: Secretaría de Educación Publica, 1973), presents a much more positive view of the role and situation of modern Mayan women of Yucatán than Lombardo Otero does of Mayan women of Chiapas, and this may be due to the fact that there was less economic misery in Yucatán in the 1960s than there was in mountainous Chiapas in the 1940s.

The early Mexican anthropologist, Manuel Gamio, who, by the way, took a very dim view of feminism in his age, insists in *Forjando patria* (México: Librería de Porrua Hnos., 1916) that Aztec women enjoyed power and prestige in their society. However, the noted student of Aztec culture and society, Miguel

León-Portilla in "La mujer en la cultura nahuatl," *Nicaragua Indígena* 2d epoch, 21 (July-August, 1958):6-8, makes clear that Aztec women were esteemed solely as housewives, as bearers of children, and as mothers. León-Portilla also points out that the position of contemporary Nahuatl-speaking women in Mexico is unenviable: they work very hard, bear most of the responsibility for raising the children, and suffer great psychic and physical privations. However, he insists that such was not the case before the coming of the Spaniards. Ana María Flores in *México, cincuenta años de revolución* (México: Fondo de Cultura Económica, 1963), p. 219 agrees that the most oppressed women in Mexico in the 1960s were indigenous women. Yet another study by Margarita Gamio de Alba, *La mujer indígena de Centro América* (México: Inter-American Indian Institute, 1957) provides data on the subordinate role of most women in indigenous societies in Central America. Lastly, a useful general survey of the status of indigenous women among the Seri, Tarahumara, Huichol and other Indian groups in Mexico is found in Carlos A. Echánove Trujillo, *Sociología mexicana*, 2d ed. (México: Editorial Porrua, 1963), chapter 7.

Women in Colonial Mexico

The view that the Spanish conquest was a boon for Mexico is very unpopular, so it is not surprising that only a handful of writers argue that the introduction of Catholicism after the conquest redeemed and dignified Mexican women. Priests like José Castillo y Pina, *Cuestiones sociales* (México: Impresores, S.A., 1934) and José Cantú Corro, *La mujer a través de los siglos* (México: Ediciones Botas, 1938) view the pre-Columbian past as barbarous, and they are equally negative about modern secular movements, especially feminism in Mexico in the 1920s and 1930s. They and the lay Catholic writer, Carlos Hernández, author of *Mujeres célebres de México* (San Antonio, Texas: n.p., 1918), reflect the extreme conservatism of the Mexican Church in the first forty years of the twentieth century.

A general introduction to women in colonial Latin America is found in William L. Schurz, *This New World* (New York: E.P. Dutton & Co., 1954), chapter 8, "The Woman." An excellent chapter on the contributions of Spanish-born women to the forging of a new society after the conquest is found in James Lockhart, *Spanish Peru, 1532-1560: Colonial Society* (Madison, Wis.: University of Wisconsin Press, 1968). See also section 1 of June Hahner, ed., *Women in Latin American History: Their Lives and Views* (Los Angeles: Latin American Center Publications, 1976), for letters written by elite women, including an excerpt from the famous autobiographical letter of Sor Juana Inés de la Cruz to "Sor Filotea."

For works by and about Sor Juana the reader is referred to footnotes eight through sixteen in chapter 1. Still the best critical study of the life and writings of

Sor Juana is the work of the Cuban scholar, Anita Arroyo, *Razón y pasión de Sor Juana* (México: Editorial Porrua, 1952). Incidentally, Sor Juana was not the only gifted woman poet in the colonial period. See José M. Vigil, ed., *Poetisas mexicanas* (México: Oficina Tip. de la Secretaría de Fomento, 1893), for an anthology of talented woman poets from the sixteenth to the nineteenth centuries.

No doubt one of the reasons why Sor Juana has attracted so much attention is that she was one of the few women in all of Latin American history whose autobiographical work has been printed. A perusal of the section on "Biography and Autobiography," in *Women in Spanish America*, ed. Meri Knaster, pp. 3-9, reveals that very few Mexican women have written autobiographies that have been published. If women in colonial Mexico kept diaries or wrote letters, these have not seen their way into print. This is why Edith B. Couturier's essay on "Women in a Noble Family: The Mexican Counts of Regla, 1750-1830," in *Latin American Women: Historical Perspectives*, Asunción Lavrin, ed. (Westport, Conn.: Greenwood Press, 1978):129-49 is of great interest, since much of Mrs. Couturier's information about the women related to the Count of Regla is derived from their private correspondence. For an excellent introduction to the problems involved and the opportunities available in doing original research on colonial women, see Asunción Lavrin, "In Search of the Colonial Woman in Mexico: the Seventeenth and Eighteenth Centuries," in the same anthology. Asunción Lavrin and Edith Couturier have collaborated on a study of dowries and wills in colonial Mexico which demonstrates that dowries provided economic security for married women. At the same time the writers point out that the lack of a dowry was not always a deterrent to marriage. See Edith B. Couturier and Asunción Lavrin, "Dowries and Wills: A View of Women's Socioeconomic Role in Colonial Guadalajara and Puebla, 1640-1790," *Hispanic American Historical Review* 59 (1979):280-304. Mrs. Lavrin has published a number of excellent essays on conventual life in New Spain. See pages 143-44 of Meri Knaster's bibliographical guide for a complete list of Lavrin's essays on nuns and nunneries in colonial Mexico. Of related interest is the fine essay by Ann Miriam Gallagher, R.S.M., "The Indian Nuns of Mexico City's *Monasterio* of Corpus Christi, 1724-1821," in the Lavrin anthology on Latin American women.

Women in Mexico from the Independence Period to 1876

Until recently little primary research had been done on the varied and active role women played in the independence movement from 1808 to 1821. An exception is Janet R. Kentner, "The Socio-Political Role of Women in the Mexican Wars of Independence, 1808-1821." (Ph.D. diss., Loyola University, 1975). Earlier, María Luisa Leal C. in "Mujeres insurgentes," *Boletín del Archivo General de la Nación* 20 (1949):543-604, revealed that there is considerable documentation at the National Archives in Mexico on women insurgents other than the famous heroines, La Corregidora, Leona Vicario, and Gertrudis Bocanegra. But even these famous women of the independence movement have been studied exclusively by male historians who view them as exceptions to the general rule of feminine passivity and subordination. See, for example, Luis Rubio Siliceo, *Mujeres célebres de la independencia de México* (México: Talleres Gráficos de la Nación, 1929); C. A. Echánove Trujillo, *Leona Vicario: La mujer fuerte de la independencia*, Vidas Mexicanas, no. 21 (México: Ediciones Xochitl. 1945); and Carlos Hernández, *Mujeres célebres de México* (San Antonio, Texas: n.p., 1918). Only Genaro García, *Leona Vicario, Heroína insurgente* "Biblioteca Enciclopédica Popular no. 36 (México: Secretaría Pública, 1945) is sympathetic to the idea of the equality of the sexes. As a result, García sees Leona Vicario from a somewhat feminist point of view. The others extol the feminine virtues of these heroines and emphasize that they returned to their roles as dutiful and self-effacing daughters, wives, and mothers once the war was over.

The subject of women in Mexico from 1821 to 1876 has yielded few published monographs, and one must turn primarily to official documents and contemporary newspapers and periodicals for scattered references to women. Among the few monographs on Mexican women in this unsettled period is Silvia Arrom's *La mujer mexicana ante el divorcio eclesiástico* (México: Secretaría de Educación Pública, 1976). Another key work by Ms. Arrom is her "Women and the Family in Mexico City: 1800-1851" (Ph.D. diss., Stanford University, 1977).

The role of women during the French intervention is the subject of Adelina Zendejas's work, *La mujer en la intervención francesa* (México: Sociedad Mexicana de Geografía y Estadística, 1962). For a well-researched biography of the wife of President Benito Juárez, see Angeles Mendieta Alatorre's *Margarita Maza de Juárez* (México, 1972). A rare autobiographical work by the wife of a leading conservative is Concepción Lombardo de Miramón, *Memorias*, La Biblioteca Porrua, no. 74 (México; Editorial Porrua, 1980).

An indispensable source on working-class women in nineteenth-century Mexico is the publication of the Centro de Estudios Históricos del Movimiento Obrero Mexicano, *La mujer y el movimiento obrero mexicano en el siglo XIX: Antología de la prensa obrera* (México: Centro de Estudios Históricos del Movimiento Obrero Mexicano, 1975). The anthology includes articles from socialist and working-class newspapers on the "social function of women" which reveal that the romantic and idealized view of females so common in the nineteenth century was shared by the most politically radical men in Mexico. Most Mexican socialists exhorted women to concentrate on homemaking and child-rearing. An exception was the socialist José Romero Cuyas, who in 1874 vigorously defended feminist goals. He also wished to see Mexican women enter medicine and other professions. See his article on "La emancipación de la mujer," in *La mujer y el movimiento obrero mexicano* cited above. An important monograph on the industry that employed a significant number of women in the nineteenth century is Dawn Keremitsis's *La industria textil mexicana en el siglo XIX*, SEP SETENTAS no. 67 (México: Secretaría de Educación Pública, 1973).

Fanny Calderón de la Barca's *Life in Mexico* provides some lively and impressionistic accounts of Mexican society women in the late 1830s and early 1840s, excerpted by June Hahner, ed., *Women in Latin American History*, 39-42. For an idyllic picture of the domestic life of primarily upper-class women in the 1880s, see chapter 7 of Fanny Chambers Gooch, *Face to Face with the Mexicans* (New York: Fords, Howard & Hulbert, 1887).

Interest in the education of women in the decades after independence sparked ideas of equality and led to the development of feminist sentiment in Mexico by the end of the nineteenth century. A well-researched introduction to elementary education in early nineteenth-century Mexico City is Dorothy Tanck Estrada's *La educación ilustrada (1786-1836)* (México: El Colegio de México, 1977). The *Proyecto de decreto sobre enseñanza libre de Jalisco* (Guadalajara, Jal.: Imprenta del C. Urbano Sanroman, 1826), demonstrates that interest in female education was not confined to the capital city. However, the first projected normal school for women was planned in Mexico City while Valentín Gómez Farías was vice-president in 1833. See Manuel Eduardo de Gorostiza's *Leyes y reglamento para el arreglo de la instrucción pública en el Distrito Federal* (México: Imprenta de la Dirección de Instrucción Pública, 1834). The plan was annulled when Santa Anna returned to the presidency.

The appearance, in 1841, of the *Semanario de las señoritas mexicanas; Educación científica, moral y literaria del bello sexo* indicates that by that date there were enough women desirous of higher education to launch a journal intended to enlarge the intellectual horizons of young Mexican women of the leisured class. The appearance of the *Semanario* also indicates that there were young women in Mexico interested in education beyond the primary level. However, after the failure of the reform effort of 1833, it was not until 1856 that the national government set out to establish a secondary school for girls. The *Decree of President Ignacio Comonfort Establishing a Secondary School for Girls in Mexico City* (México: Secretaría de Gobernación, 1856) is found in the April 14, 1856, issue of the liberal newspaper, *El Monitor Republicano*. This journal was ambivalent about changes in the status of Mexican women. On the one hand the editors applauded the idea of secondary education for women, while on the other hand contributors to the journal ridiculed bluestockings.

Officials in Jalisco established a girl's lyceum at Guadalajara by 1862, some seven years before a secondary school for females was established in Mexico City. The Biblioteca de México has a rare copy of the *Memoria de la Junta Directiva de Enseñanza Pública sobre el estado que guarda este ramo en fin del año de 1862* (Guadalajara: Tipografía de José María Brambila, 1863), which details the lyceum's first year. For data on the lyceum in 1866, during Maximilian's brief tenure as Emperor of Mexico, see the article by Angélica Peregrina, "Noticia de establecimientos para la educación de niñas en el departamento de Jalisco en 1866," *Boletín del Archivo Histórico de Jalisco* 2 (1978):17-22. Documents on the lyceum in the 1870s and 1880s are found at the Archivo Histórica de Jalisco in the printed *Colección de los decretos, circulares y ordenes de los poderes legislativo y ejecutivo del Estado de Jalisco*, 38 vols. (Guadalajara: Tip. de M. Pereztete [and others], 1874-1910.

Information about vocational education for women in Jalisco is found in Mario Aldana Rendón, "La Escuela de Artes y Oficios y la educación artesanal en Jalisco, 1867-1877," in the aforementioned *Boletín del Archivo Histórico de Jalisco* 2 (1978):2-10. Juan de Dios Peza, "La beneficencia en México," *Boletín de la Sociedad Mexicana de Geografía y Estadística* 5 (1881):684-93, provides important information on the Vocational School for Women in Mexico City from 1871 to 1881.

An indispensable source for tracing the increasing emphasis on female education in Mexico is a work published by the Secretariat of Public Education, *La educación pública en México a través de los mensajes presidenciales desde la consumación de la independencia hasta nuestros días* (México: Secretaría de Educación Pública, 1926). An excellent secondary source on female education in the 1860s and 1870s is by Luis González y González, Emma Cosío Villegas, and Guadalupe Monroy, *La república restaurada: La vida social*, vol. 4 of *Historia moderna de México,* ed. Daniel Cosío Villegas (México: Editorial Hermes, 1957). For a Marxist perspective on the education provided women from 1880 to 1928, see the interesting essay by Mary K. Vaughan, "Women, Class and Education in Mexico, 1880-1928," *Latin American Perspectives* 4 (1977):63-80.

A well-researched study of nineteenth-century Mexican women is by Barbara Ann Bockus, "La mujer mexicana en el siglo XIX vista a través de la novela." (M.A. thesis, Universidad Nacional Autónoma de México, 1959), which provides useful data on the growth of interest in female education as reflected in nineteenth-century Mexican novels. Of related interest is Teresa Rulfo de Rosenzweig's "Las heroínas de la novela mexicana del siglo XIX" (M.A. thesis, Universidad Nacional Autónoma de México, 1954), which reveals how the best-known Mexican writers of the nineteenth century portrayed women in their novels. According to Rulfo, some were outright misogynists (Lizardi and Inclán, for example) while only a few (Payno and Gamboa) portrayed their female characters in a favorable or positive light.

Mexican Women during the Porfiriato, 1876-1910

The best introduction to Porfirian society and culture is Moisés González Navarro's *El porfiriato: La vida social*, vol. 5 of *Historia moderna de México,* ed. Daniel Cosío Villegas (México: Editorial Hermes, 1957). Professor González Navarro presents indispensable data on women of all classes, and he emphasizes the hard lot of working-class women in Mexico City. During the Porfiriato, as women eagerly sought both higher education and vocational training, influential men began to publicize the achievements of women. One of the most important was José María Vigil, Professor of Logic at the Escuela Nacional Preparatoria and for years Director of the Biblioteca Nacional de México. Vigil's desire to publicize the achievements of talented women was first seen in his study, *Doña Isabel Prieto de Landázuri. Estudio biográfico y literario* (México: Imprenta de Francisco Díaz de Léon, 1882), a moving account of a very fine poet who lived from 1833 to 1876. To demonstrate the abilities of Mexican women to his countrymen and to foreigners, Vigil then edited a massive anthology of poems by Mexican women from the sixteenth through the nineteenth century for presentation at the Chicago Exposition of 1893. See José M. Vigil, ed., *Poetisas mexicanas. Siglos XVI, XVII, XVIII y XIX. Antología formada por encargo de la Junta de Señoras Corespondiente de la Exposición de Chicago.* (México: Oficina Tip. de la Secretaría de Fomento, 1893). Finally, Vigil published *La mujer mexicana* (México: Oficina Tip. de la Secretaría de Fomento, 1893), an essay that stressed the progress women were making as a result of the Porfirian peace. Vigil saw only the positive aspects of the Porfirian regime with respect to women, while Genaro García, one of Mexico's best-known historians in the early twentieth century, denounced the legal inequality of women in two essays, *La desigualdad de la mujer* (México: Imprenta de Francisco Díaz de Léon, 1891) and *La condición de la mujer* (México: Compañía Limitada de Tipográficos, 1891). Genaro García was also highly critical of the unequal opportunities available for education in Mexico. See his *La educación nacional en México* (México: Tipografía Económica, 1903). On the other hand, Rafael de Zayas Enríquez in *El estado de Yucatán* (New York: Little and Ives, 1908) emphasized how much had been done to raise Yucatán's literacy rate among men and women to 16 percent in one generation.

In contrast to José María Vigil and Genaro García, other intellectuals of this period were hostile to feminism and to higher education for women. See, for example, the journalist Ignacio Gamboa's diatribe, *La mujer moderna* (Mérida, Yuc.: Imprenta Gamboa Guzmán, 1906) and the sociologist José Hernández's disparaging remarks as quoted in Paula Alegría, "La educación de la mujer," (thesis, Escuela Nacional de Maestros, México, 1930). The educator Felix Palavicini joined them in denouncing higher education for women in *Problemas de educación* (Valencia: F. Sempere y Cia., 1910), but after the revolution began he seemed to have had a change of heart with respect to feminism. When he founded *El Universal* in 1916 he was one of the few newspaper editors to support woman suffrage in Mexico. However, Palavicini never adjusted well to the changing role and situation of women, and in his two novels, *¡Castigo!* (México:

n.p., 1926) and *Miga* (México: Tallleres Linotipográficos de "Excelsior," 1932), the female characters are warped and destructive.

Two essential works that catalog the undoubted progress middle-class women made in Porfirian Mexico are by Laureana Wright de Kleinhans, *Mujeres notables mexicanas* (México: Tipografía Económica, 1910) and the journal *La Mujer Mexicana* (1904-1908). Señora Wright includes biographical sketches of over one hundred women from pre-Columbian times to 1910, but of interest to this study are the data she gives on Mexico's leading female teachers, the country's first women doctors, and the sole female practicing law in 1910. A number of the women singled out by Señora Wright edited or contributed to *La Mujer Mexicana*. The main concern of the editors of the journal was to overcome male hostility to female education and to middle-class women working outside the home. The editor's tepid feminism indicates that traditional attitudes concerning woman's place were slow to change in Mexico.

Charles Cumberland in *Mexico: The Struggle for Modernity* (New York: Oxford University Press, 1968), has much to say about the degradation of Mexican men through alcohol during the Porfirian era, but he has nothing to say about the degradation of women in a society that sacrificed the material well-being of the masses in order to modernize the economy. Dr. Luis Lara y Pardo's *La prostitución en México* (México: Librería de la Vda. de Charles Bouret, 1908) provides some startling data on the high incidence of prostitution in Mexico in the early twentieth century. One wonders what impelled Dr. Lara y Pardo to write the only work we have on prostitution during the Porfirian regime. His contempt, and in fact, his hatred for women prostitutes is apparent on every page. After reading his work one can more clearly understand why "los de abajo" ("the underdogs") who took up arms in 1910 viewed all educated and well-dressed persons with suspicion. One of the worst consequences of the Porfirian regime was the intensification of class hatred that the uneven development of the country engendered.

WOMEN AND THE MEXICAN REVOLUTION, 1910-1920

Angeles Mendieta Alatorre's *La mujer en la revolución mexicana* (México: Talleres Gráficos de la Nación, 1961), is based largely on primary research and provides a mine of information on the multifaceted participation of women in the Mexican Revolution. The writing and organization, however, are distinctly inferior to the scholarship. A more recent attempt at evaluating the role of women in the Mexican Revolution is the fine essay by Frederick C. Turner, "Los efectos de la participación femenina en la revolución de 1910," *Historia Mexicana* 16 (1966-1967):603-20. For the English version of this well-written essay see his *The Dynamic of Mexican Nationalism* (Chapel Hill: University of North Carolina

Press, 1968). Shirlene Ann Soto's *The Mexican Woman: A Study of Her Participation in the Revolution, 1910-1940* (Palo Alto, Cal.: R & E Research Associates, Inc., 1979) includes some interesting data and an excellent bibliography,
but the writing and organization are flawed. In addition, there are some factual
errors in the text. For information about the role of Carmen Serdán and other
Poblanas in the revolution, see David G. LaFrance's, "The Maderista Rebellion
in the State of Puebla, 1909-1911." (M.A. thesis, University of the Americas,
1976).

Mexican men in favor of women's rights have stressed the active involvement
of women in Mexico's wars since 1810. See, for example, Miguel Alessio
Robles's *Voces de combate* (México: Imp. Manuel León Sánchez, 1929) and José
María Vigil's *La mujer mexicana* (México: Oficina Tip. de la Secretaría de
Fomento, 1893). The modern feminist, Adelina Zendejas, has written an exhaus-
tive account of the role of women during the French intervention in Mexico. See
her *La mujer en la intervención francesa* (México: Sociedad Mexicana de
Geografía y Estadística, 1962). These works make clear that there were precedents for women acting as *soldaderas* and even soldiers during the Mexican
Revolution. However, only Zendejas finds evidence that Mexican women made
an intellectual contribution to the struggles between liberals and conservatives in
the decade 1857-1867.

Information about Juana Belén Gutiérrez de Mendoza (1875-1942) is fragmen-
tary, for only scattered copies of the newspapers she edited from 1900-1942,
Vesper, *El Desmonte*, and *Alma Mexicana*, survive in the Hemeroteca Nacional
in Mexico City. The most reliable secondary source on the career and ideas of
Señora Gutiérrez between 1900 and 1920 is Angeles Mendieta Alatorre's *La
mujer en la revolución mexicana*. Artemisa Saénz Royo, a feminist journalist
from Vera Cruz who wrote under the pen name of "Xochitl," has a short essay on
Juana Gutiérrez in her *Semblanzas mujeres mexicanas: Revolucionarias y guerrreras,
revolucionarias ideológicas* (México: M. León Sánchez, 1960), but her work
must be used with caution. Ms. Saénz Royo was a sincere and enthusiastic
feminist, but she was not a historian. Both the *Semblanzas* and an earlier work,
Historia político-social-cultural del movimiento femenino en México, 1914-1950
(México: M. León Sánchez, 1954), contain gross factual errors about events,
such as the Second Feminist Congress of Yucatán in 1916, in which Ms. Saénz
Royo herself participated. A brief but reliable account of Juana Gutiérrez's
revolutionary activities is by the contemporary feminist María Antonieta Rascón,
"La mujer y la lucha social," in *Imagen y realidad de la mujer*, ed. Elena Urritia,
SEP-SETENTAS, no. 172 (México: Secretaría de Educación Pública, 1975).
Ms. Rascón reveals that Juana Gutiérrez died in such poverty that her relatives
sold her only possession, a typewriter, to pay her funeral expenses.

Angeles Mendieta Alatorre, who has been mentioned, is the best source on
Dolores Jiménez y Muro, providing us with data on her revolutionary activities

from 1910 to 1920. James D. Cockcroft pays tribute to her work in the years immediately before the revolution in his *Intellectual Precursors of the Mexican Revolution, 1900-1913* (Austin: University of Texas Press, 1968). Gildardo Magaña, a close associate of Zapata, was the first writer to publish Jiménez y Muro's "Political and Social Plan of March 1911" and to publicize her contributions to the revolution. See his *Emiliano Zapata y el agrarismo en México*, 2 vols. (México: n.p., 1934). For her role as editor of a feminist journal in the years before the revolution, see the aforementioned *La Mujer Mexicana* from July 15 to December 31, 1905.

In her brief (1916-1919) career, Hermila Galindo published more books and essays than did any other feminist of her time or after, largely because she had official support from President Carranza and General Salvador Alvarado. Her controversial ideas on women are fully developed in two essays written for presentation at the First and Second Feminist Congresses held in Mérida, Yucatán, in January and November 1916. The first is *La mujer en el porvenir* (Mérida, Yuc.: Imprenta y Litografía de "La Voz de la Revolución," 1915) and the second is *Estudio de la Srita. Hermila Galindo con motivo de los temas que han de absolverse en el Segundo Congreso Feminista de Yucatán* (Mérida, Yuc.: Imprenta del Gobierno Constitucionalista, 1916). It is interesting to note that Srita. Galindo did not venture to appear at either congress and read her work in person. Her ideas on sex and religion so outraged her audience that one woman, a mathematics teacher, suggested that *La mujer en el porvenir* be burned on the spot. Hermila Galindo's political writings, *La doctrina Carranza y el acercamiento indolatino* (México: n.p., 1919) and *Un presidenciable: El general don Pablo González* (México: Imprenta Nacional, 1919), have little to say about Mexican women, but they are of interest to the student of Mexican feminism because women have rarely published political tracts in Mexico. *La doctrina Carranza* reveals that Galindo was an able propagandist for Carranza's dream of forging a Latin American alliance against the United States, while *Un presidenciable* is an above-average example of campaign literature. Strangely enough, no copies of the feminist journal, *Mujer Moderna*, which Hermila Galindo is supposed to have edited from 1915 to 1919, have turned up at the Hemeroteca Nacional de México nor in other public collections, which leads one to suspect that it must have appeared sporadically and must have had a very limited readership. Despite her active feminism during the revolutionary years, Hermila Galindo has attracted little scholarly attention. The most complete account of her brief career as a feminist and political writer is in Angeles Mendieta Alatorre's *La mujer en la revolución mexicana*.

For brief biographies of Julia Nava de Ruisánchez, Elisa Acuña y Rossetti, and María Arias Bernal, all of them normal school teachers in Mexico City, one must turn once again to Angeles Mendieta Alatorre. Additional information about María Arias Bernal is found in Vito Alessio Robles's *Voces de combate* (México: Imp. Manuel León Sánchez, 1929).

Our only source of information on the printer María Hernández Zarco and the normal school principal Beatriz González Ortega is Aurora Fernández's *Mujeres que honran a la patria* (México: n.p., 1958), an excellent collection of brief biographies of exemplary but little-known Mexican women by one of Mexico's most distinguished feminists of the 1930s and 1940s.

With the exception of Angeles Mendieta Alatorre and Frederick C. Turner, historians have had little to say about *soldaderas*, for they simply do not appear in conventional historical sources. One must turn to foreign observers, like John Reed, *Insurgent Mexico* (New York: D. Appleton & Co., 1914); Rosa E. King, *Tempest Over Mexico* (New York: Howes Publishing Co., 1944); and Vincent Starret, "Soldier-women of Mexico," *Open Court* 32 (June 1918):376-82, for vivid but impressionistic accounts of the *soldadera*. Gustavo Casasola's *Historia gráfica de la revolución mexicana: 1900-1960*, 4 vols. (México: Editorial F. Trillas, 1960) is a monumental pictorial record of Mexico in the twentieth century, and his photographs of *soldaderas* reveal that they were neither whores nor saints but simply harried women trying to survive under the worst of circumstances. Though ignored by historians, the *soldadera* has fascinated novelists, as shown by Mary Scalise Regoli in "La mujer en la novela de la revolución" (M.A. thesis, Universidad Nacional Autónoma de México, 1963).

Angeles Mendieta Alatorre and Gustavo Casasola are the chief secondary sources for material on Mexican women who served as soldiers during the revolution. Anita Aguilar and Rosalind Rosoff Beimler, authors of *Así firmaron el Plan de Ayala* (México: Secretaría de Educación Pública, 1976) which is based on taped interviews with surviving veterans of Zapata's army, made it possible for me to listen to Colonel María de la Luz Espinosa Barrera's engrossing account of her life as a soldier during the revolution.

A basic introduction to the conflict between church and state in modern Mexico is Frank Tannenbaum's *Peace by Revolution: An Interpretation of Mexico* (New York: Columbia University Press, 1933). Robert E. Quirk's monograph, *The Mexican Revolution and the Catholic Church, 1910-1920* (Bloomington, Ind.: University of Indiana Press, 1973), provides useful background for the conflict between church and state that reached such an acute stage during the revolution. The activities of Catholic women during the revolution in defense of the church are well-documented in contemporary religious publications. See especially J. Ignacio Dávila Garibi's *Memoria histórica de las labores de la Asociación de Damas Católicas de Guadalajara* (Guadalajara, Jal.: Tipografía, Litografía y Encuadernación de J. M. Yguiniz, 1920), and the anonymous, *La cuestión religiosa en Jalisco* (México: n.p., 1918). These and other rare works on the religious conflict in Mexico are found in the Basave Collection of the Biblioteca de México in Mexico City, one of the most important repositories of printed sources on late-nineteenth and early-twentieth-century Mexico.

YUCATÁN AND THE WOMEN'S MOVEMENT, 1870-1920

The best general introduction to Yucatán and its unique problems and characteristics is Fernando Benítez's *Ki: El drama de un pueblo y de una planta* (México: Fondo de Cultura Económica, 1956). Another important work of a general nature is Antonio Bustillos Carrillo's *Yucatán al servicio de la patria y de la revolución* (México: Casa Ramírez Editores, 1959). A superlative study of Yucatán in the nineteenth century is Nelson Reed's *The Caste War of Yucatán* (Stanford: Stanford University Press, 1964). Howard F. Cline in "The 'Aurora Yucateca' and the Spirit of Enterprise in Yucatan, 1821-1847," *Hispanic American Historical Review* 27 (February 1947) demonstrates that the modernizing impulse began in Yucatán in 1821, immediately after independence was achieved from Spain. Mary Wilhelmine Williams, "Secessionist Diplomacy of Yucatán," *Hispanic American Historical Review* 9 (May 1929) is useful for gauging the strongly separatist sentiments in Yucatán that help to explain why "outsiders" like Alvarado have always been resented by Yucatecans. The revolutionary period is the subject of David A. Franz's "Bullets and Bolshevists: A History of the Mexican Revolution and Reform in Yucatán, 1910-1924" (Ph.D. diss., University of New Mexico, 1973).

Rodolfo Menéndez in his study *Rita Cetina Gutiérrez* (Mérida, Yuc.: Imprenta Gamboa Guzmán, 1909) makes clear that the revered poet and educator had an enormous influence in the promotion of education for women in Yucatán, while Efrem Leonzo Donde, "Páginas históricas. La educación pública en Yucatán. El Instituto Literario de Niñas (1877-1912)," *La Revista de Yucatán* (Mérida, Yuc.), May 13, 1923, chronicles the development of the secondary school for girls in Mérida that Rita Cetina Gutiérrez directed for sixteen years.

In a work intended to attract foreign investment in Yucatán, Rafael de Zayas Enríquez's *El estado de Yucatán* (New York: Little and Ives, 1908) provides useful information on educational progress in Yucatán in the late nineteenth and early twentieth centuries. Zayas Enríquez also provides interesting figures on the number of legitimate and illegitimate births in that state. In 1901 Yucatán had one of the lowest percentages of illegitimate births in all of Mexico, 21.6 percent. The state also had one of the highest marriage rates (9.61 per 1,000 inhabitants) in the republic. The impression one gets from Zayas Enríquez is one of considerable social stability in Yucatán. However, for evidence of oppression of the rural peasantry in Yucatán see the work of Fernando Benítez and Nelson Reed cited earlier and the 1910 study of John Kenneth Turner, *Barbarous Mexico* (Austin: University of Texas Press, 1969).

Salvador Alvarado still awaits a biographer; there is ample material for a study of this man, who tried to reform Yucatán overnight. Alvarado took great pains to publicize his ideas and his actions, and the interested student will find many useful references to works by and about Alvarado in Felipe Texidor, comp., *Bibliografía Yucateca* (Mérida, Yuc.: Talleres Gráficos del Sureste, 1937). See notes 50 through 75 in chapter 3 of this study for the titles of Alvarado's most important publications while he was governor of Yucatán.

After Alvarado left Yucatán in 1918, he continued to publish articles, pamphlets, and books. In *La traición de Carranza* (New York: privately printed, 1920) he turned against the man who had appointed him governor of Yucatán and denounced Carranza for betraying the revolution. Alvarado then went on to publish a work intended to promote his presidential ambitions. *La reconstrucción de México* 2 vols. (México: J. Ballesca y Cia., 1919) is a detailed examination of Mexico's ills in 1919 and is full of high-minded ideas about reform. The work contains an important chapter on Mexican women, which summarizes Alvarado's views on the role and situation of his countrywomen. His views on prostitution are especially interesting, since few of his revolutionary colleagues gave the problem serious attention.

La reconstrucción de México attracted little attention at the time of its appearance and won few votes for Alvarado. The general lacked the skills of a practical politician; he also lacked the common touch. As a result, his bid for national office came to naught, and he died an obscure death in 1924 during the De la Huerta uprising. His ideas, however, continue to interest Mexicans, as evidenced by the recent SEP-SETENTAS publication, *Salvador Alvarado, Antología ideológica* edited by Antonio Pompa y Pompa, SEP-SETENTAS no. 305 (México: Secretaría de Educación Pública, 1976). Section 7 of the anthology is devoted to the problems of Mexican women.

For favorable evaluations of Alvarado, see Carlo de Fornaro, "General Salvador Alvarado: Fighter and Administrator," *Forum* 55 (January 1916):69-78; numerous articles in the pro-Alvarado newspaper, *La Voz de la Revolución*, published in Yucatán, from March 1915 to March 1918; the previously cited work of Fernando Benítez, *Ki*; and Frank Tannenbaum's *Peace by Revolution*. A highly critical view of Alvarado's tenure as governor of Yucatán is by Percy Alvin Martin, "Four Years of Socialistic Government in Yucatan," *The Journal of International Relations* 10 (1919-1920):209-22. The work of two Yucatecans, Luis Rosado Vega, *El desastre: Asuntos yucatecos. La obra revolucionaria del General Salvador Alvarado* (Havana: Imprenta "El Siglo XX," 1919) and [Carlos R. Menéndez], *Las seis coronas del General* (Mérida, Yuc.: Imprenta "La Amadita," 1917) reveal the deep resentment that Alvarado stirred among even prorevolutionary Yucatecans.

For the profeminist views of one of Alvarado's chief aides, see J. D. Ramírez Garrido, *Al margen del feminismo* (México: Talleres "Pluma y Lapiz," 1918). The only work by a woman who attended the Second Feminist Congress of Yucatan, Artemisa Saenz Royo's *Historia político-social-cultural del movimiento femenino en México, 1914-1950* (México: M. León Sánchez, 1954) is disappointingly inaccurate. For a reliable and at the same time sympathetic account of what transpired at the two congresses, one must turn to *La Voz de la Revolución*, found at the Hemeroteca Pino Suárez in Mérida, Yucatán. See also *Primer Congreso Feminista de Yucatán, Anales de esa memorable asamblea* (Mérida, Yuc.: Talleres Tipográficos del "Ateneo Peninsular," 1916) for a record of the transactions of the first congress. Oddly enough, the annals of the second congress were never published, and the only source for the meetings are articles in *La Voz de la Revolución* from November 23 to December 2, 1916. In the work of Antonio Bustillos Carrillo cited earlier there are rare photographs of Consuelo Zavala, Rosa Torres, and other women who attended the two feminist congresses of Yucatán. An excellent evaluation of the first feminist congress is the essay by Alaíde Foppa, "El Congreso Feminista de Yucatán, 1916," *Fem* 3 (November-December 1979):55-9. Foppa notes that in 1975 the Grupo de Voluntarios del Instituto del Fondo Nacional de la Vivienda para Trabajadores published a facsimile edition of the *Anales* of the first congress. This is good news, since the original edition of 1916 was printed on paper of such poor quality that the copy used by the author literally fell apart as she turned the pages.

FELIPE CARRILLO PUERTO AS CHAMPION OF WOMEN'S RIGHTS IN YUCATÁN, 1922-1923

Unlike his predecessor Alvarado, Felipe Carrillo Puerto wrote little in his lifetime. In his less than two years as governor of Yucatán, he delivered only one message to the legislature that was printed, the *Informe rendido por el Gobernador Constitucional de Yucatán, C. Felipe Carrillo Puerto ante la H. XXVII Legislatura del Estado, el 1° de enero de 1923* (Mérida, Yuc.: Imprenta y Litografía Gamboa Guzmán, 1923). His ideas about socialism, however, are faithfully reflected in *Tierra*, the organ of the Socialist party while he was governor. The May 1924 issue of *Survey*, devoted entirely to Mexico, has an essay by Carrillo Puerto entitled "The new Yucatan," which he wrote shortly before his death. Incidentally, the same issue of *Survey* includes two articles by Mexican women, one by Elena Landázuri, an associate of the Young Women's Christian Association in Mexico, and another by Esperanza Velázquez Bringas, a lawyer, educator, and writer from Yucatán who shared Carrillo Puerto's ideas on divorce and birth control. In "Why we are different" Elena Landázuri sought to define Mexican character, and concluded, as have many Mexicans, that "our individual life is rich and full; our collective life exceedingly poor." Esperanza Velázquez Bringas wrote an essay on "The Educational Missionary," detailing her travels in Yucatán and Jalisco as inspector of the educational missions that sought to wipe out Mexico's illiteracy rate as rapidly as possible.

Edmundo Bolío Ontiveros is the author of an affectionate and anecdotal biography of the radical governor, *De la cuna al paredón* (Mérida, Yuc.:

Talleres de la Compañía Periodista del Sureste, n.d.). Ernest Gruening, author of the classic *Mexico and Its Heritage* (New York: D. Appleton-Century Company, 1928) did much to publicize Carrillo Puerto's ideas in the United States and elsewhere in a number of published essays. These include "Felipe Carrillo Puerto," *The Nation*, 16 January 1924; "A Maya Idyl: A Study of Felipe Carrillo, Late Governor of Yucatan," *The Century Illustrated Monthly Magazine* 107 (November 1923-April 1924):832-36; "The Assassination of Mexico's Ablest Statesman," *Current History* 19 (October 1923-March 1924):736-40; and *Un viaje a Yucatán* (Guanajuato: Talleres Gráficos de *Los Sucesos*, 1924). A favorable evaluation of Carrillo Puerto's ideas on birth control and easy divorce is Mary Turner Mason's "The Russian Experiment in Yucatan," *The Outlook* 133 (January 1923):86-9. Mason insisted that schools in Yucatán were not teaching birth control methods or socialism to children, as the enemies of Carrillo Puerto had charged. A later and very favorable view of Carrillo Puerto as a "true idealist" is by Erna Fergusson in *Mexico Revisited* (New York: Alfred A. Knopf, 1955), pp. 114-17.

Both Ernest Gruening and Frank Tannenbaum viewed Carrillo Puerto as an unblemished champion of the oppressed, but the Yucatecan's right-wing enemies charged that he had his political enemies murdered, that he was corrupt, that he spent lavish sums of money on clothing and cars, and that he had some 142 relatives on the public payroll. An early indictment that is seldom documented is Anastasio Manzanilla's *El bolchevismo criminal de Yucatán* (México: Ediciones de "El Hombre Libre," 1921). Another political enemy of Carrillo Puerto, Dr. Adolfo Ferrer, in *El archivo de Felipe Carrillo* (New York: Carlos López Press, 1924), published letters stolen from the assassinated governor's office in an attempt to discredit his memory. These include letters Carrillo Puerto received from the American Birth Control League in New York. Bernardino Mena Brito's *Bolshevismo y democracia en México*, 2d ed. (México: n.p., 1933), is a venomous attack on Carrillo Puerto by a Mexican Fascist. A balanced view of Carrillo Puerto is found in John W. F. Dulles's *Yesterday in Mexico: A Chronicle of the Revolution, 1919-1936* (Austin: University of Texas Press, 1961). For a penetrating study of Felipe Carrillo Puerto's strategies in his attempt to consolidate control in Yucatán, see Gilbert M. Joseph's "The Fragile Revolution: Cacique Politics and Revolutionary Process in Yucatan," *Latin American Research Review* 15 (1980):39-64. The essay contains an excellent bibliography of primary and secondary sources on Carrillo Puerto and Yucatán. Students of the period are well advised to consult Mr. Joseph's doctoral dissertation "Revolution from Without: The Mexican Revolution in Yucatan, 1915-1940," (Ph.D. diss., Yale University, 1978) for a fuller treatment of Carrillo Puerto's failure to establish a truly popular government in Yucatán.

The periodical *Tierra*, copies of which are found in the Carlos Menéndez

Library and the Hemeroteca Pino Suárez of Mérida, is the primary source of information on Elvia Carrillo Puerto and the activities of the Ligas Feministas in promoting social reform in Yucatán. The press of Mérida, led by Carrillo Puerto's estranged friend, Carlos R. Menéndez, was very conservative and printed only negative reports about Carrillo Puerto's government. Only *Tierra* reported the election of Elvia Carrillo Puerto and other women to the state legislature in November 1923, and only *Tierra* gave an accurate account of Carrillo Puerto's birth control program in Yucatán. Margaret Sanger's pamphlet on birth control methods, translated as *La regulación de la natalidad, o la brújula del hogar* (Mérida, Yuc,: Imp. "MAYAB," 1922), was widely distributed to adults in Yucatán in 1922 and 1923 but is now a rare item. Only one copy turned up at the Basave Collection of the Biblioteca de México. An enlightening examination of birth control in contemporary Latin America is Nora Scott Kinzer's "Priests, Machos, and Babies, or Latin American Women and the Manichean Heresy," *Journal of Marriage and the Family* 35 (May 1973):300-312.

Two booklets provide information on the papers and the resolutions of the 1923 Feminist Congress held in Mexico City. They are the *Primer Congreso Feminista de la Liga Pan-Americana de Mujeres* (México: Talleres Linotipográficos "El Modelo," 1923) and *Sección Mexicana de la Liga Pan-Americana para la elevación de la mujer* (México: Talleres Linotipográficos "El Modelo," 1923). Newspaper coverage of the May 1923 Pan American Congress of Women by *El Universal* and *El Demócrata* provides additional information about the participants and the resolutions of the congress. In November 1922 *Excelsior* gave full and sympathetic coverage to a Catholic women's congress held in Mexico City but refused to send reporters to the Pan American Conference the next May. *Excelsior* maintained its antifeminist and conservative stance for twenty years after the revolution.

MEXICAN WOMEN ON THEIR OWN, 1924-1930

In 1923 Carrie Chapman Catt, in an essay entitled "Anti-Feminism in South America," *Current History* 18 (April-September 1923):1028-36, concluded that the struggle for women's rights in Latin America "is a difficult one, and the women leading the organized groups with definite aims find the outlook dark and unpromising." (p. 1036). Her discouraging view was not shared by Ida Clyde Clark and Lillian Ballance Sheridan, editors of *Women of 1924 International* (New York: Women's News Service, Inc., 1924). They reported some feminist activity in practically every Latin American country. And interestingly, the editors had more to report about feminist activities in Mexico than in any other Latin American country, including Argentina. Argentina had previously been the leader in women's emancipation and had hosted the first feminist congress in Latin America in 1910.

Another indispensable source for evidence of the active role women were playing in the reconstruction of Mexico in the 1920s is the *Bulletin of the Pan American Union*. For example, Helen Bowyer, who provided Clark and Sheridan with the data on Mexican women they used in *Women of 1924 International*, contributed an article on "Social Welfare Work in Rural Mexico," to volume 56 (January-June 1923):453-59 of the *Bulletin*. Elena Landázuri, mentioned earlier, contributed an essay on "New Tendencies in the Public Instruction of Mexico," to the November 1922 issue of the *Bulletin*. Especially useful is the data on the large number of women enrolled in day and night classes in technical schools in Mexico City. Shorter articles on women's activities in Mexico are to be found in practically every issue of the *Bulletin of the Pan American Union* in the 1920s and 1930s.

Yet another source for the activities of Mexican women in the 1920s is the Pan American International Women's Committee, *Proceedings and Report of the Columbus Day Conferences* (New York: Inter-American Press, 1926). These conferences were held in twelve Latin American countries on October 12, 1923. The report of the conferences in Mexico, which were attended by Mexico's leading feminists and professional women, is found on pages 38-44 of the *Proceedings*.

The data found in *Women of 1924 International*, the *Bulletin of the Pan American Union*, and the Pan American International Women's Committee *Proceedings* confirm the views of R. B. Brinsmade and M. C. Rolland, *Mexican Problems* (New York: n.p., 1916), that the Mexican Revolution was accelerating the women's movement in Mexico. However, Ernest Gruening in his chapter on women in *Mexico and Its Heritage* (New York: D. Appleton-Century Co., 1928) found that the vast majority of Mexican women had experienced no improvement in their status as a result of the revolution.

Sofía Villa de Buentello's *La mujer y la ley* (México: Imprenta Franco-Americana, 1921) indicates that Carranza's Law of Family Relations of 1917 providing for greater legal equality for married women had not been implemented. Señora de Buentello's book and her activities from 1922 to 1926 in favor of legal equality appear to have influenced the decision of the Calles government to revise the civil code in 1927 and to improve the legal status of women.

For a time Buentello collaborated with Elena Arizmendi, who in 1922 founded the International League of Iberian and Latin American Women. The league, perhaps the only attempt in the 1920s at uniting all Spanish-speaking feminists, had its headquarters in New York, where Arizmendi lived. There she published a short-lived feminist journal, *Feminismo Internacional* (December 1922 to November 1923), to which Buentello contributed at least one article. Buentello's "Libros y periódicos para la mujer," is found in the April 1923 issue of *Feminismo Internacional*. I found no copies of this journal while in Mexico, but Asunción

Lavrin, who is researching the feminist movement in four South American countries, found an almost complete set of Arizmendi's journal at the Library of Congress.

By 1925 there was a falling out between Arizmendi and Buentello, and the former disavowed the international congress Buentello was organizing. From July 2 to July 16, 1925, *Excelsior* gleefully reported the difficulties encountered at, and the ultimate failure of, the International Congress of Iberian and Hispanic American Women which Sofía organized. A more balanced account of the meetings of the ill-fated congress can be found in *El Universal* and *El Demócrata* in their issues of July 2 to July 16, 1925. The ambitious agenda of the congress, most of which was never debated, is found in *Gran Congreso Internacional convocado por la Liga de Mujeres Ibéricas e Hispano-Americanas y que debe celebrarse en esta Ciudad* (México: Imprenta Comercial, 1925).

Although Elena Torres was one of Mexico's leading feminists from 1917 to 1924, information about her activities must be pieced together from scattered sources. *Women of 1924 International* provides information about her feminist and professional activities found nowhere else, and the sources on the 1923 Pan American Congress of Women cited earlier reveal the leading role she played in that conference. A summary of the paper she delivered on teaching citizenship in Mexico is found in Secretaría de Educación Pública, *Memorias del segundo congreso del niño* (México: Secretaría de Educación Pública, 1925). We shall probably never know why Elena Torres dropped out of the women's movement after 1924 to devote herself exclusively to educational reform in Mexico. Perhaps public apathy, ideological differences with other feminists, and the unrelenting hostility of influential conservative groups led Torres to give up the struggle after seven years of intensive effort on behalf of women.

Elvia Carrillo Puerto's attempt to run for national office is detailed in Ernest Gruening's *Mexico and Its Heritage*. See also Ward M. Morton's *Woman Suffrage in Mexico* (Gainesville: University of Florida Press, 1962), the only monograph in English on the subject. Some biographical data and a photograph of Elvia Carrillo Puerto are found in Antonio Bustillos Carrillo's *Yucatán al servicio de la patria y de la revolución* (México: Casa Ramírez Editores, 1959).

The Bulletin of the Pan American Union provides what little information we have concerning the Pestalozzi-Froebel Society, founded by Professor María Rosaura Zapata. *Women of 1924 International* and Ifigenia M. de Navarrete, *La mujer y los derechos sociales* (México: Ediciones Oasis, 1969) mention the establishment of the Asociación de Mujeres Cristianas, the Temperance Society, the Association of Mexican University Women, and the Association of Mexican Women Doctors during the 1920s. *Mujer*, edited by María Ríos Cárdenas from 1926 to 1929 and found only at the Hemeroteca Nacional de México, is the chief source of information for feminist activities, primarily in Mexico City, at the end of the 1920s. Shirlene Ann Soto provides a general survey of women's activities in the 1920s and 1930s in *The Mexican Woman: A Study of her Participation in the Revolution, 1910-1940* (Palo Alto, Cal.: R & E Research Associates, 1979), pp. 74-105.

THE FEMINIST MOVEMENT IN THE 1930s

The single most important source for the period from 1930 to 1940 is María Ríos Cárdenas's *La mujer mexicana es ciudadana. Historia, con fisonomía de una novela de costumbres, 1930-1940* (México: Epoca, 1940). Since funds were apparently not available to publish the minutes and resolutions of the three congresses held from 1931 to 1934, our only sources of information on these meetings are Ríos Cárdenas's book and newspaper accounts in *El Universal* and *Excelsior* in Mexico City, and *El Informador* in Guadalajara, Jalisco.

A contemporary evaluation in English of the women's movement in Mexico is found in Verna Carleton Millan's *Mexico Reborn* (Boston: Houghton Mifflin Co., 1939). For a carefully researched study of the fight for woman suffrage from 1934 to 1940, see Ward M. Morton's *Woman Suffrage in Mexico*, chapter 3. Another important secondary source on feminism in the 1930s is Lillian E. Fisher's "The Influence of the Present Mexican Revolution Upon the Status of Mexican Women," *Hispanic American Historical Review* 22 (February 1942):211-28. Brief biographies of leading feminists of the 1930s are found in María Efraína Rocha's *Semblanzas biográficas de algunas luchadoras mexicanas contemporáneas* (México: Ediciones del Comité Coordinador Femenino, 1947). A recent evaluation of the 1930s feminist movement is by María Antonieta Rascón, "La mujer y la lucha social," in *Imagen y realidad de la mujer* ed. Elena Urritia, SEP-SETENTAS no. 172 (México: Secretaría de Educación Pública, 1975), pp. 139-174, who points out the relevance of the views of left-wing feminists of the 1930s to contemporary Mexican feminism.

Margarita Robles de Mendoza's *La evolución de la mujer en México* (México: Imp. Galas, 1931), tells us little about Mexican women, but the book does reveal that the author either knew nothing about or was not interested in publicizing the work of Elena Torres, Sofía Villa de Buentello, María Ríos Cárdenas, and other feminists active in the 1920s and early 1930s. Señora Robles de Mendoza's *Silabario de la ciudadanía de la mujer mexicana* (Jalapa: Talleres Tipográficos del Gobierno, 1932) is a typical example of official revolutionary rhetoric. María Efraína Rocha in *Semblanzas biográficas* presents Margarita Robles de Mendoza in a most favorable light, but Juana B. Gutiérrez de Mendoza exposed her upper-class prejudice against the poor in her newspaper *Alma Mexicana: Por la Tierra y Por la Raza*, 15 November 1935, pp. 7-8. Scattered copies of *Alma Mexicana* are found in the Hemeroteca Nacional in Mexico City.

It is clear from the 1933 and early 1934 campaign speeches of Lázaro Cárdenas published in *La gira del General Lázaro Cárdenas: Sintesis ideológica* (México: Secretaría de Prensa y Propaganda del CEN del PNR, 1934) that his interest in women's rights and in woman suffrage dates from after his election. Ward M. Morton is probably correct in attributing Cárdenas's change of heart to the influence of his friend, Francisco J. Múgica. Múgica's interest in feminism can be gleaned from Armando de María y Campos's *Múgica: Crónica biográfica* (México: Compañía de Ediciones Populares, 1939).

For a brief biography of Palma Guillén, see Consuelo Colon's *Mujeres de México* (México: Imprenta Gallarda, 1944). Information about Alexandra Kollontay's six-months residence in Mexico as Russian ambassador is detailed in *El Universal, Excelsior*, and the *New York Times* from December 1926 to June 1927.

These same newspapers document the efforts of Lázaro Cárdenas to grant women the vote, as do the works of María Ríos Cárdenas and Ward M. Morton. Ms. Ríos Cárdenas and other Mexican commentators are not clear as to why woman suffrage was defeated in 1939, but contemporary foreign observers unhesitatingly agree that support of General Juan A. Almazán's candidacy by right-wing women doomed the movement to enfranchise women before the end of Cárdenas's term. For evidence of this see works by Virginia Prewett, Betty Kirk, Lillian E. Fisher, and Ward M. Morton, cited in note 97 in chapter 6.

INDEX

Acuña y Rossetti, Elisa, 38, 106
Adultery, 4, 15, 99
AFL, 28
Aguascalientes, city of, 29
Aguilar, Anita, 55 n.94
Alamán, Lucas, 20 n.24
Alcoholic beverages: consumption
  of, in Díaz period, 113;
  consumption of, in post-revolutionary
  period, 113. *See also* Pulque
Alegría, Juana Armanda: *Psicología
  de las mexicanas*, 3, 18 n.2
Almázan, Juan Andreu: candidate for
  the presidency, 144; defeated
  by Ávila Camacho, 145;
  gains support of Feminine
  Idealist party, 144, 150 n.97
Alvarado, Ernestina, 113
Alvarado, Gov. Salvador, xiv, 44,
  46, 77, 87, 91, 96, 104,
  127, 153, 156; and anticlericalism,
  67, 69, 70, 79; early life,
  65; and expenditures on education,
  68; and Felipe Carrillo
  Puerto, 90; and the First Feminist
  Congress, 70-72; ideas of, on
  women, 65-67; and *Ligas
  Femeniles*, 92; political

ambitions of, 79, 86, 88; *Mi
  sueño*, 91; *La reconstrucción
  de México*, 90; and reforms in
  Yucatán, 65-70; supports
  "rationalist education," 70;
  unpopularity in Yucatán of, 79-80;
  on woman suffrage, 78-79
Amasiato, 13
Anticlericalism, 26, 35, 45, 46, 48,
  75; in Yucatán, 67, 69, 70,
  79, 90
Antifeminism, 16, 17, 72, 73
Anti-Reelectionist party, 27
Apatzingán constitution, 6
Archivo Histórico de Jalisco, 22 n.43
Arias Bernal, María, 38
Arizmendi, Elena, 115
Ascanio, Francisca, 77
Asociación de Mujeres Cristianas
  (YWCA), 35, 114, 115
Asociación Femenina de Temperancia,
  113
Association of Catholic Women
  (Guadalajara, Jalisco), 47
Association of Mexican University
  Women, 114
Association of Mexican Women
  Doctors, 114

Ateneo Peninsular, 69
Ávila, Gov. Eleuterio, 64
Ávila Camacho, Manuel: elected,
    145; presidential nominee of
    PRM, 144, 145
Ávila de Rosado, Porfiria, 75
Aztec society, 4; and sexual double
    standard, 4
Azuela, Mariano, 28, 41; *The
    Underdogs*, 41

Balmaceda, Doctora, 141
Barbarous Mexico (John Kenneth
    Turner), 64
Bassols, Narciso, 126
Beimler, Rosalind Rosoff, 55 n.94
Belén, prison of, 27, 29, 38
Benítez, Fernando, 79
Bermúdez, María Elvira, 3; *La vida
    familiar del mexicano*, 99
Betancourt, Susana, 98
Birth control, 97, 100; in Yucatán,
    93
Bishop of Puebla, 5
Bloque Nacional de Mujeres
    Revolucionarias, 127, 135;
    petitions Congress for woman
    suffrage, 130-31
Bocker, Dr. Dorothy, 94
Bolío Ontiveros, Edmundo, 89
Boston Transcript, The, 78
Bowyer, Helen, 114

Cabo Rodríguez, Matilde, 140
Calles, Plutarco Elías, 46, 58, 111,
    115, 116, 137, 138, 154,
    156; founds the Partido Nacional
    Revolucionario, 112; puppets of,
    138; and woman suffrage,
    137-38
Campfollowers. See *Soldaderas*

Cano, Gov. Abel, 111
Canto y Pastrana, Dominga, 62
Cantú Corro, José, xiv
Cárdenas, Lázaro, xv, 136, 140,
    141, 142, 143, 144, 150 n.97,
    155, 157, 158; appoints first
    woman ambassador, 140;
    candidate for the presidency, 112,
    138; and Inter-American
    Commission on Women, 132;
    interest of, in women's rights,
    127; and land reform, 127;
    quoted on woman suffrage,
    xv, 36, 139, 141, 143, 144; quoted
    on women's rights, 138-139
Carlota, Empress of Mexico, 21
Carranza, Venustiano, 27, 28, 30,
    33, 48, 64, 65, 77, 157; and
    divorce decree, 35, 94, 107;
    government of, 153; and
    Law of Family Relations, 36, 37,
    76, 80, 85-86 n.115, 94
Carrillo Puerto, Elvia, 97, 110, 111,
    116, 131, 132-33, 142, 157;
    arguments of, for woman suffrage,
    131; elected to state
    legislature in Yucatán, 91; and
    Feminist Leagues of Yucatán, 92;
    founds Liga Orientadora de Acción
    Femenina, 112; refused seat
    by Congress, 112; role of,
    at the first Congress of
    the Pan American League for the
    Elevation of Women, 97,
    99; runs for Congress in San Luis
    Potosí, 111
Carrillo Puerto, Felipe, xiv, 91, 95,
    96, 104, 112, 156, 157; and
    birth control, 92; and divorce law,
    94, 95; early years of, 89;
    elected governor of Yucatán,

89-90; evaluation of, as
feminist advocate, 100; as
governor of Yucatán, 87,
88; ideas of, on women's
liberation, 97; as leader of
Socialist Party of Yucatán, 89; as
leader of the Yucatecan Socialist
Party, 80; as organizer of Peasant
Leagues of Resistance, 89; and
relationship with Salvador
Alvarado, 90
Casa del Obrero Mundial, 48
Casasola, Gustavo, 40, 41-42;
*Historia gráfica de la
revolución*, 54 n.77, 150 n.97
Casas y Miramón, María, 107,
108
Castelum, Dr. Bernardo J., 120
Caste War of Yucatan, The (Nelson
Reed), 64, 69
Castillo Ledón, Amalia, 132
Castillo y Pina, José, xiv
Castro Morales, Carlos, 89
Catholic church, 25, 35; 1857
constitutional restrictions
against, 45-46; 1917 constitutional
restrictions against, 46;
during the Porfiriato, 45-46;
in Jalisco, 47-49; and Revolution
of 1910-1920, 45-49; and women's
support of, xiii, 46-49, 69
Catholic women, 138, 139, 154; in
defense of the church, 138,
154, 156; demonstrations against
government by, 135, 139;
organizations of, 35, 47-49
Cedillo, Gen. Saturnino, 111
Census: of 1910, 31; of 1921, 105;
of 1930, 125
Central League of Resistance of
Mérida, 89

Cetina Gutiérrez, Rita, 14, 61, 62,
69; and Feminist League, 92
Chapa, Dr. Esther, 136, 141, 146
"Chata, La," 43
Chiapas, state of, 63
Children of Sánchez, The (Oscar
Lewis), xi, xii
Church-state conflict: and women,
xiv, 46-49
Círculos de Estudios Femeninos
(Guadalajara, Jalisco), 47
Civil Code of 1884, 13, 15, 36,
75
Civil Code of 1927, 104, 119-21,
137
Cline, H. F., 60
Cockroft, James D., 29; *Intellectual
Precursors of the Mexican
Revolution: 1900-1913*, 29,
50 n.5
Communists: barred from Congress
on Prostitution, 135; at First
Congress of Women
Workers and Peasants, 129; at
Second Congress, 134, 135;
views of, on prostitution, 136
Comonfort, President Ignacio, 9
"Complot de Tacubaya," 29
Confederation of Catholic Associations
of Mexico, 56
Congress of Women Workers and
Peasants: First (1931), 127,
128-29; Second (1933), 127,
130, 133, 134; Third (1934), 127,
135, 137, 148 n.55
Consensual unions: in contemporary
Mexico, 100, 103 n.61
Constitution of 1857, 45, 46, 52 n.48
Constitution of 1917, 35, 37, 52 n.48;
article 34, 143, 144; and woman
suffrage, 111

Contigo Pan y Cebolla (Guillermo Prieto), 8
Convention on the Nationality of Women: signed by Cárdenas, 140
Convents, 8
Cooperative Women's Union. *See* Union Cooperativa 'Mujeres de la Raza'
Coronela, La. *See* Espinosa Barrera, Coronela María de la Luz
Correa Zapata, Dolores, 13, 74
"Corredora, La," 43
"Cuca." *See* García, María del Refugio
Cuellar, José T. de: *Ensalada de Pollos*, 8
Cuernavaca, 41, 42
Cumberland, Charles C., 41, 82 n.36, 113

Damas Católicas (Union of Catholic Women), 114
Day care centers, need for, 119
Debt peonage in Yucatán, 59, 63
Depression, Great: and effects on women, 125-26, 127, 133-34
d'Erzell, Catalina, 117
Desmonte, El, 27
Díaz, Porfirio, 10, 11, 17, 22, 26, 27, 28, 29, 38-39, 46, 47, 153
Diéguez, Gen. Miguel, 46, 48, 49
Divorce, 16, 34, 35, 94, 95, 97, 99, 107, 121
Divorce law of 1914 (Carranza), 94
Divorce law of 1923 (Carrillo Puerto), 94, 95, 100
Domestic servants, 12, 13, 63, 66, 99, 125
Domínguez, Belisario, 38
Domínguez, Corregidor Miguel, 6

Dynamic of Mexican Nationalism, The (Frederic C. Turner), 44, 54 n.77
Dzib, Raquel, 91

Eagle and the Serpent, The (Martín Luis Guzmán), 46, 56
Economic role of women, 3; in Díaz period, 12, 13, 14, 31-32; during the Great Depression, 125-26; after the Revolution, 105-6
Education of women: arguments in favor of, 5, 7, 10, 74-75; in colonial period, 5, 6; in Díaz period, 10-11, 22 n.50, 61-62; in early national period, 7, 8-9, 21 n.39, 61; normal schools, 11, 62; in Revolutionary period, 30, 67-69; secondary schools, 9-10, 11, 62; and sexual education in Yucatán, 67-69, 92; urged by Liberals, 8-10, 21 n.43; vocational schools, 10, 11. *See also* Teachers, women
Election law (June 1918), 37, 112
Encina, Luz, 135
Ensalada de Pollos (José T. de Cuellar), 8
Ensign Nun, The, 43
Escuela de Artes y Oficios de Mujeres (Vocational School for Women), 10
Espinosa Barrera, Coronela María de la Luz, 42-43, 158
Eugenia (Eduardo Ursaíz), 88
Excelsior, xv, 103 n.64, 125, 139

Farfán, Cristina, 61
Farrera, Remedios, 42
Feminine Idealist party, 144

Feminine Leagues. See *Ligas
Femeniles*
Feminine Temperance Association.
See Asociación Femenina de
Temperancia
Feminism: in the Díaz period, 13-16;
general issues of concern,
13-16, 34, 35, 36, 73, 74, 75, 76,
77, 98-100, 116-17, 118,
119, 128, 133, 134, 136, 143;
origins of, in Mexico,
xii-xiii, 4, 18; opposition to,
xiii-xv, 16-17, 18; and
Socialism, 21 n.34, 66, 157; and
woman suffrage, 16, 36-37,
77-78, 90-91, 99, 110, 112, 137,
142, 143, 144, 152-55; in
Yucatán, 61-62, 73-79, 91-92,
95-96, 100. *See also*
Alvarado, Salvador; Carrillo
Puerto, Felipe; Galindo, Hermila;
Ríos Cárdenas, María; Torres,
Elena; Villa de Buentello, Sofía;
Zavala y Castillo, Consuelo
Feminist Congresses. *See* Congress
of Women Workers and
Peasants, First, Second, Third;
Feminist Congress of
Yucatán, First, Second; International
Congress of the League of
Iberian and Spanish-American
Women; International
Feminine Congress of the Republic
of Argentina, First; Pan
American Conference of Women,
First; Pan American League
for the Elevation of Women, First
Congress of
Feminist Congress of Yucatán, First,
36, 53, 70-77, 80, 90, 156
Feminist Congress of Yucatán,

Second, 70, 77-78, 79, 80,
96, 106-7
Feminist Council of Mexico, 106
Feminist Leagues. See *Ligas
Feministas*
Feminist Revolutionary party, 127
Ferrer y Guardia, Francisco, 70; and
"rationalist education," 76
Flores Magón, Ricardo, 26, 30
Flores Magón brothers, 65
Fornaro, Carlo de, 65
Franco, Agustín, 71
"Free love," 97, 157; advocated in
Yucatán, 94, 98
Frente Unico Pro-Derechos de la
Mujer, 121 n.8, 127, 137, 141,
142, 144, 145, 156;
program of, 142
Freud, Sigmund, 14

Gaither, R. B., 95
Galindo, Concepción D. de, 114
Galindo, Hermila, 13, 26, 32, 33,
70, 75, 96, 106, 111, 116, 131,
142, 153; "La mujer en el
porvenir," 36, 73-74; as supporter
of Carranza, 34; views of, on
the Catholic Church, 34, 35,
46; views of, on divorce
decree, 35, 74; views of, on sex
education, 35, 36, 37
Galván, Florencio, 111
Gamboa, Ignacio, 16, 72; *La mujer
moderna*, 16
Gamio, Manuel, 16, 156
García, Genaro, 152, 156; on legal
status of women, 109
García, María del Refugio, 141, 142,
145; at the Congress on
Prostitution, 136; at First Congress
of Women Workers and

Peasants, 129; refused seat by Congress, 142-43; runs for Congress in Uruapán, 142; secretary general of the Frente Unico Pro-Derechos de la Mujer, 129, 137, 142; stages hunger strike, 143

García Ortiz, Francisca, 74

Génesis del crimen en México (Julio Guerrero), 40-41

George, William R: as founder of the George Junior Republic, 82

Gimeno de Flaquer, Concepción, 14

González, Cesar A., 73

González, Pablo, 34, 46

González, Soledad, 117

González Navarro, Moisés, 23

González Ortega, Beatriz, 39

González y González, Luis, 10, 51

Graves, Robert, 19

Gruening, Ernest, 58, 100 n.2; and birth control in Yucatán, 93; *Mexico and Its Heritage*, 111

Guadalajara, city of, 21, 47, 48

"Güera Carrasco, La," 43

Guerrero, Julio: *La génesis del crimen en Mexico*, 40-41

Guillén, Palma, 140

Gutiérrez de Mendoza, Juana Belén, 26, 27, 29, 37-38, 46, 106, 132, 142 n.30, 152, 158

Guzmán, Martín Luis: *The Eagle and the Serpent*, 28, 46, 56

Havana, 33

Hembrismo, 3

Henequen, 60, 63, 79, 88, 91

Heraldo de Motul, El, 89

Hernández, Adela, 118

Hernández, José, 16

Hernández Zarco, María, 38

Hidalgo, state of, 10

Hidalgo y Costilla, Miguel, 6

Hijas de Cuauhtémoc, 39

Historia gráfica de la revolución (Gustavo Casasola), 40, 41, 54 n.84

"Hombres necios" (Sor Juana Inés de la Cruz), 4

Housing, 30, 31

Huerta, Gen. Victoriano, 29, 33, 38, 46, 47, 48

Huidobro de Azua, Esther, 14

Illegitimacy, 43

Infant mortality, 98

Informador, El (Guadalajara), 148 n.55

Instituto Literario de Niñas of Mérida, Yucatán, 61, 62

Insurgent Mexico (John Reed), 40

Intellectual Precursors of the Mexican Revolution: 1900-1913 (James D. Cockroft), 29, 50 n.5

Inter-American Commission on Women, 131

International Conference of American States in Montevideo, Seventh, 140

International Congress of the League of Iberian and Spanish-American Women, 110

International Feminine Congress of the Argentine Republic, First, 71

International Harvester Company, 79

International League of Iberian and Spanish-American Women. *See* Liga Internacional de Mujeres Ibéricas e Hispanoamericanas

Iturbe, Gen. Ramón F., 56

Jalisco, state of, 6; educational
project, 7; during revolution
of 1910-1920, 47-49
Jara, Gen. Heriberto, 46
Jerome, Saint, 5
Jesús Soto, María de, 10
Jiménez y Muro, Dolores, 26, 29-32,
37, 46; as author of
"Political and Social Plan" of
1911, 29, 31
Juana Inés de la Cruz, Sor, xii-xiii,
4, 12, 18 n.8, 19 n.9, 19 n.13,
74
Juárez, President Benito, 9, 10, 155
Journals, feminist. *See Mujer; Mujer
Mexicana, La; Mujer Moderna, La*
Juvenile courts, 99

Kennedy, Anne, 93, 102 n.24
King, Rosa E.: *Tempest Over
Mexico*, 40, 41, 42
Kinzer, Nora Scott, 98
Kollontay, Alexandra, 140
Komarowsky, Mirra: *Women in the
Modern World*, 31

Labor code of 1931, 126
Landázuri, Elena, 52, 114
Lara, Guadalupe, 91
Lara y Pardo, Dr. Luis: *La
prostitución en México*,
44, 45
Latin American Bureau of the Third
International, 96
Lavrin, Asunción, 6, 22 n.43, 158
Law, women in, 12, 13, 105, 116,
118, 119
Law of Family Relations (Venustiano
Carranza), 36, 76, 80, 98,
108, 119, 120

League of Women Voters, 115; 1922
Baltimore meeting, 106
Legal status of women, 13, 15, 36,
67, 75-76, 109, 119-21
Lesbianism, 16
Lerdo de Tejada, Miguel, 9
Lerner, Gerda, 3
"Letter to Sor Filotea" (Sor Juana
Inés de la Cruz), 4, 5
Lewis, Oscar: *The Children of
Sanchez*, xi, xii
Liberals, 7, 9, 10
Liceo de Niñas, Guadalajara,
21 n.43
Liga Internacional de Mujeres
Ibéricas e Hispanoamericanas,
110, 115, 135
Liga Nacional de Mujeres, 116
Liga Orientadora de Acción
Femenina, 132-33, 142 n.32;
founded by Elvia Carrillo
Puerto, 112
Ligas Femeniles (Feminine Leagues):
advocated by Alvarado, 92
Ligas Feministas (Feminist Leagues):
founded by Carrillo Puerto, 92
Literacy, among women, 105; in
Yucatán, 62

Machismo, xiii, 3, 4, 118
Madero, Angela, 27
Madero, President Francisco I., 27,
29, 32, 36, 38, 153; Plan de
San Luis Potosí, 29
Madre Conchita, La, 138
Magaña, Gildardo, 32
Malvaéz, Inés, 108
Manrique, Gov. Aurelio, 111
Margen del feminismo, Al (J. D.
Ramírez Garrido), 71

Marriage, 13, 15, 74, 76, 94, 97, 98.
    See also Divorce
Martínez, María, 78
Mason, R. H., 41
Maximilian, Emperor of Mexico, 9,
    21
Maya cities, 59
Maya Indians, 58-59, 63-64, 79-80
Medicine, women in, 10, 11-12,
    23 n.59, 96
Menéndez, Carlos R., 84 n.78, 89,
    94
Mérida, Yucatán, 39, 58, 59, 61, 62,
    88
Mesa, Aurora, 143
Mexican Congress, 10
Mexican Congress on the Child,
    Second, 107
Mexican Feminine Confederation of
    Veracruz, 143
Mexican Liberal party, 65
Mexico and Its Heritage (Ernest
    Gruening), 111
Mexico City, 9, 11, 12, 19 n.20,
    23 n.64, 30, 32, 33, 38, 39,
    96, 97, 104, 116, 118, 119, 120,
    127, 128
Michel, Concepción, 129, 145,
    149 n.81; at First Congress of
    Women Workers and Peasants,
    129
Michoacán, state of, 138, 140
Millan, Verna Carleton, 142
Mistral, Gabriela, 107
Mi sueño (Salvador Alvarado),
    91-92
Mójica Bobadilla, Rosa, 43
Monitor Republicano, El, 16
Monogamy, 15
Montessori School, in Mérida, 96
Montoya, Dr. Matilda P., 11, 12, 96

Morality, and feminism, 14-15, 97,
    98-99
Morelos, state of, 38, 41
Moreno Canton, Delio, 89
Morrow, Dwight, 116, 148 n.58
Morton, Ward M.: *Woman Suffrage
    in Mexico*, xii, 141, 150 n.97
Múgica, Francisco J., 46, 140,
    144
Mujer, 116-19, 128
"Mujer en el porvenir, la" (Hermila
    Galindo), 36
Mujeres Libres, Las, 107
Mujer Mexicana, La, 13, 14, 15, 17,
    29, 62, 74, 152, 156
Mujer Moderna, La, 16, 32, 34
Mujer Moderna, La (Ignacio
    Gamboa), 16

National Bloc of Revolutionary
    Women. *See* Bloque
    Nacional de Mujeres Revolucionarias
National Council of the American
    Birth Control League, Inc., 93
National Council of Mexican
    Women, 106, 117
National League of Women. *See* Liga
    Nacional de Mujeres
National Revolutionary party. *See*
    Partido Nacional Revolucionario
    (PNR)
National School of Medicine, 12
Nava de Ruisánchez, Julia, 96, 131,
    147 n.23; involvement of, in
    feminist movement from 1904-
    1940, xiv, 38
Navarro, Canon Luis, 47
Negra Angustias, La (Francisco
    Rojas González), 42-43
Nelken, Margarita, 144
Nervo, Amado, 4

Newspapers. *See Desmonte, El;*
    Excelsior; Heraldo de
    Motul, El; Informador, El;
    Monitor Republicano, El;
    New York Times, The; Revista de
    Mérida, La; Revista de
    Yucatán, La; Tierra; Universal,
    El; Universal Ilustrado, El;
    Vesper; Voz de la Revolución, La
New York Times, The, 107, 141
Nieto, Gov. Rafael, 111, 112
Normal School for Men, 22 n.46
Normal School for Women, 11,
    22 n.46, 22 n.50

Obregón, President Alvaro, 30, 34,
    46, 48, 90, 107, 115, 138; on
    Yucatán, 80 n.2
Ocampo, María Luisa, 117-18
Ocampo, Melchor, 9
Orozco, José Clemente, 40, 44
Orozco y Jiménez, Archbishop
    Francisco, 47, 48
Ortíz Argumedo, Colonel, 64
Ortíz de Dominguez, Josefa (La
    Corregidora), 6, 19
Ortíz Rubio, President Pascual, 128,
    129, 130, 138

Pachuca, city of, 10
Palavicini, Felix, 17, 37, 156
Palma, Isabel, 95
Pan American Conference of
    Women, First, in Baltimore, 96
Pan American Congress of Public
    Health Officers, First, 120
Pan American League for the
    Elevation of Women, 95, 96, 106,
    110; First Congress of, 95,
    96-100, 108, 113, 117, 127, 129;
    founding of, 115

Pan American Round Table of
    Mexico, The, 115
Pardo Bazán, Emilia, 26
Partido Femenino Idealista, 150 n.97
Partido Feminista Revolucionario,
    129
Partido Liberal Mexicano, 30
Partido Nacional Revolucionario
    (PNR), 112, 130, 139, 142, 154
Partido Revolucionario Mexicano
    (PRM), 114
Paul, Saint, 5
Peace by Revolution (Frank
    Tannenbaum), 56 n.114,
    87, 88
Pedagogical Congress of Yucatán,
    Second, 69
Peniche, Beatriz, 91
Pérez, Isolina, 74
Pérez Treviño, Gen. Manuel, 130
Pfandl, Ludwig, 4
Pino Suárez, José María, 64
Pistache, 17
"Plan de Ayala," 28
"Political and Social Plan Proclaimed
    by the States of Guerrero,
    Michoácan, Tlaxcala, Campeche,
    Puebla, and the Federal
    District," 29
Polygamy, 15
Population: in Chiapas in 1910, 63;
    in Mexico in 1921, 49 n.2,
    105; in Yucatán in 1910, 62, 63
Portes Gil, President Emilio, 132,
    138, 141, 142
Posada, José Guadalupe, 40, 54
Precursor Movement (1900-1910),
    29, 38, 65
Prieto, Guillermo, 155; *Contigo Pan
    y Cebolla*, 8, 9, 21 n.38
Progreso, Yucatán, 79, 88

"Project of a Decree Concerning
Public Education in the Free State
of Jalisco," 6
Prostitutes: and contraception, 92;
in Yucatán, 92
Prostitution, 8, 13, 23, 34, 55,
66-67, 100, 106; Congress
on, 135-36; during the Porfiriato,
44
Protestants, xiv, 114
Psicología de las mexicanas (Juana
Armanda Alegría), 3
Public administration, women in, 12,
125-26
Pulque, 113-14

Querétaro, city of, 138; Constitutional
Convention in, 17, 153
Quintana Roo, Andrés, 21 n.38
Quirk, Robert, 40

Ramírez Garrido, Col. J. D.: *Al
margen del feminismo*, 71
Ramírez Vázquez, Pedro, 56
Rape, 110, 118-19
"Rationalist" education, 72
Reconstrucción de México, La
(Salvador Alvarado), 90
Reed, Alma, 95
Reed, John: *Insurgent Mexico*, 40
Reed, Nelson: *The Caste War of
Yucatán*, 64, 69
Regeneración, 26, 65
Registro Yucateco, 60
Regulación de la natalidad, La
(Margaret Sanger), 92, 93, 94
Revista de Merida, La, 89
Revista de Yucatán, La, 84 n.78,
86 n.130, 89, 94
Revolutionary Party of National
Unification, 150 n.97

Revolutionary songs, 40
Revolution of Ayutla, 9
Reyes, Alfonso, 4
Ríos Cárdenas, María, xiv; as
architect of Congress of Women
Workers and Peasants, 127;
calls for a feminist confederation,
129; edits *Mujer*, 116-19; at
First Congress of Women Workers
and Peasants, 128; at
Second Congress, 134, 135; at
Third Congress, 137
Rivera, Dr. Columba, 12, 13, 74,
96
Rivera, Librado, 30
Robles, Amelia, "El Güero" of Río
Balsas, 43
Robles de Mendoza, Margarita,
131-32, 141, 142, 147 n.30;
Mexican representative to the
Inter-American Commission
on Women, 132; repudiated by
Mexican feminists, 132;
urges women to vote in 1932
elections, 131-32
Rodríguez, President Abelardo, 134,
138
Rojas González, Francisco: *La Negra
Angustias*, 42
Román, Refugio, 118
Romero Cuyas, José: "La
emancipación de la mujer,"
21 n.34, 23 n.59
Roy, Evelyn, 108

Saénz Royo, Artemisa, 70, 84 n.79
Sánchez Facio, María Elena de
García, 117
Sandino revolution in Nicaragua, 115
Sandoval de Zarco, María, 12, 13,
74, 116

Sanger, Margaret, 92-93; invited to Yucatán, 93; pamphlet on birth control, 92-94; *Women and the New Race*, 93

San Luis Potosí, state of, 111, 112; grants women restricted suffrage, 111; rescinds woman suffrage, 112

Santibáñez, María, 118

Sarabia, Juan, 30

School of Domestic Arts, Mérida, 68

School of Medicine, Mérida, 96

Semanario de las Señoritas Mexicanas, 8

Sexual education, 35, 36, 97, 98; in Yucatán, 92

Sexuality, 34, 36

Sexual standard: advocacy of a single sexual standard, 14, 98, 100; double, 4, 17

Siempreviva, La (feminist newspaper), 61, 152

Siempreviva, La (feminist society), 61

Siempreviva school, La, 61-62, 69

Sierra, Justo, 15, 152, 156

Six Year Plan, 138; and "socialist education," 135

Socialism and Feminism, 21 n.34, 23 n.59, 66, 94, 157

"Socialist education," 135, 139

Socialist Party of the Southeast, 88, 91, 157

Sociedad Obstétrica Mexicana, 116

Sociedad Protectora de la Mujer, 14, 38, 96, 131

Soldaderas, 40-41, 43, 49, 158

Sole Front for Women's Rights. *See* Frente Unico Pro-Derechos de la Mujer

Spencer, Herbert, 17

Staël, Madame de, 7

Suárez, María, 118

Suffrage, women's, xiii, 16, 36, 37, 99, 104, 139, 145, 152, 154-55; advocacy of, in 1920s, 110; arguments in favor of, 130-31; debated in Yucatán in 1916, 77-78; favored by *El Universal*, 128; in Republican Spain, 128; in Yucatán, 90-91

Superior Council of Health, 97

Syphilis: incidence of, 120

Tannenbaum, Frank, 65; *Peace by Revolution*, 56 n.114, 87, 88

Teachers, women, 10, 11, 12, 22 n.46, 62, 69, 72, 74, 76, 78, 96, 105, 106, 107, 113, 126

Tejeda, Adalberto, 111, 157

Tempest Over Mexico (Rosa E. King), 40, 41, 42

Tenorio Zavala, Gertrudis, 61

Tierra (Yucatecan Socialist newspaper), 93

Topete, Hermila Galindo de. *See* Galindo, Hermila

Topete, Manuel de, 34

Torres, Elena, 95-96, 97, 98, 99, 106, 121, 131, 147 n.24, 157; on divorce, 108; founds first Montessori school in Mérida, 68, 107

Torres, Rosa, 90

Toussaint, Manuel, 4

Turner, Frederick C.: *The Dynamic of Mexican Nationalism*, 40, 44, 54 n.77

Turner, John Kenneth: *Barbarous Mexico*, 64

Underdogs, The (Mariano Azuela), 41, 43
Unemployment, female, 106
Union Cooperativa 'Mujeres de la Raza,' 108
Union of Catholic Women. *See* Damas Católicas
Universal, El, 37, 110, 113, 116, 128, 133
Universal Ilustrado, El, 118
Uranga, Consuelo, 134-35
Urquizo, Francisco L., 40
Ursáiz, Dr. Eduardo: *Eugenia*, 88
Ursúa, Dr. Antonia de, 115, 116
Uruápan, Michoacán, 142, 143

Valladolid, Yucatán, 60
Vasconcelos, José, 107
Vera, Luz, 106
Veracruz, city of, 141, 143; Carranza's government in, 33; Carranza's propagandists in, 33
Vesper (Guanajuato), 26, 27, 38, 106
Vicario, Leona, 6, 19 n.22, 21 n.24, 21 n.38
Vigil, Jose María, 50 n.3, 155-56
Villa, Pancho, 28, 33, 39, 46
Villa de Buentello, Sofía, 115, 131; on birth control, 94; on divorce, 107-9; *La mujer y la ley*, 108, 109, 110; on legal inferiority of women, 109
Vizcaínas, Las, 6, 19 n.20
Voz de la Revolución, La, 70, 72-73, 84

Washington, Booker T., 65
Westrup de Valesco, Berthe, 113
White slave traffic, 97

Woman Suffrage in Mexico (Ward M. Morton), xii, 141, 150 n.97
Women: as bureaucrats, 12, 125-26; during Cárdenas era, 137-46; in Díaz period, 10-16; in early national period, 6-10; and higher education, 85 n.107; during independence movement, 6; in post-Revolutionary period, 104-21, 125-37; in pre-Columbian and colonial Mexico, 3-6; in Revolutionary period, 26, 37-42, 47-49; in work force, 8, 14, 31, 32, 105, 125; in Yucatán, 61-62, 65-69, 70-78, 90-92, 95-100. *See also* Civil Code of 1884; Civil Code of 1927; Divorce; Divorce law of 1914; Divorce law of 1923; Domestic servants; Economic role of women; Education of women; Feminism; Feminist Congresses; Law, women in; Legal status of women; Marriage; Medicine, women in; *Mujer*; *Mujer Mexicana, La*; Prostitution; *Soldaderas*; Suffrage, women's; Teachers, women
Women and the New Race (Margaret Sanger), 93
Women in the Modern World (Mirra Komarowsky), 31
Women of 1924 International, 107
Women's International League for Peace and Freedom, Mexican branch, 115; meeting in Mexico, 112
Women's Protective Society. *See* Sociedad Protectora de la Mujer
Wright de Kleinhans, Laureana, 14

Yautepec, Morelos, 42, 43
Young Women's Christian Association. *See* Associación de Mujeres Cristianas
Yucatán, state of, 49, 58, 77, 78, 97, 157; Alvarado, as governor of, 44, 64-70, 79-80; Carrillo Puerto, as governor of, 89-95; in the Díaz period, 62-64; early feminist movement in, 61-62; in early national period, 60-61; in the early Revolutionary period, 64; secessionist movement in, 60; work force in, 63. *See also* Debt peonage; Feminist Congress of Yucatán; Henequen
Yucatán Peninsula, 58-59, 63; in the pre-Columbian and colonial period, 59-60

Zacatecas, state of, 39, 40
Zamarrón, Hermila, 111
Zapata, Emiliano, 27, 29, 32, 33, 38, 88; assassination of, 32; meeting with Madero, 42; "Plan de Ayala," 28
Zapata, María Rosaura, 113
Zapata Vela, Licenciada Elisa, 136
Zapatistas, 41, 42
Zavala, Lorenzo de, 62
Zavala y Castillo, Consuelo, 62, 69, 70, 72-73, 75, 76, 77, 78
Zendejas, Adelina: *La mujer en la intervención francesa*, 50

About the Author

ANNA MACÍAS is Professor of History at Ohio Wesleyan University in Delaware, Ohio. She is the author of *Genesis del gobierno Constitucional en Mexico, 1808-1820*.